EXPERIMENTAL

Cognitive
Psychology
AND ITS APPLICATIONS

EXPERIMENTAL
Cognitive
Psychology
AND ITS APPLICATIONS

EDITED BY Alice F. Healy

DECADE
of BEHAVIOR
2000-2010

American Psychological Association
Washington, DC

Published by
American Psychological Association
750 First Street, NE
Washington, DC 20002
www.apa.org

To order
APA Order Department
P.O. Box 92984
Washington, DC 20090-2984

Tel: (800) 374-2721; Direct: (202) 336-5510
Fax: (202) 336-5502; TDD/TTY: (202) 336-6123
Online: www.apa.org/books/
E-mail: order@apa.org

In the U.K., Europe, Africa, and the Middle East, copies may be ordered from
American Psychological Association
3 Henrietta Street
Covent Garden, London
WC2E 8LU England

Typeset in Century Schoolbook by World Composition Services, Inc., Sterling, VA

Printer: United Book Press, Inc., Baltimore, MD
Cover Designer: Naylor Design, Washington, DC
Technical/Production Editor: Emily Leonard

The opinions and statements published are the responsibility of the authors, and such opinions and statements do not necessarily represent the policies of the American Psychological Association.

Library of Congress Cataloging-in-Publication Data

Experimental cognitive psychology and its applications / edited by Alice F. Healy.
        p. cm.—(Decade of behavior)
    Includes bibliographical references and index.
    ISBN 1-59147-183-4
    1. Cognitive psychology.   2. Psychology, Experimental.   I. Healy, Alice F.
II. Series.

BF201.E945 2004
153—dc22   2004008268

British Library Cataloguing-in-Publication Data
A CIP record is available from the British Library.

Printed in the United States of America
First Edition

APA Science Volumes

Attribution and Social Interaction: The Legacy of Edward E. Jones

Best Methods for the Analysis of Change: Recent Advances, Unanswered Questions, Future Directions

Cardiovascular Reactivity to Psychological Stress and Disease

The Challenge in Mathematics and Science Education: Psychology's Response

Changing Employment Relations: Behavioral and Social Perspectives

Children Exposed to Marital Violence: Theory, Research, and Applied Issues

Cognition: Conceptual and Methodological Issues

Cognitive Bases of Musical Communication

Cognitive Dissonance: Progress on a Pivotal Theory in Social Psychology

Conceptualization and Measurement of Organism–Environment Interaction

Converging Operations in the Study of Visual Selective Attention

Creative Thought: An Investigation of Conceptual Structures and Processes

Developmental Psychoacoustics

Diversity in Work Teams: Research Paradigms for a Changing Workplace

Emotion and Culture: Empirical Studies of Mutual Influence

Emotion, Disclosure, and Health

Evolving Explanations of Development: Ecological Approaches to Organism–Environment Systems

Examining Lives in Context: Perspectives on the Ecology of Human Development

Global Prospects for Education: Development, Culture, and Schooling

Hostility, Coping, and Health

Measuring Patient Changes in Mood, Anxiety, and Personality Disorders: Toward a Core Battery

Occasion Setting: Associative Learning and Cognition in Animals

Organ Donation and Transplantation: Psychological and Behavioral Factors

Origins and Development of Schizophrenia: Advances in Experimental Psychopathology

The Perception of Structure

Perspectives on Socially Shared Cognition

Psychological Testing of Hispanics

Psychology of Women's Health: Progress and Challenges in Research and Application

Researching Community Psychology: Issues of Theory and Methods

The Rising Curve: Long-Term Gains in IQ and Related Measures

Sexism and Stereotypes in Modern Society: The Gender Science of Janet Taylor Spence

Sleep and Cognition

APA Decade of Behavior Volumes

Contents

Contributors

John R. Anderson, PhD, Department of Psychology, Carnegie Mellon University, Pittsburgh, PA

Harry P. Bahrick, PhD, Department of Psychology, Ohio Wesleyan University, Delaware, OH

Daniel M. Bernstein, PhD, Department of Psychology, University of Washington, Seattle

David M. Bloome, PhD, Department of Language, Literacy, and Culture, The Ohio State University, Columbus

Lyle E. Bourne, Jr., PhD, Department of Psychology, University of Colorado, Boulder

Scott Douglass, PhD, Department of Psychology, Carnegie Mellon University, Pittsburgh, PA

Susan Dumais, PhD, Microsoft Research, Redmond, WA

Gilles O. Einstein, PhD, Department of Psychology, Furman University, Greenville, SC

Alinda Friedman, PhD, Department of Psychology, University of Alberta, Edmonton, Canada

Morton Ann Gernsbacher, PhD, Department of Psychology, University of Wisconsin—Madison

Susan R. Goldman, PhD, Department of Psychology and College of Education, University of Illinois at Chicago

Arthur C. Graesser, PhD, Department of Psychology, University of Memphis, TN

Elena L. Grigorenko, PhD, PACE Center, Yale University, New Haven, CT

Alice F. Healy, PhD, Department of Psychology, University of Colorado, Boulder

Xiangen Hu, PhD, Department of Psychology, University of Memphis, TN

Peder Johnson, PhD, Department of Psychology, University of New Mexico, Albuquerque

Janice M. Keenan, PhD, Department of Psychology, University of Denver, CO

Ronald T. Kellogg, PhD, Department of Psychology, Saint Louis University, St. Louis, MO

Walter Kintsch, PhD, Institute of Cognitive Science, University of Colorado, Boulder

Darrell Laham, PhD, Knowledge Analysis Technologies, Boulder, CO

Thomas K. Landauer, PhD, Department of Psychology, University of Colorado, Boulder

Elizabeth F. Loftus, PhD, Department of Psychology and Social Behavior and Department of Criminology, Law, and Society, University of California, Irvine

Gordon D. Logan, PhD, Department of Psychology, Vanderbilt University, Nashville, TN

Mark A. McDaniel, PhD, Department of Psychology, Washington University, St. Louis, MO

Danielle S. McNamara, PhD, Department of Psychology, University of Memphis, TN

James S. Nairne, PhD, Department of Psychological Sciences, Purdue University, West Lafayette, IN

Douglas L. Nelson, PhD, Department of Psychology, University of South Florida, Tampa

Raymond S. Nickerson, PhD, Department of Psychology, Tufts University, Medford, MA

Vimla Patel, PhD, Departments of Biomedical Informatics and Psychiatry, Columbia University, New York, NY

Walter Perrig, PhD, Institute of Psychology, University of Bern, Switzerland

Robert W. Proctor, PhD, Department of Psychological Sciences, Purdue University, West Lafayette, IN

Yulin Qin, PhD, Department of Psychology, Carnegie Mellon University, Pittsburgh, PA

Timothy C. Rickard, PhD, Department of Psychology, University of California, San Diego

David A. Robertson, PhD, School of Psychology, Georgia Institute of Technology, Atlanta

Ernst Z. Rothkopf, PhD, Teachers College, Columbia University, New York, NY

Roger W. Schvaneveldt, PhD, Applied Psychology Unit, Arizona State University East, Mesa

Richard M. Shiffrin, PhD, Department of Psychology, Indiana University, Bloomington

Robert J. Sternberg, PhD, PACE Center, Yale University, New Haven, CT

Mark Steyvers, PhD, Department of Cognitive Sciences, University of California, Irvine

Lynn Streeter, PhD, Knowledge Analysis Technologies, Boulder, CO

Kim-Phuong L. Vu, PhD, Department of Psychology, California State University, Northridge

Charles A. Weaver III, PhD, Department of Psychology and Neuroscience, Baylor University, Waco, TX

Erica L. Wohldmann, MA, Department of Psychology, University of Colorado, Boulder

Foreword

In early 1988, the American Psychological Association (APA) Science Director-ate began its sponsorship of what would become an exceptionally successful activity in support of psychological science—the APA Scientific Conferences program. This program has showcased some of the most important topics in psychological science and has provided a forum for collaboration among many leading figures in the field.

The program has inspired a series of books that have presented cutting-edge work in all areas of psychology. At the turn of the millennium, the series was renamed the Decade of Behavior Series to help advance the goals of this important initiative. The Decade of Behavior is a major interdisciplinary campaign designed to promote the contributions of the behavioral and social sciences to our most important societal challenges in the decade leading up to 2010. Although a key goal has been to inform the public about these scientific contributions, other activities have been designed to encourage and further collaboration among scientists. Hence, the series that was the "APA Science Series" has continued as the "Decade of Behavior Series." This represents one element in APA's efforts to promote the Decade of Behavior initiative as one of its endorsing organizations. For additional information about the Decade of Behavior, please visit http://www.decadeofbehavior.org.

Over the course of the past years, the Science Conference and Decade of Behavior Series has allowed psychological scientists to share and explore cutting-edge findings in psychology. The APA Science Directorate looks forward to continuing this successful program and to sponsoring other conferences and books in the years ahead. This series has been so successful that we have chosen to extend it to include books that, although they do not arise from conferences, report with the same high quality of scholarship on the latest research.

We are pleased that this important contribution to the literature was supported in part by the Decade of Behavior program. Congratulations to the editors and contributors of this volume on their sterling effort.

Steven J. Breckler, PhD
Executive Director for Science

Virginia E. Holt
Assistant Executive Director for Science

Preface

The primary purpose of this volume is to bring together contributions by some of the most significant contemporary experimental psychologists working in cognition, including the areas of learning, memory, information processing, discourse, and knowledge representation. They share their perspectives and their recent research findings so that these ideas and results can be integrated for use by practitioners in the field, including those in training, education, and testing. Such integration should also be of value to students and other researchers concerned with the core issues of human cognition.

A secondary purpose of this volume is to serve as a triple Festschrift in honor of three distinguished faculty members from the University of Colorado (CU) who are recently retired from teaching at the university: Lyle Bourne, Walter Kintsch, and Thomas Landauer. All three of these individuals throughout their careers have done basic research on a wide range of topics in experimental cognitive psychology. In recent years all three have made important contributions to the understanding of learning, memory, information processing, discourse, and knowledge representation, and findings from these studies have direct practical implications for training, education, and testing. In the case of Lyle Bourne, his research has most recently focused on the long-term retention and transfer of knowledge and skills with applications concerning military and industrial training. In the case of Walter Kintsch, his most recent research has been largely on text comprehension with applications concerning the teaching of reading and writing. Finally, in the case of Thomas Landauer, his recent research has been on the representation of knowledge, with applications concerning educational testing.

The primary chapter authors are all eminent contemporary experimental psychologists and theorists in the core areas within cognitive psychology. Each of them has his or her own program of empirical research that, like those of the honorees, has had a significant practical impact on everyday life. Thus, the contributors present summaries of their basic research programs with a focus on the applications of their findings.

The study of cognition has experienced rapid growth in the last decade. This topic is fundamental both to the science of psychology and to its applications to real-world problems. However, there has traditionally been a huge gap between the basic research findings in this area and practice in the field. There, thus, remains a crucial need to bridge from the laboratory to the real world. This volume brings together individuals who not only have a distinguished record as experimental psychologists but also have tried to show how their findings can be applied in the field.

This volume was preceded in May 2003 by a conference at CU. There were two types of sessions at the conference. First, there were keynote addresses by eight of the distinguished researchers contributing chapters to the volume (Anderson, Bahrick, Healy, Loftus, McDaniel, Nickerson, Schvaneveldt, and

Sternberg). Second, there were three symposia, each focusing on the career and contributions of one of the three Festschrift honorees. These symposia included discussions of those aspects of the honorees' work that speak most strongly to the theme of basic research on cognition with applications to real-world problems. Four former students or collaborators served as the participants in each symposium. The primary authors of the remaining chapters in the volume served as session chairs at the conference.

The present volume starts with short biographical sketches of the three honorees, followed by the chapters summarizing the symposia in their honor. The subsequent chapters are organized into five sections, each representing a different major topic in cognitive psychology: learning, memory, information processing, discourse, and knowledge representation. Some of the chapters were arbitrarily assigned to one of these topics although they span several of them.

The conference and volume were made possible by the generous financial support of a number of groups, including the American Psychological Association and four groups at CU: the Institute of Cognitive Science, the Coleman Institute for Cognitive Disabilities, the Department of Psychology, and the Council on Research and Creative Work of the Graduate School. Many individuals, primarily from CU, also generously devoted their time and effort to the conference or the volume: Ellena Andrus (financial management), Bob Bjork (from the University of California at Los Angeles, session chair at conference), Marilyn Hughes Blackmon (conference poster), Jean Bowen (conference catering and organization), David Braddock (conference planning), Carolyn Buck-Gengler (conference posters), Donna Caccamise (conference planning and conference poster), Shana Carpenter (from Colorado State University, conference poster), Debbie Clawson (from Catholic University, conference photos), Ron Cole (special address at conference), Tim Curran (guest editor of chap. 5 in this volume), Simon Dennis (conference posters), Nancy Edwards (financial management), Gregg Emmel (conference Web site), Bruce Healy (emotional support), Charlotte Healy (clarinet choir at conference reception), Eileen Kintsch (conference poster), Knowledge-Analysis Technologies, Incorporated (T-shirt funding), James Kole (audiovisual at conference and conference posters), Bob Levin (plaques for honorees), Carol Lynch (opening remarks at conference), Ernie Mross (computer advice), Jim Parker (photograph of honorees), José Quesada (conference posters), Carolyn Rickard (name tags at conference), Jon Roberts (computer advice), Jerry Rudy (introductory remarks at conference), Vicki Schneider (travel expense disbursement and poster at conference), and Rita Yaroush (T-shirt design).

It has been my pleasure and honor to work with the three honorees as a colleague and collaborator and to know them as friends. On a broad scale, they have helped shape the field of cognitive psychology. On a more narrow scale, they have helped shape my own research and career. I have been stimulated and inspired by them, and I will be forever indebted to them for guiding and enriching my life. Thank you Lyle, Walter, and Tom!

About the Honorees:
Lyle E. Bourne, Jr., Walter Kintsch, and Thomas K. Landauer

From left to right: Walter Kintsch, Thomas K. Landauer, and Lyle E. Bourne, Jr.

Lyle E. Bourne, Jr.

Lyle E. Bourne, Jr., received his bachelor's degree at Brown University in 1953 and his PhD in psychology from the University of Wisconsin in 1956. He has been a member of the faculty of the Departments of Psychology of the University of Utah (1956–1963) and of the University of Colorado at Boulder (1963–present), where he is presently professor emeritus. Bourne spent 2 years as a visiting faculty member at the University of California, Berkeley (1961–1962, 1968–1969). He served as director of the Institute of Cognitive Science at the University of Colorado from 1980 to 1983 and as chairman of the Department of Psychology from 1983 to 1991. Professionally, Bourne is a member of the Rocky Mountain Psychological Association and a charter member of the Psychonomic Society and the Cognitive Science Society. He is also a fellow of the American Psychological Association (APA) and the American Psychological Society. He was elected to membership in the Society of Experimental Psychologists in 1972. He received a Research Scientist Award from the National Institutes of Health for the period 1971–1976. Bourne is the author of over 125 journal articles, 23 book chapters, and 14 books.

During his career, Bourne has served on the editorial board of a number of journals, including the *Journal of Experimental Psychology*, the *Journal of Experimental Child Psychology*, the *Journal of Verbal Learning and Verbal Behavior*, the *Journal of Clinical Psychology*, and *Memory & Cognition*. He served as associate editor for the *Journal of Experimental Psychology* and, when that journal was divided, became editor of the *Journal of Experimental Psychology: Human Learning and Memory* (1975–1980). He has also been the Science Watch editor of *American Psychologist* (1992–2000). Bourne has made various service contributions to the APA, as member of the Council of Representatives (two terms, from Division 3), Publication and Communications Committee (two terms), Council of Editors, and Board of Scientific Affairs (two terms, chair in second term). He has also been a member and chairman of the Publication Committee (1980–1985) and Governing Board of the Psychonomic Society (1976–1982). He was the chair of the Science Seminar Series of the Federation of Behavioral, Psychological, and Cognitive Sciences (1987–1990). Bourne was elected president of the Rocky Mountain Psychological Association (1988), chair of the Society of Experimental Psychologists (1987–1988), president of Division 3 (Experimental Psychology) of the APA (1991–1992), chair of the Governing Board of the Psychonomic Society (1981–1982), president of the Federation of Behavioral, Psychological and Cognitive Sciences (1995–2000), and president of Division 1 (Society for General Psychology) of the APA (2000–2001). Bourne was a member of the Psychobiology Panel of the National Science Foundation from 1972 to 1976.

Bourne's scholarly interests lie largely in the area of human skill learning, memory, and cognitive processes, including their neurophysiological correlates. He is also engaged in research on political decision making, interpersonal relationships, and stress effects on memory. A good reference to his learning–memory research is the first chapters in Healy and Bourne's (1995, 1998) books cited below. Generally speaking, this work focuses on conditions of learning and types of learning material that optimize original learning, enhance the durability of long-term memory, and provide for generalizability and the broadest transfer possible. The studies are done in a variety of contexts, ranging from target detection and simple list learning to mental multiplication and foreign language acquisition. The processes under examination include perceptual discriminations, cognitive skills, and the parameters of motor performance. The theoretical framework in which much of this research is conducted rests on a fundamental principle called the principle of procedural reinstatement: The extent to which learned material is retained over time and transfers to other tasks depends on the degree of overlap between encoding and retrieval procedures and the similarity of the originally learned factual information to that required by the transfer task. Bourne has recently used brain imaging techniques based on event-related potentials in EEG and MEG (magnetoencephalographic) recordings to study separable components of skill in a target identification task and in mental arithmetic.

Selected Publications

Healy, A. F., & Bourne, L. E., Jr. (Eds.). (1995). *Learning and memory of knowledge and skills: Durability and specificity*. Thousand Oaks, CA: Sage.

Healy, A. F., & Bourne, L. E., Jr. (Eds.). (1998). *Foreign language learning: Psycholinguistic experiments on training and retention*. Mahwah, NJ: Erlbaum.

Pauli, P., Schleichert, H., Bourne, L. E., Jr., & Birbaumer, N. (1998). Effects of cortical polarization on mental arithmetic. *Cognitive Brain Research, 7*, 49–56.

Bourne, L. E., Jr., Healy, A. F., Parker, J. T., & Rickard, T. C. (1999). The strategic basis of performance in binary classification tasks: Strategy choices and strategy transitions. *Journal of Memory and Language, 41*, 223–252.

Bourne, L. E., Jr., Pauli, P., Fendrich, D. W., Rickard, T. C., & Healy, A. F. (2001). Deliberate and automatic processes in mental arithmetic. *Cognitive Processing, 2*, 487–522.

Clawson, D. M., Healy, A. F., Ericsson, K. A., & Bourne, L. E., Jr. (2001). Retention and transfer of Morse code reception skill by novices: Part–whole training. *Journal of Experimental Psychology: Applied, 7*, 129–142.

Healy, A, F., Hoffman, J. M., Beer, F. A., & Bourne, L. E., Jr. (2002). Factors influencing reactions to international military and terrorist attacks. *Political Psychology, 23*, 439–468.

LaVoie, N., Bourne, L. E., Jr., & Healy, A. F. (2002). Memory seeding: Representations underlying quantitative estimations. *Journal of Experimental Psychology: Learning, Memory, and Cognition, 28*, 1137–1153.

Schneider, V. I., Healy, A. F., & Bourne, L. E., Jr. (2002). What is learned under difficult conditions is hard to forget: Contextual interference effects in foreign vocabulary acquisition, retention, and transfer. *Journal of Memory and Language, 46*, 419–440.

Bourne, L. E., Jr., Healy, A. F., & Beer, F. A. (2003). Military conflict and terrorism: General psychology informs international relations. *Review of General Psychology, 7*, 189–202.

Walter Kintsch

Walter Kintsch graduated from the Teachers' Training College in Feldkirch, Austria, in 1951. He taught in rural schools in the province of Vorarlberg, first a second-grade class, then for 3 years in a one-room school with Grades 1 to 8. He came to the United States with a Fulbright scholarship to the University of Kansas in 1955–1956 to study psychology, where he received an MA degree. After a year at the University of Vienna, he returned to Kansas, receiving a PhD degree in 1960. His dissertation under the direction of Edward L. Wike investigated motivational factors in rats in a straight-alley runway. A National Institute of Mental Health postdoctoral fellowship allowed him to study the then emergent mathematical psychology with William K. Estes at Indiana University. He held faculty positions in the Department of Psychology at the University of Missouri (1961–1965) and the University of California, Riverside (1965–1967). In 1967–1968 he was visiting professor at Stanford University. He came to the University of Colorado at Boulder in 1968 as professor of psychology. Since 1983 he has also been director of the Institute of Cognitive Science at the University of Colorado. He became professor emeritus in 2004.

Kintsch has been editor of *Psychological Review* from 1988 to 1994 and the *Journal of Verbal Learning and Verbal Behavior* (now *Journal of Memory and Language*) from 1976 to 1980. He has also been an associate editor for *Cognition and Instruction* and has been at various times a member of the editorial board of 12 other journals.

Kintsch is a founding member of the Cognitive Science Society and has been a member of its Governing Board and its chair. He also has been a member of the Governing Board of the Psychonomic Society and its chair. He is a fellow of the American Psychological Association (APA) and has been president of its

Division 3 (Experimental Psychology). He is a member of the National Academy of Education.

Kintsch received the Distinguished Scientific Contribution Award of APA in 1992. In 2001, he was awarded an honorary doctorate from Humboldt University in Berlin. In 2002, the German Society of Psychology bestowed on him its Lifetime Achievement Award.

Kintsch's early research focused on mathematical learning theory, in particular Markov models of paired-associate learning and conditioning. During the 1960s this focus shifted toward an interest in memory, especially recall and recognition. As it became more and more obvious that meaning was a decisive factor in memory, Kintsch started to investigate meaningful materials more directly. Thus began a lifelong concern with memory for text, text comprehension, and learning from text. The first product of this work was the 1974 book *The Representation of Meaning in Memory*. Along with other researchers at that time, Kintsch proposed that propositions are the units of mental representation of meaning. This informal notion of proposition became a very useful and influential tool for the analysis of texts as well as subject protocols and helped bring about a surge of interest in the experimental investigation of discourse comprehension.

At that time, Kintsch started an intensive, decade-long collaboration with the Dutch linguist Teun van Dijk. In 1978, they published an article in *Psychological Review* that shifted the focus of research from text analysis and representational issues to the question of how people process text, that is, text comprehension. Their 1978 process model became the basis for much of the research on discourse comprehension in the decades to come. The van Dijk–Kintsch cooperation culminated in the 1983 book *Strategies of Discourse Comprehension*, which elaborated their process model and introduced another influential concept, that of the situation model.

The year of 1988 brought the publication, again in *Psychological Review*, of the construction–integration (CI) model of comprehension, which modified the process model in important ways. The CI model views comprehension as a bottom-up process in which various alternatives are tried in parallel, resulting in an incoherent intermediate mental representation that is then cleaned up by an integration process. Integration is a constraint satisfaction process that ensures that those constructions that are linked together become strongly activated, whereas contradictory and irrelevant elements become deactivated. Thus, the end result is a holistic coherent mental structure, even though its construction may have been chaotic. In 1998, Kintsch collected the work he and others had done within the framework of the CI model in the book *Comprehension: A Paradigm for Cognition*. Kintsch argued in that book that comprehension provides an alternative paradigm for understanding many cognitive processes, not just text comprehension narrowly defined, and that this paradigm complements the historically dominant problem-solving paradigm. It does not deny the important role of problem solving and analytical thinking but points out that many cognitive processes can be usefully conceptualized as constraint satisfaction processes, more akin to perception than analytic thinking.

In recent years, Kintsch has started a collaboration with his colleague Tom Landauer, whose latent semantic analysis (LSA) has provided a realistic way of modeling the role of knowledge in comprehension. Comprehension researchers have always agreed that one cannot understand comprehension without explicitly accounting for the prior knowledge of the comprehender. Before LSA, such accounts were limited to small, artificial illustrative examples, often more misleading than useful. LSA changed all that: Comprehension researchers now have a way of dealing with human knowledge on a realistic scale (even though LSA has, as yet, its own limitations), making it possible to model the role of knowledge in comprehension.

LSA also made it possible for Kintsch to return to the elementary school classroom he left so many years ago. With support from the National Science Foundation/Interagency Education Research Initiative, Kintsch and a large group of his colleagues and coworkers are busy introducing LSA-based technology into schools all over the state of Colorado. The Colorado Literacy Tutor is an ambitious project that develops technology in cooperation with teachers, that helps them to teach reading–decoding as well as comprehension, that makes available this technology statewide, and that carefully evaluates its effectiveness in education.

Selected Publications

Kintsch, W. (1970). *Learning, memory and conceptual processes*. New York: Wiley.

Kintsch, W. (1974). *The representation of meaning in memory*. Hillsdale, NJ: Erlbaum.

Kintsch, W., & van Dijk, T. A. (1978). Towards a model of text comprehension and production. *Psychological Review, 85,* 363–394.

van Dijk, T. A., & Kintsch, W. (1983). *Strategies of discourse comprehension*. New York: Academic Press.

Kintsch, W. (1988). The role of knowledge in discourse comprehension: A construction–integration model. *Psychological Review, 95,* 163–182.

Ericsson, K. A., & Kintsch, W. (1995). Long-term working memory. *Psychological Review, 102,* 211–245.

Kintsch, W. (1998). *Comprehension: A paradigm for cognition*. New York: Cambridge University Press.

Kintsch, W. (2000). Metaphor comprehension: A computational theory. *Psychonomic Bulletin & Review, 7,* 257–266.

Kintsch, W. (2001). Predication. *Cognitive Science, 25,* 173–202.

Thomas K. Landauer

Thomas K. (Tom) Landauer received a BA from the University of Colorado (CU) in 1954 and a PhD from Harvard in 1960. He taught at Harvard (1959–1960) and Dartmouth (1960–1963); was at the Center for Advanced Study in the Behavioral Sciences at Stanford in 1964, Stanford (1965–1969), and Princeton (1978–1979, and part time 1979–1981); and worked at Bell Laboratories (1969–1984), Bell Communications Research (1985–1994), and CU (1994–present), where he is now a research professor. At Harvard he did research on acquired reinforcement in rats under Richard Solomon and cross-cultural research with John W. M. Whiting and taught in the Graduate School of Education.

At Dartmouth he did research in rat reinforcement, human paired-associate learning, and the biochemistry of memory. His most cited work from that period is a one-page article on the rate of implicit speech. At Stanford, he did research on social development and continued brain research, and adding, with collaborator Jonathan Freedman in the late 1970s, research into semantic cognition, including the first studies of category size effects on reaction time. While at Stanford he taught introductory, physiological, and developmental psychology, which led to his somewhat idiosyncratic textbook *Psychology: A Brief Overview*, and a book of classical readings in the biological bases of behavior.

In 1969, after a half year in Kenya with Whiting initiating a controlled longitudinal study to test the effects of early physiological stress on physical, emotional, and cognitive growth, Landauer moved to the research department of AT&T's Bell Telephone Laboratories (Bell Labs) in Murray Hill, New Jersey. There he worked exclusively on human learning and memory, including developing a random storage model of memory with surprisingly wide ability to simulate learning and memory phenomena, estimating the amount of learned information in human memory (10^9 bits), and studying the effects of repetition spacing. Learning research included applications in "real-world" settings to test completeness of understanding and set problems, a strategy that has guided much of his work. These included demonstrations that an optimal schedule of expanding intervals between rehearsals works as well as repeated presentations for remembering names, phone numbers, and course content. Brought to fruition in collaborations with Bob Bjork, the phenomenon is widely used for amelioration of dementia.

At Bell Labs he also continued investigations of semantic category effects, an extensive series of experiments on lexical naming and semantic categorization as a function of frequency, recency, masking, and sublexical structure, and research on word frequency as a function of similarity neighborhoods pioneered with Lynn Streeter. In 1980, he formed and led one of the first laboratories devoted to human computer interaction. The group's work focused on understanding how people use words to refer to things, with the goal of making computers better understand what people want. From 1979 to 1981 he also served as a lecturer at Princeton.

With the breakup of AT&T in 1984, Landauer's group, renamed Cognitive Science Research, moved to the spun-off Bell Communications Research (Bellcore). Their best-known accomplishment grew out of failures to find effective solutions to the "vocabulary problem" in information retrieval. Search for a computational model fueled the invention, development, and application of latent semantic analysis (LSA). The assumption behind LSA is that the meaning of a semantically coherent passage can be approximated by the sum of the meanings of its words. Recent evidence suggests that LSA captures over 80% of the variability in similarity of textual meaning experienced by people. It has been used extensively for modeling psycholinguistic phenomena and in educational applications, including automatic scoring and feedback for expository writing.

Another area of his research was the so-called computer productivity paradox. Landauer's 1994 book, *The Trouble With Computers*, reviewed a wide range of evidence that computers had not improved work productivity and that iterative behavioral test and fix yielded dramatic improvement, and it gave research-based advice on how to go about it.

In 1994, Landauer retired from Bellcore and became a half-time professor at CU. Since then, his research has focused on applying LSA to further psycholinguistic phenomena and educational technologies and on increasing its accuracy, scalability, and scope as a cognitive tool. In 1998, with two CU PhDs, Darrell Laham and Peter Foltz, he founded a company that develops applications of LSA and delivers them over the Internet.

Landauer also served 6 years on the National Research Council Committee on Human Factors, on several conference committees, and on 10 publication boards. He is a fellow of the American Association for the Advancement of Science, Divisions 3 and 21 of the American Psychological Association, the American Psychological Society, and the Society of Experimental Psychologists. He won the Association of American Publishers "best scholarly book in computer science" award for *The Trouble With Computers*, the Association for Computing Machinery's Rigo award for research in documentation, and the CU Psychology Department faculty research award, and he was elected to the Human Computer Interaction Academy. He has published well over 100 refereed articles and chapters and given dozens of keynote addresses. His research has been supported by the National Science Foundation, National Institute of Mental Health, Institute of Educational Sciences, National Aeronautics and Space Administration, Defense Advanced Projects Research Agency, Office of Naval Research, Army Research Institute, Air Force Research Laboratory, and others.

Selected Publications

Landauer, T. K. (1962). Rate of implicit speech. *Perceptual and Motor Skills, 15,* 646.

Landauer, T. K. (1964). Delay of an acquired reinforcer. *Journal of Comparative and Physiological Psychology, 68,* 374–379.

Landauer, T. K., & Whiting, J. W. M. (1964). Infantile stimulation and adult stature of human males. *American Anthropologist, 66,* 1007–1028.

Moyer, R., & Landauer, T. K. (1967). The time required for judgments of numerical inequality. *Nature, 216,* 159.

Landauer, T. K., & Freedman, J. L. (1968). Information retrieval from long-term memory: Category size and recognition time. *Journal of Verbal Learning and Verbal Behavior, 7,* 291–295.

Landauer, T. K., & Streeter, L. A. (1973). Structural differences between common and rare words. *Journal of Verbal Learning and Verbal Behavior, 12,* 119–131.

Landauer, T. K. (1974). Consolidation in human memory: Retrograde amnestic effects of confusable items in paired associate learning. *Journal of Verbal Learning and Verbal Behavior, 13,* 45–53.

Landauer, T. K. (1975). Memory without organization: Explorations of a model with random storage and undirected retrieval. *Cognitive Psychology, 1,* 495–531.

Landauer, T. K., & Ross, B. H. (1978). Memory for at least one of two items: Test and failure of several theories of spacing effects. *Journal of Verbal Learning and Verbal Behavior, 17,* 669–680.

Landauer, T. K. (1986). How much do people remember? Some estimates of the quantity of learned information in long-term memory. *Cognitive Science, 10,* 477–493.

Landauer, T. K. (1994). *The trouble with computers*. Cambridge, MA: MIT Press.

Landauer, T. K., & Dumais, S. T. (1997). A solution to Plato's problem: The latent semantic analysis theory of the acquisition, induction, and representation of knowledge. *Psychological Review, 104,* 211–240.

Landauer, T. K. (2002). On the computational basis of cognition: Arguments from LSA. In B. H. Ross (Ed.), *The psychology of learning and motivation* (Vol. 41, pp. 43–84). San Diego, CA: Academic Press.

Part I

Symposia

1

Domain-Specific Knowledge in Intellectual Skills: A Symposium in Honor of Lyle E. Bourne, Jr.

Ronald T. Kellogg, Alinda Friedman,
Peder Johnson, and Timothy C. Rickard

Intellectual skills embody the human capacity for thinking and acquiring knowledge. Discovering and understanding the cognitive processes underlying these skills formed the basis of a career spanning nearly five decades. Lyle E. Bourne, Jr., published his first book, *Human Conceptual Behavior,* in 1966. This monograph summarized a decade of his and others' work on human thinking, as revealed in concept identification and rule-learning tasks. His latest books, coedited with Alice Healy in 1995, *Learning and Memory of Knowledge and Skills,* and in 1998, *Foreign Language Learning: Psycholinguistic Studies on Training and Retention*, broke important new ground in basic and applied research on cognitive skills. The body of Bourne's work has shown that high-level thinking processes are both amenable to rigorous experimental research and fundamental to the field of cognitive psychology and its applications. It was under his leadership that the Institute of Cognitive Science in Boulder, Colorado, was created from its predecessor, the Institute for the Study of Intellectual Behavior. Here, Bourne's 35 doctoral students learned that there is more to the field than the study of memory and language, narrowly conceived. We trace our current interests and expertise to the training and insights we received from Bourne and are privileged to honor his legacy in the present chapter.

Cognitive skills are well retained for long periods of time when the task used to acquire them is reinstated at the time of performance (Healy & Bourne, 1995; chap. 5, this volume). This finding suggests that skills can be domain or even task specific, with retrieval of relevant knowledge tightly linked to the original learning context. In this chapter, we conjecture that (a) an individual's understanding of the conceptual content of a domain can be measured using reliable and valid techniques, (b) the categorical representations of a given domain strongly shape thinking skills, (c) domain expertise alleviates a severe working memory constraint on thinking skill through retrieval from long-term memory, and (d) practice at a given task causes a shift from relying on computations in working memory to long-term memory retrieval that can be formally modeled. We illustrate these points through reasoning, writing, and mathematics tasks but propose them as applicable to all intellectual skills.

Domain-Specific Conceptual Understanding

When students learn a new domain in classroom instruction, they often fail to understand the conceptual content in the manner of an expert (Chi, Glaser, & Rees, 1981). A detailed representation of a learner's conceptual understanding of a domain can now be inferred with a method developed over the past 12 years and guided by five basic assumptions (Goldsmith, Johnson, & Acton, 1991). First, conceptual knowledge involves an understanding of how the important concepts within a domain are interrelated. Second, as individuals move toward expertise within a domain, they begin to share a core understanding. Third, with the appropriate techniques this understanding can be objectively elicited and represented. Fourth, once an "expert representation" of a domain has been defined, it can be used as a referent to assess students' conceptual understanding of the domain. Fifth, the structural organization of these representations becomes more internally consistent or coherent with expertise.

These assumptions served as the basis for a methodology to study the conceptual representations of domain knowledge that involves elicitation, representation, and evaluation. Knowledge is elicited by simply having students and experts rate the relatedness of pairs of those concepts that are deemed most important on the basis of textbooks and experts' input. To derive a representation, one submits the matrix of proximity data from these ratings to the Pathfinder scaling algorithm (Schvaneveldt, 1990; see also chap. 16, this volume), which generates a connected graph of the concepts. The sophistication of each student's graph is then evaluated in terms of its graph similarity (SIM) to an expert network and its internal consistency or coherence (Goldsmith & Davenport, 1990), which is measured in terms of minimizing the frequency of triangle inequalities (e.g., if A is close to B and B is close to C, then A should be close to C).

A *coherence score* is defined as the correlation between an individual's ratings of similarity and a set-theoretic measure of concept similarity. The latter refers to similarity in the neighborhoods of a pair of concepts. It is based on the ratio of the intersection of common neighbors divided by the union of the two sets. For example, if Concept A has Concepts C, D, E, and F as neighbors, and Concept B has C, D, E, and G as neighbors, then the intersection of common neighbors is 3, and the union is 5, resulting in a similarity of .6. For a domain of concepts, a set-theoretic measure is computed on all pairs of concepts, and this value is correlated with the raw rating of similarity to provide a coherence score.

The Validity Issue

These methods are effective and reliable in mapping a learner's domain knowledge. In addition, the knowledge networks generated by Pathfinder are extremely effective means of communicating the relational structure among concepts (Smith, Best, Stubbs, Bastiani, & Roberson-Nay, 2002). Moreover, the knowledge networks have good face validity with experts and communicate clearly to students how their understanding compares with an expert's. However, there remained two important questions regarding the validity of the measures. First, do SIM and coherence scores truly measure conceptual understanding, and, second, why is this kind of domain-specific knowledge important?

Some support for the validity of these measures was provided by the finding that SIM and coherence scores increased with expertise. SIM was tracked in the statistics domain using the same set of concepts across several courses: from introductory to an advanced undergraduate and graduate-level statistics classes. The results showed that the average SIM and coherence score increased with expertise (Acton, Johnson, & Goldsmith, 1994). Further, exam performance was positively correlated with SIM and coherence across several classroom domains, including statistics, cognitive psychology, computer programming, and research techniques (Johnson, Goldsmith, & Teague, 1995). However, to demonstrate that SIM and coherence are truly measures of conceptual understanding and that conceptual understanding is an important type of knowledge, we need a domain in which competence requires both a conceptual and a nonconceptual type of knowledge.

The College Algebra Domain

In examining the content of algebra exams, it appeared that performance was almost entirely based on computational skills in which students were simply required to apply a rote-learned algorithm to familiar class problems. This conjecture was supported by the math education literature in which a number of educators and researchers believe there is far too much of an emphasis on computational skills to the neglect of a conceptual understanding (Bransford, Brown, & Cocking, 1999). Moreover, the magnitude of the correlations between SIM and exam performance (.25) was considerably lower for a college algebra course than an upper-division cognitive class.

It was hypothesized that to solve novel problems in algebra requires a conceptual network of the relationships among the important semantic concepts in algebra that presumably mediates the relationship between algebra problems and the algorithms used to solve the various problems. Thus, to be competent in algebra, a student must not only possess basic computational skills but also have a well-formed knowledge network of core algebra concepts and then have problem-specific concepts linked appropriately to this knowledge network.

Kristin Umland, a math professor at the University of New Mexico, compiled a library of conceptual types of questions while authoring a college algebra textbook (Umland, 2002). One conceptual class is word problems, which Polya (1962) believed required the single most important ability in secondary school math instruction. This is the ability to set up the equations to solve the problems. The task of translating a real situation into mathematical terms that

allow for algorithmic solution is where most students have the greatest difficulty, as evidenced by chemistry and physics faculty lamenting students' inability to understand basic algebraic applications. A second class of problems
required some type of translation, for example, is $\{f(x) = 2 - 3x\}$ a linear
function? Both of these conceptual types of problems differed from nonconceptual, purely computational problems in that they were judged by experts to
relate to more of the semantic concepts in the algebra domain.

If conceptual knowledge mediates the transfer of computational skills,
then it should be possible to demonstrate that SIM and coherence are predictive
of better performance on word problems and algebra problems with novel
surface structures. Most important, it is predicted that transfer of algebra
competence to novel contexts, such as higher math or physics courses, will be
superior for students with better conceptual understanding.

The SIM and coherence measures provide a theoretically grounded means
of defining conceptual understanding within a specific domain. Without a detailed representation of conceptual understanding, it is difficult to tell when
thinking skills will transfer to novel situations. We argue that these measures
have wide applicability in specifying a uniquely important property of an individual's knowledge in a given domain.

Domain-Specific Categories in Reasoning

Given that one can assess an individual's conceptual understanding of a domain, how do the acquired categories shape thinking skills, such as reasoning?
This section addresses how the representation of geographic knowledge in
relatively abstract, nonoverlapping categories affects geographic reasoning and
influences the biases observed in people's location judgments.

Geographical Categories

In most of the experiments on this topic, people were asked for their most
accurate estimates of the latitudes of various cities around the world, after
being reminded of the metric. When the data were plotted in order of the mean
estimated latitude for each city, clear categories and subcategories emerged
on both sides of the Atlantic, with boundary zones between them and little
discrimination among the locations of the cities within them (Friedman &
Brown, 2000a, 2000b). These two features were taken as the hallmarks of
regionalization.

To determine whether the regions had functional significance for geographical reasoning, two groups of people estimated latitudes of European and African cities (Friedman & Brown, 2000a). Their estimates showed clear breaks
between northern and southern Europe and between southern Europe and
northern Africa, and both southern European and African cities were underesti-
mated to a large degree. They were then provided with seed facts: One group
learned that Lisbon and Athens are at 39 and 38 degrees of latitude, respectively, and the other learned that Tunis and Algiers are both at 37 degrees.

Thus, both groups were given nearly identical information, but the implications were different for each region. In particular, when a person learns that the real latitude of Tunis is further north than he or she initially thought, it implies that the southern boundary of Europe must also be further north. But learning that they misjudged Athens carries no necessary implications about the northern boundary of Africa. In line with these implications, African seeds affected both southern European and African estimates, whereas southern European seeds affected only European estimates.

Friedman and Brown's (2000b) findings further showed that the regions may be linked according to their real or imagined conceptual similarity, even if they are many miles apart. Location estimates for cities in the Old and New World made before and after people received seed facts from the southern subregions of either Europe or the United States were compared. The numerical information in the seed facts was again identical. As hypothesized, the cities in North America and Europe were conceptually linked, with the seeds from the Old World affecting estimates in the New World and vice versa. Thus, when people learned the actual location of Athens and Lisbon, they moved both southern Europe and the southern United States north and vice versa.

Reinterpreting Tversky's Finding

The discovery that geographic representations of separate northern and southern regions were coordinated across the Atlantic led to the reexamination of one of the seminal findings in the spatial cognition literature. Tversky (1981) published an experiment in which people made bearing estimates between cities in North America and Europe. About 60% of American university students presented with five pairs of cities placed the European city to the south of the U.S. city when, in fact, the cities within each pair were located at about the same actual latitude. The classic view of this finding is that the bias to locate European cities to the south of their North American counterparts occurs because of a seriously distorted representation of the relative size, shape, and location of continents around the globe. The distortion is alleged to occur through the unconscious application of an "alignment heuristic" based on the Gestalt principle of physical proximity. The shapes of Europe and North America are "straightened" so that, for example, Rome is moved south of Chicago when in fact they are at the same actual latitude. But Tversky's finding might have been due to a serendipitous pairing of cities from what was discovered to be the northern region of the United States with cities from Mediterranean Europe, or cities from the southern region of the United States with cities from north Africa. In fact, this situation characterized four of the five original stimulus pairs.

To test this interpretation, researchers conducted two experiments using the bearing estimate paradigm (Friedman, Brown, & McGaffey, 2002). The conditions were defined by the factorial combination of cities selected in the northern and southern regions of the United States and the northern and southern regions of Europe. If regionalization and conceptual coordination rather than perceptual distortion account for the tendency to place North

American cities to the north of European cities at the same latitude, then that pattern should appear in only the northern United States–southern Europe condition. The results verified this prediction and constrained Tversky's interpretation.

Cross-Cultural Comparisons of Domain-Specific Reasoning

At this point, it was of interest to examine what was causing some of the biases repeatedly observed. In all the cases thus far, there was a clear tendency for estimates to become more biased as the cities being estimated were located increasingly further south. Because all the subjects had been Canadians, a physical proximity hypothesis was first entertained: Estimation bias should increase with increasing physical distance from one's own home region, in part because similarity decreases and uncertainty increases with increasing distance from a landmark.

The most direct way to distinguish this hypothesis from virtually any other alternative was to have people who live in different places estimate the same locations. Thus, Canadians from Edmonton, Alberta, and Americans from San Marcos, Texas, estimated latitudes of 10 cities in each of the four major regions of North America (Friedman, Kerkman, & Brown, 2002). If proximity is the primary cause of bias in estimated locations, Texans should be relatively less biased in their estimates of locations in the southern United States and Mexico but more biased in their estimates of locations in Canada. But instead, the Texan data looked very similar to the Albertan data in two important respects: There were the same four regions, and the largest bias was to the Mexican estimates.

Recently, university students from Ciudad del Victoria, Mexico, which is about the same distance from the border as San Marcos, were tested (Kerkman, Friedman, Brown, Stea, & Carmichael, 2003). The Mexicans looked like the Texans in their estimates for Canadian cities and like the Canadians in their estimates of most of the Mexican locations. Unlike either group, the Mexicans did not distinguish between the northern and southern U.S. regions and were also relatively accurate about the locations of a few cities in northern Mexico. But all three groups still placed the majority of Mexican cities at or below the equator. Because it is unlikely that the three sets of subjects were using different estimation strategies, the data imply that the physical proximity hypothesis—intuitive as it seems—is simply wrong.

In conclusion, geographical knowledge comes from a variety of sources learned over the life span. These sources result in an aggregate representation that is primarily discrete, region based, accurate in some respects, and biased in others. Geographic knowledge not only is about where things are located but also includes information about climate, agriculture, politics, time zones, and so on. Further, people have beliefs about the placement of regions and subregions relative to global landmarks (e.g., the equator and poles) and about a city's regional membership. These beliefs feed plausible reasoning processes to yield judgments about geography.

Domain Expertise and the Limits of Working Memory

Domain-specific knowledge not only shapes reasoning in distinct ways but also alleviates a central constraint on effective thinking: namely, the limited resources of working memory. Our third point is well-illustrated in a writing task, because composing an effective text is a major intellectual challenge. It demands the language skills of comprehension and production as well as the thinking skills of problem solving, reasoning, and decision making. Writing skill is the single best predictor of student achievement in college freshmen (Geiser & Studley, 2001), perhaps because it involves so many intellectual abilities. This section briefly documents that writing processes overload working memory and suggests that domain expertise can alleviate this demand through automatic access to domain-specific knowledge stored in long-term memory.

Overloading Working Memory

The architecture of working memory involves multiple components that temporarily store specific types of information and a set of executive attentional functions that control these (Jonides & Smith, 1997). These include (a) a verbal component that stores and rehearses phonologically coded words, (b) a semantic component that stores the meaning of words and objects, (c) a visual component that stores perceptual appearances of objects, and (d) a spatial component that stores the locations of objects in space. Executive functions include focusing attention, response scheduling, inhibiting alternative responses, and retrieval from long-term memory.

The demands of writing on executive functions can be assessed by measuring reaction time (RT) to an auditory probe presented during writing. The secondary RT task competes with writing processes for executive functions, such as focusing attention and scheduling a response. Increases in RT during writing in relation to baseline, single-task RT measurements index the degree of momentary cognitive effort required by writing processes. The more RT interference, the more momentary cognitive effort these processes consume. The data show that planning conceptual content, generating sentences, and reviewing the conceptual content and language already produced are highly effortful. Writing processes cause markedly greater RT interference compared with incidental and intentional learning of word lists and reading simple and complex syntactic constructions (Kellogg, 1994).

Further, the mean length of written sentences in a text systematically declines as the concurrent load on working memory increases (Ransdell, Levy, & Kellogg, 2002). Irrelevant speech occupies the phonological store of verbal working memory but reduces sentence length only slightly until writers are forced to pay attention to the speech to detect embedded targets. The largest drop in sentence length is found when both the executive and the verbal components of working memory are heavily loaded by the requirement to store and rehearse six digits.

Long-Term Working Memory

Ericsson and Kintsch (1995) proposed a domain-specific expansion of working memory called *long-term working memory*. Experts in a domain develop retrieval structures that allow rapid and reliable access to knowledge required for task performance. The classic short-term working memory system needs only to maintain the necessary retrieval cues for ready access to domain-specific knowledge. They reviewed findings showing that concurrent tasks that use the transient components of working memory do not interfere with an expert's access to long-term memory. Thus, writers skilled in a particular topic domain could retrieve propositions from long-term memory without adding to the burden on short-term working memory.

One interpretation of such findings is that retrieval from long-term memory for experts in a domain is automatic. The effort to retrieve information stored in long-term memory can be a conscious, effortful process that shares the frontal lobe circuitry associated with executive attention (Cabeza et al., 2003). Craik, Govoni, Naveh-Benjamin, and Anderson (1996) found that retrieval markedly interferes with RT to a secondary task. However, the process dissociation procedure has identified automatic retrieval processes as well (Kane, Picton, Moscovitch, & Winocur, 2000). Unlike conscious retrieval, automatic memory retrieval does not activate frontal regions and presumably would not interfere with a secondary RT task.

The semantic, verbal, and possibly other components of working memory are arguably needed to maintain representations temporarily for planning conceptual content, linguistically encoding this content, and monitoring the developing text. The ability to retrieve information automatically from long-term memory without further straining transient working memory would provide a significant advantage to domain experts. If so, then one would expect less RT interference to the tone detection task for high-knowledge compared with low-knowledge writers.

Some evidence now supports this view (Kellogg, 2001). College students wrote narratives describing a half-inning of a baseball game. In Experiment 1, subjects were divided into high and low verbal ability crossed with high and low baseball knowledge. As expected, a high degree of domain knowledge facilitated elaboration of the conceptual content planned by the writer. The narratives contained more game actions and relevant-nongame actions for high-knowledge compared with low-knowledge writers. By contrast, the low-knowledge writers generated texts with a high proportion of irrelevant nongame actions. It made no difference whether the writers were high or low in verbal ability for these effects to emerge, whereas the opposite pattern held for an analysis of grammatical errors. Low-verbal writers generated more errors overall than did high-verbal writers. Thus, verbal ability and domain knowledge appeared to make unique contributions to the writing task, and reliable, independent effects were obtained for these factors in judges' ratings of the quality of the texts.

These effects were replicated in Experiment 2 in which secondary RT was measured as writers composed. If relevant knowledge is retrieved directly from long-term memory rather than maintained in working memory during composition, then high-knowledge writers ought to show less RT interference compared with low-knowledge writers. The results verified this prediction. Individuals with domain expertise, regardless of their verbal ability, were able to write a text with less load on the executive functions of working memory than that experienced by novices. Domain knowledge, therefore, helps to overcome a major constraint on writing skill, the limited capacity of working memory.

Modeling the Shift to Memory Retrieval

Expertise in a domain, then, can reduce the need to carry out all processing steps in a controlled manner within working memory. Retrieval from long-term memory is an alternative, single-step solution to problems that may require multiple computations when thought out in working memory. For example, in mentally adding 8 + 12, one could compute the answer for the units column, carry the 1 to the tens column and arrive at the solution. With sufficient practice, one might retrieve the solution from long-term memory and avoid computations in working memory. A number of studies have shown that practice in a specific task causes a shift from multistep, algorithmic processing to single-step, memory-based processing. Tasks exhibiting this effect include arithmetic, mnemonically mediated retrieval (Rickard & Bajic, 2003), element counting (Palmeri, 1999), and word reading (Tao & Healy, 2002), among many others. Although this strategy shift appears to be one of the more common effects of practice, it has been studied directly only recently, starting with seminal work by Logan (1988; also chap. 10, this volume) and Siegler (e.g., Siegler & Shrager, 1984).

Attentional Demands of Retrieval

An ongoing theoretical debate concerns the nature of strategy execution in such tasks. On the one hand, several theorists have argued that memory retrieval is an automatic process that can be executed in parallel with other more controlled processes (e.g., Logan, 1988). The simplest version of such a model assumes a race between the two strategies, with each strategy being executed with the same speed and accuracy as if it were executed by itself. As formally developed to date, these models assume that memory retrieval gradually becomes faster with practice, eventually replacing the algorithm as the winning strategy in a probabilistic fashion over the course of multiple performance trials. This gradual strategy replacement model predicts that the overall speedup curve for an item follows a smooth function such as a power function or some other similar function (Palmeri, 1999; Rickard, 2004).

On the other hand, there may be a fundamental attentional limitation that precludes parallel execution of algorithm and retrieval strategies, at least prior to extensive practice (Rickard, 1997, 2004). Retrieval can require executive attention, as noted in the previous section. Given an attentional limitation, either the algorithm is selected and the retrieval strategy is completely suppressed or retrieval is selected and the algorithm is completely suppressed. In the *component power laws* (CMPL) simulation model, the algorithm solely determines performance for the first n practice trials. However, the association that supports memory retrieval gradually strengthens over trials for each item. On Trial $n + 1$, the retrieval strategy is strong enough to win the early-stage competition with the algorithm, and it continues to govern performance exclusively thereafter.

The CMPL simulation model generates power function expected value speedup for the memory retrieval strategy. Ignoring the asymptote parameter, the equation is

$$\mu_{retrieval} = b*(n - 1)^{-c}, \tag{1}$$

where b and c are parameters of the power function, and n is the trial number. The model also allows for power function speedup in execution of the algorithm with practice. However, provided that the algorithm does not speed up much with practice, a simplified CMPL equation governing overall speedup in the population mean, $\mu_{overall}$, is

$$\mu_{overall} = \mu_{algorithm} \text{ if } n < shift, \text{ (algorithm trials)} \tag{2}$$
$$\mu_{overall} = b(n - 1)^{-c} \text{ if } n \geq shift, \text{ (retrieval trials)}$$

Here, *shift* refers to the first practice trial on which the retrieval strategy is selected. This equation is depicted graphically in Figure 1.1. Its most prominent feature is the step-function RT drop at the point of the strategy shift. Provided that the algorithm is sufficiently time consuming, the model must predict this abrupt RT shift for expected RTs for each item, although the trial number of the shift should vary over items and subjects. Also shown in Figure 1.1 are curves generated from a gradual strategy replacement model, with five free parameters, which is based on Logan's (1988; see also Palmeri, 1999) instance theory (see Rickard, 2004, for more details). Clearly, at the level of individual item speedup curves, the strategy selection and gradual strategy replacement models make very distinct predictions.

The Law of Practice

The law of practice, then, may be best modeled as a step function rather than the smooth function traditionally assumed. The CMPL versus strategy race predictions were tested using a serial addition task. On each trial, subjects were first presented with a letter cue. Beneath the letter, five digits were then sequentially presented at a rate of about one digit per second, followed by a question mark that prompted a vocal response. For each of the 10 letter cues, the answer to the serial addition was the same throughout all practice trials, although the particular digits that were presented varied from trial to trial for each letter to prevent any anticipatory transition to retrieval based on

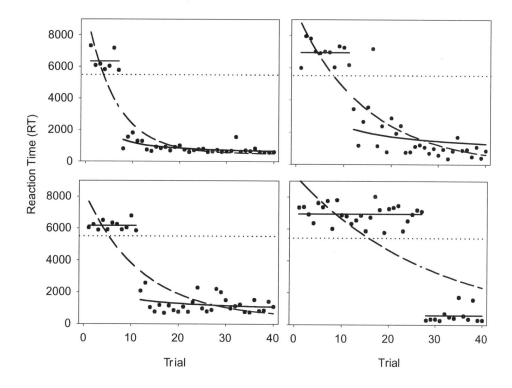

Figure 1.1. Four example item speedup curves, along with the best fits of the component power laws or CMPL (solid line) and strategy race or gradual strategy replacement models (dashed line). The horizontal dotted line represents the fastest possible performance on the algorithm.

intermediate sums arrived at during the serial addition. Thus, there are only two ways to complete these problems: (a) use of the algorithm as originally taught or (b) retrieval of the response, using the letter as the only effective cue.

Results for four example item speedup curves (these are raw data with no averaging), along with the best fits of the CMPL and strategy race models, are shown in Figure 1.1. Pronounced step-function RT drops are clearly evident, and the fit of the CMPL model is good. These visual patterns held for most items, and for 202 of the 220 items the r^2 value was higher for the CMPL model fit. For this task at least, a strategy selection model such as CMPL provides the better account.

The step-function RT shifts observed here also have implications for the long-running effort by psychologists to discover a universal empirical law of practice. All functions that have been proposed to date, most prominently the power and exponential functions, have predicted smooth speedup throughout practice for any task. The current results appear to eliminate all of those candidate functions. Rather, a step-function speedup parameter must be included in any truly general practice law.

Conclusion

Lyle E. Bourne, Jr., has championed the study of intellectual skills throughout his career. In recent years, he and his collaborators have shown the degree to which such skills depend on domain-specific knowledge. Highly durable skills require reinstating the learning context of a specific task at the time of retrieval. Here, we have extended this view in four ways by drawing on evidence from different labs, tasks, and domains.

First, it should be possible with existing methods to measure reliably and validly conceptual structures in a specific knowledge domain. Second, the categories of a particular domain strongly influence reasoning and other thinking skills. Third, thinking skills make heavy demands on working memory, but the automatic retrieval of domain-specific knowledge from long-term memory gives experts an edge. Fourth, as skill in a domain advances with practice, the shift to a memory retrieval strategy may be best modeled by a step function rather than the smooth function typically assumed. We conjecture that testing all four hypotheses in a single task and domain would significantly advance the science of intellectual skills.

References

Acton, W. H., Johnson, P. J., & Goldsmith, T. E. (1994). Structural knowledge assessment: Comparison of referent structures. *Journal of Educational Psychology, 85*, 88–96.

Bourne, L. E., Jr. (1966). *Human conceptual behavior.* Boston: Allyn & Bacon.

Bransford, J. D., Brown, A. L., & Cocking, R. (1999). *How people learn: Brain, mind, experience, and school.* Washington, DC: National Academy Press.

Cabeza, R., Dolcos, F., Prince, S. E., Rice, H. J., Weissman, D. H., & Nyberg, L. (2003). Attention-related activity during episodic memory retrieval: A cross-function fMRI study. *Neuropsychologica, 41*, 390–399.

Chi, M. T. H., Glaser, R., & Rees, E. (1981). Expertise in problem solving. In R. J. Sternberg (Ed.), *Advances in development of human intelligence* (Vol. 1, pp. 7–75). Hillsdale, NJ: Erlbaum.

Craik, F. I. M., Govoni, R., Naveh-Benjamin, M., & Anderson, N. D. (1996). The effects of divided attention on encoding and retrieval processes in human memory. *Journal of Experimental Psychology: General, 125*, 159–180.

Ericsson, K. A., & Kintsch, W. (1995). Long-term working memory. *Psychological Review, 102*, 211–245.

Friedman, A., & Brown, N. R. (2000a). Reasoning about geography. *Journal of Experimental Psychology: General, 129*, 193–219.

Friedman, A., & Brown, N. R. (2000b). Updating geographical knowledge: Principles of coherence and inertia. *Journal of Experimental Psychology: Learning, Memory, and Cognition, 26*, 900–914.

Friedman, A., Brown, N., & McGaffey, A. (2002). A basis for bias in geographical judgments. *Psychonomic Bulletin & Review, 9*, 151–159.

Friedman, A., Kerkman, D. D., & Brown, N. (2002). Spatial location judgments: A cross-national comparison of estimation bias in subjective North American geography. *Psychonomic Bulletin & Review, 9*, 615–623.

Geiser, S., & Studley, R. (2001). *UC and the SAT: Predictive validity and differential impact of the SAT I and SAT II at the University of California.* Retrieved March 15, 2002, from http://www.ucop.edu/sas/research/researchandplanning/pdf/sat—study.pdf

Goldsmith, T. E., & Davenport, D. (1990). Assessing structural similarity of graphs. In R. Schvaneveldt (Ed.), *Pathfinder associative networks: Studies in knowledge organization* (pp. 75–86). Norwood, NJ: Ablex.

Goldsmith, T. E., Johnson, P. J., & Acton, W. H. (1991). Assessing structural knowledge. *Journal of Education Psychology, 83,* 88–96.

Healy, A. F., & Bourne, L. E., Jr. (Eds.). (1995). *Learning and memory of knowledge and skills: Durability and specificity.* Thousand Oaks, CA: Sage.

Healy, A. F., & Bourne, L. E., Jr. (Eds.). (1998). *Foreign language learning: Psycholinguistic studies on training and retention.* Mahwah, NJ: Erlbaum.

Johnson, P. J., Goldsmith, T. E., & Teague, K. W. (1995). Similarity, structure, and knowledge: A representational approach to assessment. In P. Nichols, S. Chipman, & R. L. Brennan (Eds.), *Cognitively diagnostic assessment* (pp. 221–249). Hillsdale, NJ: Erlbaum.

Jonides, J., & Smith, E. E. (1997). The architecture of working memory. In M. D. Rugg (Ed.), *Cognitive neuroscience* (pp. 243–276). Cambridge, MA: MIT Press.

Kane, K. A., Picton, T. W., Moscovitch, M., & Winocur, G. (2000). Event-related potentials during conscious and automatic memory retrieval. *Cognitive Brain Research, 10,* 19–35.

Kellogg, R. T. (1994). *The psychology of writing.* New York: Oxford University Press.

Kellogg, R. T. (2001). Long-term working memory in text production. *Memory & Cognition, 29,* 43–52.

Kerkman, D. D., Friedman, A., Brown, N. R., Stea, D., & Carmichael, A. (2003). The development of geographic categories and biases. *Journal of Experimental Child Psychology, 84,* 265–285.

Logan, G. D. (1988). Toward an instance theory of automatization. *Psychological Review, 95,* 492–527.

Palmeri, T. J. (1999). Theories of automaticity and the power law of practice. *Journal of Experimental Psychology: Learning, Memory, and Cognition, 25,* 543–551.

Polya, G. (1962). *Mathematical discovery* (Vol. 1.). New York: Wiley.

Ransdell, S., Levy, C. M., & Kellogg, R. T. (2002). The structure of writing processes as revealed by secondary task demands. *L1—Educational Studies in Language and Literature, 2,* 141–163.

Rickard, T. C. (1997). Bending the power law: A CMPL theory of strategy shifts and the automatization of cognitive skills. *Journal of Experimental Psychology: General, 126,* 288–311.

Rickard, T. C. (2004). Strategy execution in cognitive skill learning: An item-level test of parallel versus selection models. *Journal of Experimental Psychology: Learning, Memory, and Cognition, 30,* 65–82.

Rickard, T. C., & Bajic, D. (2003). Automatic mediation or absence of mediation: Commentary on Crutcher and Ericsson (2000). *Journal of Experimental Psychology: Learning, Memory, and Cognition, 29,* 1381–1386.

Schvaneveldt, R. W. (1990). *Pathfinder associative networks: Studies in knowledge organization.* Norwood, NJ: Ablex.

Siegler, R. S., & Shrager, J. (1984). A model of strategy choice. In C. Sophian (Ed.), *Origins of cognitive skills* (pp. 229–293). Hillsdale, NJ: Erlbaum.

Smith, L. D., Best, L. A., Stubbs, D. A., Bastiani, A. B., & Roberson-Nay, R. (2002). Constructing knowledge: The role of graphs and tables in hard and soft psychology. *American Psychologist, 57,* 749–761.

Tao, L., & Healy, A. F. (2002). The unitization effect in reading Chinese and English text. *Scientific Studies of Reading, 6,* 167–197.

Tversky, B. (1981). Distortions in memory for maps. *Cognitive Psychology, 13,* 407–433.

Umland, K. (2002). *College algebra.* Dubuque, IA: Kendall/Hunt.

2

Walter Kintsch:
A Psychology Beyond Words

Charles A. Weaver III, Janice M. Keenan,
Walter Perrig, and Vimla Patel

Were association norms—or in more contemporary terms, latent semantic analysis (LSA)—available for researchers, "Walter Kintsch" and "text comprehension" would clearly appear together. His models of comprehension remain widely cited and influential: His 1978 article with Teun van Dijk is arguably the most influential comprehension article of the past 30 years, but his academic achievements extend well beyond those publications. Although the depth of Kintsch's career in text comprehension is nothing less than breathtaking, the breadth of his career is just as impressive. In a career that spans more than 40 years, Kintsch published on an astonishing range of topics, and to focus exclusively on comprehension is to miss the scale of his contributions.

Kintsch began his professional life as a school teacher in Austria in the early 1950s, coming to the University of Kansas in 1955. Cognitive psychology as a discipline, of course, did not exist in the late 1950s, when Kintsch was pursuing his doctoral degree at Kansas. (Wilt Chamberlain was a record-setting basketball player at Kansas during the same years. There are numerous stories of how their paths crossed—they shared a dormitory, for example—and we are tempted to recount some of those. Given the inherent unreliability of reconstructive memory, however, these may best be left untold.) Unlike many of his 1960s' contemporaries, Kintsch's doctoral training was not in verbal learning but rather animal learning. Kintsch studied with Ed Wike (1922–1999) in the area of motivation and drive strength, at the time a very important issue in learning theory—and one in which cognitive factors played a clear role (Kintsch, 1962; Kintsch & Wike, 1957; Wike, Kintsch, & Remple, 1959). Kintsch's cognitive interests were undoubtedly influenced by this early training—Wike himself was a second-generation Tolman student, having earned his degree with H. C. Gilhousen at the University of California, Los Angeles. Gilhousen in turn completed his doctorate at Berkeley with Tolman in 1930.[1] It is worth noting

---

[1]To complete the lineage, Tolman was a student of Hugo Munsterberg, who was one of Wundt's first students.

that although Kintsch published with nearly 100 different coauthors, his most frequent remained Ed Wike.

Kintsch would continue to publish articles in animal learning and behavior as late as 1970 (Premack & Kintsch, 1970). His research career, however, changed significantly during and after his postdoctoral training with William Estes at Indiana University in 1961–1962. He became a mathematical psychologist, testing Markov models of verbal learning (Kintsch, 1963a; Kintsch & Morris, 1965) and also modeling reaction times of "observing behaviors" in two-alternative choice paradigms (Kintsch, 1963b).

After spending several years as an assistant and associate professor at the University of Missouri and the University of California, Riverside, as well as a year as visiting professor at Stanford in the late 1960s, Kintsch came to the University of Colorado as a full professor in 1968. It is tempting to consider the publication of *The Representation of Meaning in Memory* (Kintsch, 1974) as the beginning of the "Kintsch era." Nothing could be further from the truth. In addition to his work in mathematical modeling, Kintsch had also published one of the earliest textbooks in cognition (Kintsch, 1970) and several articles on short-term memory coding that remain widely cited to this day (Buschke & Kintsch, 1970; Kintsch & Buschke, 1969; Kintsch, Crothers, & Jorgensen, 1971). In fact, Kintsch's citation count for research published prior to 1974 is well over 1,250.[2] Figure 2.1 displays the number of citations to Kintsch's work as a function of year of publication of cited article.

The five-year period beginning with 1974 represents the most prolific phase of Kintsch's career. This period is bounded by the two most frequently cited publications of his career: *Representation of Meaning* and his 1978 *Psychological Review* article with Teun van Dijk (Kintsch & van Dijk, 1978). In keeping with the spirit of this section, the breadth of Kintsch's career, consider again the distribution in Figure 2.1. The most striking feature about the figure may be the consistency it reflects. The sustained level of productivity, as well as the quality of the research, is nothing short of remarkable.

The arrows in Figure 2.1 indicate especially significant contributions. Several of these papers deal directly with discourse understanding: *The Representation of Meaning* (Kintsch, 1974), Kintsch's 1978 article with van Dijk (Kintsch & van Dijk, 1978), *Strategies of Discourse Comprehension* (van Dijk & Kintsch, 1983), his 1988 *Psychological Review* article on the construction–integration model (Kintsch, 1988), and most recently, the book *Comprehension* (Kintsch, 1998). Others, however, do not deal with text comprehension directly: *Learning, Memory, and Conceptual Processes* (Kintsch, 1970), Kintsch's article with Walter Perrig on spatial representations in memory (Perrig & Kintsch, 1985), his article with Jim Greeno proposing a model of word arithmetic problem solving (Kintsch & Greeno, 1985), and his article on long-term working memory with Anders Ericsson (Ericsson & Kintsch, 1995).

---

[2] All citation figures in this chapter are taken from ISI's Web of Knowledge, which searches both the Science Citation Index Expanded and the Social Science Citation Index, and are accurate as of May 2003. The citations are categorized by year of publication of the original paper and not year of citation. As a result, more recent papers will inevitably show fewer citations.

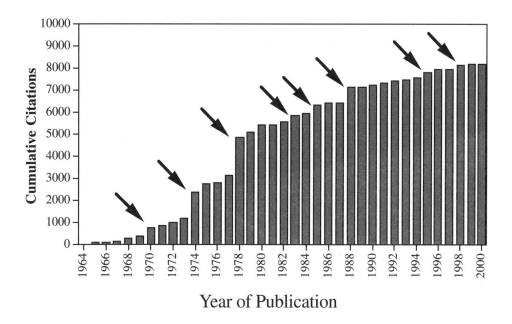

Figure 2.1. Cumulative number of citations as a function of year of publication, 1964–2000. The arrows indicate especially significant contributions.

From Propositions to Latent Semantic Analysis: The Leading Edge of Text Comprehension

One of the impressive things about Walter Kintsch is how he has been on the cutting edge of research throughout his career; in fact, in many cases his work has defined the cutting edge of comprehension research. In his model with van Dijk (Kintsch & van Dijk, 1978), he developed the *leading-edge strategy* for selecting and maintaining propositions in working memory during text comprehension. Leading-edge strategy would also be a very good name for Kintsch's career. The goal of this section is to illustrate this for his work on the representation of meaning from propositions LSA.

In the 1960s, the fact that we use language to socially connect with each other and to convey meaning was considered of much less interest, believe it or not, than the structural properties of language focused on by Chomsky and his associates (Chomsky, 1957, 1964). The Chomskyites were awed by syntax: (a) the novelty of word combinations—that is, the fact that most of the sentences we speak have never before been uttered; and (b) the recursive nature of those combinations—embeddings. But Kintsch clearly saw that, at least as psychologists, the focus needed to be more on *meaning*: How do we use language to convey thoughts? So, whereas many psycholinguists were spending their time examining the psychological reality of transformational grammar, Kintsch was opening the door to semantics—the nature of semantic memory and the units of representing meaning (Kintsch, 1974).

There were a handful of other cognitive psychologists who joined Kintsch in this semantic enterprise (Norman, 1970). What is interesting, however, is that the propositions that others proposed were still quite tied to syntactic structures; for example, Anderson and Bower's (1973) propositions in their human associative memory model represented syntactic categories, such as subject and object. Kintsch was the one who recognized the importance of having semantic relations, such as agent and instrument, in these semantic units (Kintsch, 1974; Kintsch & Keenan, 1973). Eventually, the rest of the field followed in his footsteps.

Until the 1970s, list learning was the primary paradigm for studying language—or verbal behavior, as it was called. But with the advent of propositional representations, researchers began examining comprehension and memory for whole sentences, not just pairs of associates. Most researchers were content to study comprehension with just single sentences, some of which were very thought-provoking stimuli, such as "The hippie in the park touched the debutante" (Anderson & Bower, 1973). But Kintsch recognized the importance of studying comprehension of real discourses. So, while Anderson and Bower had people reading about their hippie in the park, Kintsch was examining comprehension and memory for slightly more literary pieces, such as Boccaccio's *Decameron* (Kintsch, 1977), as well as soap operas (Bates, Kintsch, Fletcher, & Giuliani, 1980) and even jokes in his lectures (Kintsch & Bates, 1977)!

Kintsch was not just trying to be more literary or more relevant. By using such complex stimuli, he was taking on difficult issues that only arise when one moves beyond single sentences. This includes issues such as coherence: How do sentence meanings connect? Kintsch (1974) offered the field its first theory of coherence; he proposed that coherence is based on connecting propositions using argument repetition, that is, coreference. That gave other investigators an easy method of representing complex texts, and it helped move the field beyond single sentence studies to more discourse studies. Ultimately, the field came to recognize the importance of other types of coherence (Zwaan & Radvansky, 1998), but Kintsch's theory was the first clearly formulated proposal for coherence that could be subjected to experimental test.

Another issue that arises with connected discourse is the memory problem: How are all those meanings of sentences that occur early in a text retained in memory to connect with later sentences? The Kintsch and van Dijk (1978) model dealt with this question by postulating processing cycles and mechanisms for (a) selecting and maintaining propositions in working memory and (b) reinstating others. Whereas previous theorizing about text comprehension focused on the nature of the representation of meaning, Kintsch and van Dijk gave the field its first process model of comprehension for complex texts. This model represented a significant milestone in the study of discourse processing as it shifted the field from thinking about language as an object of analysis to language as process. The significance of the contribution is shown by the large number of citations it received (see Figure 2.1, second arrow), more than 1,200.

The Kintsch and van Dijk (1978) model gave the field not only its first process model but also the first simulations of complex text processing. Furthermore, the simulations opened the door to another first: the study of individual differences in comprehension. The simulations showed how the size of the "short-term memory buffer" affected the nature of inference and reinstatement processes needed for comprehension. These demonstrations of how differences in working memory capacity might affect comprehension led to a number of empirical studies of individual differences (such as Daneman & Carpenter, 1980), and it made people think about how other individual differences (e.g., inhibitory mechanisms) might affect comprehension (Gernsbacher, 1990).

In the early 1980s, the notion of mental models emerged in cognitive science, and van Dijk and Kintsch (1983) incorporated mental models into text comprehension, what they termed *situation models*. This helped bring about another very significant shift in how we think about discourse comprehension: a shift from thinking of the goal of comprehension as building a representation of the text to thinking of it as building a representation of the speaker's *knowledge*—what the speaker or writer intended the text to be about. This mental models view led to many advances in the field, such as how the notion of coherence was understood (see Graesser, Singer, & Trabasso, 1994; Keenan, Baillet, & Brown, 1984; Trabasso & van den Broek, 1985), and it accounted for previously difficult-to-explain phenomena, such as the fact that implicit information can be as easy to process as explicit information when two people know each other well and just a few words function to activate the appropriate knowledge. (Situation models are discussed extensively in the next section of this chapter.)

Kintsch has always taken a computational approach to comprehension: specifying processes in great detail and then building simulations to test them. He did that with the Kintsch and van Dijk model in 1978 and then again in 1988 with the construction–integration (C-I) model (Kintsch, 1988). The C-I model was important because it moved the field to begin incorporating principles of neural modeling and constraint satisfaction into discourse processes. It also laid the groundwork for Kintsch's recent work using LSA, an information retrieval technique developed for language processing by Tom Landauer and colleagues (see Landauer, Foltz, & Laham, 1998). Kintsch's book, *Comprehension* (1998), showed how the combination of the C-I model and LSA provided not only a theory of comprehension but also a paradigm for almost all of cognition—the grand theory! As if this was not enough, the incorporation of LSA into his theorizing has also led to some important efforts to use technology to improve reading instruction and assessment, the *Summary Street*.

This brief summary of Kintsch's comprehension research has illustrated how theoretically groundbreaking his work has been. What is important to note is that along the way many of these theoretical advances have also contributed significantly to solutions for practical problems. In other words, Kintsch's recent contributions to applied research are just the latest manifestation of a trend throughout his career. To give but one example, Kintsch offered a more meaningful way of assessing the readability of texts; he showed that coherence gaps and the load on working memory accounted for more of the difficulties in reading than previous formulas that merely considered the length of sentences and the frequency of words (Kintsch & Vipond, 1979).

Kintsch's contributions to applied research extend beyond his own efforts. To illustrate, consider these examples from Jan Keenan's laboratory of two 10-year-old children reading a sentence from the Grey Oral Reading Test (Wieder-holt & Bryant, 1992):

> Original sentence: Many American farm workers have been aided by the efforts of a shy, patient man named Cesar Chavez.
> Dyslexic child: Many American farm workers have been . . . *avev* . . . by ( ) efforts *for, for* a shy *parent* man named *Custer Cavez*. (Sentence reading time = 17 seconds)
> Comprehension deficit child: Many American farm workers have been aided by the efforts of a shy, patient man named Cesar. . . Chavez. (Sentence reading time = 9 seconds)

The dyslexic child depicted above has a word decoding ability that puts him in the lowest 4% of 10-year-olds. Accordingly, his reading is not fluent, has mispronunciations, and skipped words. This is an example of the classic reading disabled child. But thanks to the kind of research that Kintsch has done over the years, we are now identifying another class of poor readers. These children have no apparent reading problems because when they decode, they sound just fine. But, their comprehension suffers! The child labeled *comprehension deficit* (see Oakhill, Yuill, & Parkin, 1986) reads beautifully, yet she scored considerably lower (1 year 7 months) than the struggling dyslexic child on comprehension. Currently, these children do not get services because they sound so good. Thanks to research like Kintsch's, we hope to change that. He has given us (a) a theory that can help us examine component skills that may be underlying comprehension deficits, (b) methods for studying these children, and (c) potential methods for remediation, such as those incorporated in the *Summary Street* project.

Walter Kintsch's Concept of Situation Models

As noted earlier, van Dijk and Kintsch (1983) introduced the notion of situation models to discourse comprehension. In this cognitive model of discourse understanding, the reader learned about the relevance of morphology, syntax, semantics, and pragmatics. The theory, however, focused on the *understanding* from words to the understanding of clauses to complex sentences to sequences of sentences, and finally the overall textual structures. Most important, the model stressed a *functional* view, in which the reader's strategic behavior produces a stream of working hypotheses that are continuously changed, not by textual characteristics but by characteristics of the language user, such as his or her goals or world knowledge.

Situation models represent "events, actions, persons, and in general the situation, a text is about" (van Dijk & Kintsch, 1983, pp. 11–12). Situation models go beyond semantic analysis of words and verbal structures, incorporating previous experience from episodic and semantic memory. They also incorporate the context of the reading situation, given social constraints, and task demands.

The most important argument for introducing situation models into a model of discourse processing is related to their referential functions: the connection between the words in text and the world the text is about. This reference basis fills in the gaps in text where things remain unsaid, build up coherence and coreference, and allow adequate inferences. In general, situation models establish the communicative context necessary to understand what is meant by the words. Most important, situation models bring in knowledge about space and time. Thus, the explanatory power of the situation model is enormous.

As van Dijk and Kintsch (1983) acknowledged, the idea of a situational representation was not entirely new (see Clark & Marshall, 1978; Johnson-Laird, 1980; Kamp, 1981; Karttunen, 1976; Petöfi, 1982). If one traces the notion of situation models in the literature, one is confronted with two impressive facts: the quantity of citations and the diversity in the research domains in which the concept seems to play a valuable role. A PsycINFO search was conducted for the following terms: KINTSCH (AND) SITUATION* MODEL*. The search, restricted for journal articles that use the target words in title or abstract only, identified the following articles: Perrig and Kintsch (1985); Nathan, Kintsch, and Young (1992); Haenggi, Kintsch, and Gernsbacher (1995); McNamara, Kintsch, Songer, and Kintsch (1996); and Singer and Kintsch (2001).

Note several key findings. First, Kintsch's situation model work was updated regularly over the last 20 years. Second, these articles have very different objectives and approaches. Several focus on the representational view in text processing, distinguishing different levels within situation models (Haenggi et al., 1995; Perrig & Kintsch, 1985). Other work involves educational and instructional aspects of reading and solving algebra–word problems (McNamara et al., 1996; Nathan et al., 1992). Finally, there is modeling work (Singer & Kintsch, 2001). By 2003, there are about 300 journal articles that cite at least one of these five articles, covering a variety of topics: comprehension; discourse and memory; problem solving; developmental aspects; individual differences; spatial representation; imagery; reading and inferences; algebraic and mathematical reasoning; assessment, instruction, and learning environments; computer-assisted learning; multimedia learning; understanding history; and the study of the neural basis of spatial representations (route vs. survey; positron emission tomography [PET], functional magnetic resonance imaging [fMRI]).

Why are Kintsch's situation models so attractive? First, the situation model in Kintsch's work never comes alone as an isolated construct. A situation model is an element in a larger conceptual framework. In laying out the conceptual framework to study the phenomenon, Kintsch is not avoiding complexity: Many dimensions and their interactions are responsible for some final outcome in behavior. Despite this complexity—or maybe rather because of it—he is always clear and precise in what he is thinking theoretically and investigating empirically. And maybe even more important, he is equally clear and honest about restrictions and problems he cannot, or will not, solve.

Because situational knowledge is built up by experience, it deals with "embodied" cognition—knowledge that is mediated by the sensory system, by our phenomenal conscious feelings, perceptions, cognizing, and insight. For example, when reading a survey text or a route text, both describing the same spatial layout, the readers actually think of, or imagine, very different spatial scenarios. In the first case the readers take over the role of walking or driving through a spatial description; in the second case they are building up a mental map from a fixed perspective. The resulting representations differ in predictable ways, and memory performance in free recall, verification, and inference tasks vary as a function of the studied version (Perrig & Kintsch, 1985). From this experiential or phenomenological perspective, one can predict that verifying spatial configurations should become more difficult if one selects descriptions from an unfamiliar perspective. Results confirm this (Bachmann & Perrig, 1988, 1989). Even more interesting, readers are faster if the story is about a man driving through a village rather than walking through the same village. Likewise, the reader slows down when informed (in one single sentence) that the agent of a story who is heading for a date is confronted with a crowded street. Conversely, reading is speeded up if the reader is told that the agent is in a big hurry (Bachmann, Meier, & Perrig, 1990; Perrig & Bhend, 2003).

On what basis do these experiential mental processes and correlated behavior operate? Consider one study (Shelton & Gabrieli, 2002) in which researchers performed neuroimaging (fMRI) while subjects encode a spatial scenario, presented either in a route-film version or in a survey-film version. The same brain structures are activated in both film versions, but to different degrees. It is reasonable to assume that one could find similar activations in reading spatial descriptions.

Walter Kintsch says openly that the functioning of a knowledge base as rich as the situation model is difficult to model. To deal with the complexity, computers would be needed. But, he says "because computers are, by nature, very different from humans, they cannot interact with the world and learn from it in the way humans do. I see no solution to this dilemma" (Kintsch, 2000, p. 138). As a result, he often uses his world knowledge to predict behavior in experiments and to provide the inputs for formal simulations. Although readers could blame him for this subjectivity in his theorizing, few do; it is as if the scientific community understands that there are sound descriptions and solutions to understand better the phenomena in question. Just as Max Wertheimer (1945/1982) stated in the Gestalt tradition: Already common sense "feels the difference between these (ugly and senseless), and really sensible proceedings." The sensible proceedings are the ones that come close to the "insight into (the true) structural inner relatedness" of problems. In this sense, we believe, Kintsch is a real productive thinker in the "Gestalt" psychologist's sense.

Application of Kintsch's Research:
Making Sense of the Medical World

The medical world is a semantically complex and confusing place for patient and cognitive scientist alike. Communications between health professionals and patients do not inevitably lead to mutual understanding. Evidence suggests that the two subjects evolve rather different situation models. The challenge, then, is to understand these differences while attempting to develop a composite view of what the text of a dialogue is truly about.

Early problem-solving research in the medical domain was informative, but it was difficult to capture the complexity and inherent "messiness" of knowledge-rich domains within medicine. For example, early efforts in the study of medical text comprehension revealed no differences between experts' and novices' memory for text. Nearly 20 years ago Patel and Groen recognized, however, that a necessary first step was to characterize patient representations and knowledge organization (Groen & Patel, 1988; Patel & Groen, 1986). In addition, they believed that comprehension played a central role in all facets of expert performance, and their studies quickly showed that the initial understanding of a patient problem (i.e., early in a doctor–patient encounter) dictated the problem-solving maneuvers or reasoning steps that ensued.

Patel and Groen accordingly turned to the work of Walter Kintsch. First attempts by Patel and her colleagues to analyze medical texts using propositional analysis were met with skepticism. Medical texts were thought to be far too complex to be subjected to such analyses. Instead, Patel found that the unit of analysis in previous work on medical text comprehension from other laboratories had been too imprecise. Using Kintsch's propositional analysis, she reanalyzed the previous protocols. The reanalysis revealed significant and dramatic differences in recall and inferences not only as a function of expertise but also as a function of task difficulty. The power of Kintsch's theories was clear in this new approach to assessing expertise (Groen & Patel, 1988; Patel & Groen, 1986; Patel, Groen, & Frederiksen, 1986) and remained so in more recent work on expertise (Arocha & Patel, 1995; Ericsson, Patel, & Kintsch, 2000; Kintsch, Patel, & Ericsson, 1999).

Formal theories and methods of medical discourse analysis provided a means to study complex phenomena in medical cognition that extended beyond recall and text comprehension. Kintsch and van Dijk's (1978) work provided a framework based on the notion that text comprehension involves and results in multiple representations of a text. Their introduction of the situation model concept could account for how information contained in a text reflects problem-solving activity. Groen and Patel (1988) capitalized on this insight to investigate the relationship between comprehension and medical problem solving. Physicians at varying levels of expertise, plus medical students, were asked to recall and provide a pathophysiological (causal) explanation of a patient's illness. It is interesting that the propositional microstructure of a text, and the macrostructure when viewed as a network of propositions, bore a distinct resemblance to node-link representational structures of semantic networks that were common in artificial intelligence research. This representation enabled these researchers to characterize different patterns of inference and the directionality of reasoning. In addition, the pathophysiological explanations could be treated as a situation model and the development of expertise could be partly explained as a progression of these models (Patel et al., 1986).

Other research focuses on issues of cognitive performance in the use of information technologies. Theories of discourse comprehension continue to inform the studies in areas such as lay understanding of medical instructions (Patel, Eisemon, & Arocha, 1990), health literacy in vulnerable populations

(Sivaramakrishnan & Patel, 1993), and computer-mediated decision support (Patel, Arocha, & Kaufman, 1999; Patel, Kushniruk, Yang, & Yale, 2000). In recent years, there has been a growing concern about medical errors, with the implementation of computer-based clinical practice guidelines (CPGs), integrated at the locus of patient care, viewed as part of the solution (Patel, Arocha, Diermeier, Greenes, & Shortliffe, 2001). Clinical guidelines are designed to promote evidence-based practices consistent with the state of the art in medical knowledge. These guidelines use two different representational forms: narrative and algorithmic–procedural. The challenge is to translate these forms into computer-based representations that are easily accessible at the point of care and that thereby affect clinical decision making and avoidance of errors. One important factor limiting the acceptance and use of CPGs is the mismatch between a guideline's recommended actions and the physician-user's situation models of the patient's problem. In addition, guidelines can be semantically complex, often composed of elaborate collections of prescribed procedures with logical gaps or contradictions that can promote ambiguity and hence frustration on the part of users. Kintsch-inspired solutions were effective in disambiguating some of these problems with special focus on medical expertise and the relationship between comprehension and problem solving. Using these techniques, Patel and her colleagues also studied the understanding of childhood nutritional disorders by Indian mothers (Sivaramakrishnan & Patel, 1993), the comprehension of pharmaceutical instructions by Masai in Kenya (Patel et al., 1990), and intellectual performance (as a function of parasitic load) by Colombian children when performing problem-solving and comprehension tasks (Sivaramakrishnan, Arocha, & Patel, 1998). The latest challenge involves risk communication and decision making by the lay public and health professionals as they relate to threats of bioterrorism. Theories and methods of discourse analysis developed by Kintsch and colleagues appear to be fundamental in addressing these issues.

Conclusion

The year 2003 may be the year Walter Kintsch formally retires from the University of Colorado, but it will certainly not be the end of his contributions to psychology. His 10 books and more than 150 published articles and chapters—authored with 97 different coauthors—provide a tangible estimate of his scientific contribution. To those fortunate enough to know Kintsch, no such proof is needed.

References

Anderson, J. R., & Bower, G. H. (1973). *Human associative memory*. Washington, DC: Winston.

Arocha, J. F., & Patel, V. L. (1995). Construction–integration theory and clinical reasoning. In C. A. Weaver III, S. Mannes, & C. R. Fletcher (Eds.), *Discourse comprehension: Essays in honor of Walter Kintsch* (pp. 359–381). Hillsdale, NJ: Erlbaum.

Bachmann, E., Meier, D., & Perrig, W. J. (1990). *Die unterschiedlichen Repräsentationsniveaus bei der Speicherung von verbalen Ortsbe-schreibungen, Forschungsbericht* [Different levels of representations for verbal descriptions of spatial locations]. Basel, Switzerland: Institut für Psychologie, Universität Basel.

Bachmann, E., & Perrig, W. J. (1988). Die mentale Repräsentation von verbalen Ortsbeschreibungen [The mental representation of verbal descriptions of spatial locations]. *Schweizerische Zeitschrift für Psychologie, 1*, 25–36.

Bachmann, E., & Perrig, W. J. (1989). The mental representation of verbally described spatial lay-outs. *The German Journal of Psychology, 13*, 160–162.

Bates, E., Kintsch, W., Fletcher, C. R., & Giuliani, V. (1980). The role of pronominalization and ellipsis in texts: Some memory experiments. *Journal of Experimental Psychology: Human Learning and Memory, 6*, 676–691.

Buschke, H., & Kintsch, W. (1970). Rehearsal strategies and the serial-position curve in immediate free recall of ordered items. *Quarterly Journal of Experimental Psychology, 23*, 347–352.

Chomsky, N. (1957). *Syntactic structures*. The Hague, The Netherlands: Mouton.

Chomsky, N. (1964). *Aspects of the theory of syntax*. Cambridge, MA: MIT Press.

Clark, H. H., & Marshall, C. (1978). Reference diaries. In D. Waltz (Ed.), *Theoretical issues in natural language processing* (pp. 57–62). Urbana-Champaign, IL: Center for the Study of Reading.

Daneman, M., & Carpenter, P. A. (1980). Individual differences in working memory and reading. *Journal of Verbal Learning and Verbal Behavior, 19*, 450–466.

Ericsson, K. A., & Kintsch, W. (1995). Long-term working memory. *Psychological Review, 102*, 211–245.

Ericsson, K. A., Patel, V., & Kintsch, W. (2000). How experts' adaptations to representative task demands account for the expertise effect in memory recall: Comment on Vicente and Wang (1998). *Psychological Review, 107*, 578–592.

Gernsbacher, M. A. (1990). *Language comprehension as structure building*. Hillsdale, NJ: Erlbaum.

Graesser, A. C., Singer, M., & Trabasso, T. (1994). Constructing inferences during narrative text comprehension. *Psychological Review, 101*, 371–395.

Groen, G. J., & Patel, V. L. (1988). The relationship between comprehension and reasoning in medical expertise. In M. T. H. Chi (Ed.), *The nature of expertise* (pp. 287–310). Hillsdale, NJ: Erlbaum.

Haenggi, D., Kintsch, W., & Gernsbacher, M. A. (1995). Spatial situation models and text comprehension. *Discourse Processes, 19*, 173–199.

Johnson-Laird, P. N. (1980). Mental models in cognitive science. *Cognitive Science, 4*, 72–115.

Kamp, H. (1981). A theory of truth and semantic representation. In J. A. G. Groenendijk, T. M. V. Janssen, & M. B. J. Stockhof (Eds.), *Formal methods in the study of language* (Part 1, pp. 277–322). Amsterdam: Mathematical Centre Tracts.

Karttunen, L. (1976). Discourse referents. In J. D. McCawley (Ed.), *Syntax and semantics* (Vol. 7, pp. 363–385). New York: Academic Press.

Keenan, J. M., Baillet, S. D., & Brown, P. (1984). The effects of causal cohesion on comprehension and memory. *Journal of Verbal Learning and Verbal Behavior, 23*, 115–126.

Kintsch, W. (1962). Runway performance as function of drive strength and magnitude of reinforcement. *Journal of Comparative and Physiological Psychology, 55*, 882–887.

Kintsch, W. (1963a, April 19). All-or-none learning and the role of repetition in paired-associate learning. *Science, 140*, 310–312.

Kintsch, W. (1963b). A response time model for choice behavior. *Psychometrika, 28*, 27–32.

Kintsch, W. (1970). *Learning, memory, and conceptual processes*. Oxford, England: Wiley.

Kintsch, W. (1974). *The representation of meaning in memory*. Hillsdale, NJ: Erlbaum.

Kintsch, W. (1977). On comprehending stories. In M. A. Just & P. Carpenter (Eds.), *Cognitive processes in comprehension* (pp. 33–61). Hillsdale, NJ: Erlbaum.

Kintsch, W. (1988). The role of knowledge in discourse comprehension: A construction–integration model. *Psychological Review, 95*, 163–182.

Kintsch, W. (1998). *Comprehension: A paradigm for cognition*. New York: Cambridge University Press.

Kintsch, W. (2000). The control of knowledge activation in discourse comprehension. In W. J. Perrig (Ed.), *Control of human behavior, mental processes, and consciousness: Essays in honor of the 60th birthday of August Flammer* (pp. 137–146). Mahwah, NJ: Erlbaum.

Kintsch, W., & Bates, E. (1977). Recognition memory for statements from a classroom lecture. *Journal of Experimental Psychology: Human Learning and Memory, 3,* 150–159.

Kintsch, W., & Buschke, H. (1969). Homophones and synonyms in short-term memory. *Journal of Experimental Psychology, 80,* 403–407.

Kintsch, W., Crothers, E. J., & Jorgensen, C. C. (1971). On the role of semantic processing in short-term retention. *Journal of Experimental Psychology, 90,* 96–101.

Kintsch, W., & Greeno, J. G. (1985). Understanding and solving word arithmetic problems. *Psychological Review, 92,* 109–129.

Kintsch, W., & Keenan, J. M. (1973). Reading rate and retention as a function of the number of propositions in the base structure of sentences. *Cognitive Psychology, 5,* 257–274.

Kintsch, W., & Morris, C. J. (1965). Application of a Markov model to free recall and recognition. *Journal of Experimental Psychology, 68,* 372–375.

Kintsch, W., Patel, V. L., & Ericsson, K. A. (1999). The role of long-term working memory in text comprehension. *Psychologia: An International Journal of Psychology in the Orient, 42,* 186–198.

Kintsch, W., & van Dijk, T. A. (1978). Toward a model of text comprehension and production. *Psychological Review, 85,* 363–394.

Kintsch, W., & Vipond, D. (1979). Reading and comprehension and readability in educational practice and psychological theory. In L. G. Nilsson (Ed.), *Perspectives on memory research* (pp. 329–365). Hillsdale, NJ: Erlbaum.

Kintsch, W., & Wike, E. L. (1957). Habit reversal as a function of length of partial delay of reinforcement. *Psychological Reports, 3,* 11–14.

Landauer, T. K., Foltz, P. W., & Laham, D. (1998). Introduction to latent semantic analysis. *Discourse Processes, 25,* 259–284.

McNamara, D. S., Kintsch, E., Songer, N. B., & Kintsch, W. (1996). Are good texts always better? Interactions of text coherence, background knowledge, and levels of understanding in learning from text. *Cognition and Instruction, 14,* 1–43.

Nathan, M. J., Kintsch, W., & Young, E. (1992). A theory of algebra-word-problem comprehension and its implications for the design of learning environments. *Cognition and Instruction, 9,* 329–389.

Norman, D. A. (1970). *Models of human memory.* New York: Academic Press.

Oakhill, J. V., Yuill, N. M., & Parkin, A. (1986). On the nature of the difference between skilled and less-skilled comprehenders. *Journal of Research in Reading, 9,* 80–91.

Patel, V. L., Arocha, J. F., Diermeier, M., Greenes, R. A., & Shortliffe, E. H. (2001). Methods of cognitive analysis to support the design and evaluation of biomedical systems: The case of clinical practice guidelines. *Journal of Biomedical Informatics, 34,* 52–66.

Patel, V. L., Arocha, J. F., & Kaufman, D. R. (1999). Medical cognition. In F. T. Durso (Ed.), *Handbook of applied cognition* (pp. 663–693). New York: Wiley.

Patel, V. L., Eisemon, T. O., & Arocha, J. F. (1990). Comprehending instructions for using pharmaceutical products in rural Kenya. *Instructional Science, 19,* 71–84.

Patel, V. L., & Groen, G. J. (1986). Knowledge-based solution strategies in medical reasoning. *Cognitive Science, 10,* 91–116.

Patel, V. L., Groen, G. J., & Frederiksen, C. H. (1986). Differences between medical students and doctors in memory for clinical cases. *Medical Education, 20,* 3–9.

Patel, V. L., Kushniruk, A. W., Yang, S., & Yale, J. F. (2000). Impact of a computerized patient record system on medical data collection, organization and reasoning. *Journal of the American Medical Informatics Association, 7,* 569–585.

Perrig, W. J., & Bhend, D. (2003). *Auswirkungen unterschiedlicher Situationsmodelle auf die Textverarbeitung. Forschungsbericht* [Effects of different situation models on text processing]. Bern, Switzerland: Institut für Psychologie, Universität Bern.

Perrig, W. J., & Kintsch, W. (1985). Propositional and situational representations of text. *Journal of Memory and Language, 24,* 503–518.

Petöfi, J. S. (1982). Representation languages and their function in text interpretation. In S. Allen (Ed.), *Text processing* (pp. 85–122). Stockholm: Almqvist & Wiksell.

Premack, D., & Kintsch, W. (1970). A description of free responding in the rat. *Learning and Motivation, 1,* 321–336.

Shelton, A. L., & Gabrieli, J. D. E. (2002). Neural correlates of encoding space from route and survey perspectives. *Journal of Neuroscience, 22,* 2711–2717.

Singer, M., & Kintsch, W. (2001). Text retrieval: A theoretical exploration. *Discourse Processes, 31,* 27–59.

Sivaramakrishnan, M., Arocha, J. F., & Patel, V. L. (1998). Cognitive assessment and health education in children from two different cultures. *Social Science and Medicine, 47,* 697–712.

Sivaramakrishnan, M., & Patel, V. L. (1993). Reasoning about childhood nutritional deficiencies by mothers in rural India: A cognitive analysis. *Social Science and Medicine, 37,* 937–952.

Trabasso, T., & van den Broek, P. (1985). Causal thinking and the representation of narrative events. *Journal of Memory and Language, 24,* 612–630.

van Dijk, T. A., & Kintsch, W. (1983). *Strategies of discourse comprehension.* New York: Academic Press.

Wertheimer, M. (1982). *Productive thinking.* Chicago: University of Chicago Press. (Original work published 1945)

Wiederholt, J. L., & Bryant, B. R. (1992). *Gray Oral Reading Tests—Third edition.* Austin, TX: PRO-ED.

Wike, E. L., Kintsch, W., & Remple, R. (1959). Selective learning and habit reversal as a function of partial reinforcement during training and reversal. *Psychological Reports, 5,* 665–668.

Zwaan, R. A., & Radvansky, G. A. (1998). Situation models in language comprehension and memory. *Psychological Bulletin, 123,* 162–185.

3

Cherchez Le Quadrant Pasteur! A Symposium in Honor of Tom Landauer

Lynn Streeter, Darrell Laham, Susan Dumais, and Ernst Z. Rothkopf

This symposium was convened to honor Tom Landauer for his many valued contributions to psychological science and to human welfare. We owe him a debt for his important insights into language and his pioneering, ingenious invention of analytical and experimental techniques. In the course of his distinguished career, he has greatly added to our understanding of human learning, memory, and cognition. Landauer has boldly followed the verbal spoor of culture into the awesome vastness of text and found the beginnings of meaning. Above everything else, he has excelled in wedding the search for fundamental knowledge with the creation of useful tools for practical human enterprises and has provided exemplary models for the research-informed management of practical human tasks. During the past 50 years, the difficult course toward a productive psychological science has often been obscured by theoretical pretensions, unthinking empiricism, and meretricious hyperbole. Landauer has been a bright beacon in this confusing haze, always speaking clearly with an optimistic but sober voice. His work was ever elegant, focused, and utterly innocent of sham and cant.

Donald Stokes (1997) has suggested that the old Vannevar Bush conception of the sequential progression of basic science, through engineering exploration, to practical innovation was not an entirely accurate model for good progress, in either science or technology. Instead, Stokes proposed a 2×2 classification of research activities, the two dimensions being (a) whether knowledge was being sought and (b) whether the work sought to solve a practical problem. A somewhat modified version of his idea may be seen in Table 3.1.

Stokes held that the quadrant that involved both a practical problem and a search for new knowledge was the most productive. He called it *Pasteur's quadrant*, because Pasteur interwove the search for better control for the processing of agricultural products, such as a technique for producing alcohol from beets, with fundamental studies in bacteriology and chemistry. Pasteur's quadrant is clearly Landauer's turf. He has tilled it and he has managed to

Table 3.1. Donald Stokes's (1997) Conception of Scientific Research, Slightly Modified

		Importance of Practical Use	
		No consideration of use	**Problem oriented**
Importance of Basic Understanding	**Seeks basic understanding**	Pure basic research	Pasteur's quadrant
	No basic understanding sought	Random experimental walk	Pure applied research

Note. The two dimensions represent the importance of basic understanding and practical use.

produce astonishing harvests. He has demonstrated brilliantly that fundamental research and work on solutions to practical human problems can live together in interesting and useful ways.

In all candor, it must be said that the road map to Pasteur's quadrant is sometimes difficult to follow in psychological domains and their putative applications. The two criteria that define the four fields of Table 3.1 (focus on deep scientific questions and the challenge of a practical problem) harbor a tangle of uncertainties, and the distinction between good fundamental research and random-walk experimentation is not always clear. Inspiration and discriminating sensitivity to zeitgeist are often required to ask good questions of nature, but those two are not given to all. Furthermore, in psychological applications, the notion of a practical problem in keen need of a solution can betray the would-be problem solver. Psychologists sometimes find themselves offering solutions to problems for which there is little public awareness or proposing cures for problems that no one is eager to correct. As Landauer himself has pointed out, the history of human–computer interaction is replete with vexing examples of such.

The symbiosis between good fundamental research and useful practical developments can also be defeated by mismatches between the internal logic of research and that of the enterprises that our research is supposed to support. Consider, for example, the relationship between cognitive research and schooling. Most learning research focuses on efficiency—that is, how much can be learned from a given amount of effort or time? But the common schools, which are the nominal beneficiaries of most efficiency-related research, are only indirectly concerned with efficiencies. Only closed, self-contained systems, such as corporate or military training, are strongly dominated by concern about efficiencies, because both teaching and its consequences share the strong metric of cost. Such disparities between research aims and the internal logic of practical enterprises exist in other areas as well. It should not escape our attention that much of the research that has produced such very good practical results for Landauer and his coworkers has been performed under the aegis of closely managed business organizations, which were keenly aware of both the price of unsolved problems and the benefits of solutions.

Figure 3.1. Tom Landauer through the ages.

This symposium brings together three speakers, who worked closely with Landauer during their career, and whose current efforts have either stylistic or intellectual links to Landauer's research. The first section is by Lynn Streeter, who has cooperated fruitfully with Landauer in many enterprises, and who holds a unique position to comment on their intellectual and other adventures. She provides an interesting overview of Landauer's scholarly career.

A Man for All Quadrants: Tom Landauer

Tom Landauer and I have been involved personally and professionally for over 30 years. In that time he has changed dramatically, as shown in the three pictures in Figure 3.1.

In the 1960s (Figure 3.1, left), Tom's primary interest was the brain and its role in learning, memory, and growth. Those of you for whom Tom's work equates to latent semantic analysis (LSA) may thus be surprised to learn that his past accomplishments are varied, broad, interdisciplinary, and not at all similar (as measured by the cosine) with his current line of work. He has made contributions to basic psychological theory, data collection, instrumentation, and new product development, as well as having unwittingly created trends that persisted in experimental psychology. He has a respectable place in all of Pasteur's quadrants.

Given my long association with Tom, my mostly intact memory, and my ability to pilfer his various offices for interesting artifacts, I would like to cover some of Tom's accomplishments that might otherwise be lost to posterity. During this tour back in time, I will take a little time to talk about my own work in child language acquisition (Streeter, 1976).

Stress and Growth

As was common in the 1950s and 1960s, psychologists preferred the company of rodents to that of humans. It was something about their simplicity and docility that made them so lovable. In fact, Tom and Saul Sternberg would sit around the lab stroking their rats. While doing this, they observed that the fondled rats grew to be much bigger than the rats of their negligent colleagues. Did physical affection really make organisms grow bigger? Tom mentally took the rat's point of view. Perhaps the rat viewed these caresses as unwelcome overtures—as stressful events to be endured. Hence the hypothesis and resulting work that would span the next 20 years of Tom's career—stress in infancy produces physical growth (e.g., Landauer & Whiting, 1977). Tom searched the Harvard Social Relations cross-cultural files to find evidence of humans stressing their infants. As science and luck would have it, the world's cultures divided nicely into the sadistic and the overly protective parents. The sadists scarified their infants, pierced their bodies, plunged them regularly into either very hot or very cold water; tossed them high into the air, and so on. The offspring of the sadistic parents grew to be taller and more resilient than their coddled counterparts. But infant stress is not only a product of primitive societies; many things done to infants in Western societies are equally as powerful stressors as scarification. Infantile vaccination appeared to be one of them. Humans used to be short and did not start growing until the Industrial Revolution with the advent of vaccination in infancy. So, Tom and John Whiting (both short) devoted several decades of their lives to showing a causal link between infantile vaccination before age 2 and human growth. They did a controlled experiment in which 80% of randomly selected infants in one village (where everyone over age 4 in the area had been vaccinated) were vaccinated for smallpox before age 2 and the other 20% were vaccinated after age 2. Those who were vaccinated early grew taller when they became teenagers. But no one would believe Landauer and Whiting. Some were critical of their experimental design because it left too many children behind. Clearly, scientific results need to fit the current zeitgeist. One of the few articles published about these findings, "Correlates and Consequences of Stress in Infancy" (Landauer & Whiting, 1977), has little in common with "Indexing With Latent Semantic Analysis" (cosine = 0.03).

Stop the Learning

Tom has had a lifelong obsession with how the brain works and how things are learned and remembered. He reasoned that if one knew how to stop learning, then one would know a great deal about how learning proceeds. This work was done at Stanford in the 1960s and significantly predates the Nobel Prize winning work of Eric Kandel. Tom had the right instincts, the right mechanism, but the wrong dosage response curves and maybe some recalcitrant mice and rats. Tom injected rats and mice with an antibiotic (Actinomycin-D) thought to inhibit the DNA biosynthesis of RNA. Altering the RNA sequence was thought to be how learning occurred; impeding the RNA biosynthesis ought to stop learning. The drug was administered into the hearts of small mice in a shock-avoidance paradigm. But it did not really stop learning as anticipated (Landauer & Eldridge, 1966) or as Kandel would later show it did (Kandel, Schwartz, & Jessell, 2000). So, Kandel went to Stockholm, while Landauer got to marry the offspring of Scandinavian immigrants. Again, the cosine of this work with LSA is –0.02.

Methodological Contributions to the Field

Tom left the rodents behind at Stanford and moved to Bell Laboratories, turning his attention to psychology undergraduates. There he pioneered the *single point of data* experiment. Each participant contributed one and only one piece of data. There were no confounds, but thousands of undergraduates were needed to complete a single experimental design. Most important, these experiments could be done with two pieces of equipment: an IBM keypunch machine and an IBM sorter.

The punch cards were the experimental materials in the paired-associate learning experiments. Students wrote their answers on the cards, which were then keypunched in. The card contained all the necessary experimental information, so that a few passes through the old IBM sorter yielded the results, and one needed only to tally the cards in each bin after the sort. Each bin corresponded to a condition in the experiment. For Tom, the Golden Age of computing had arrived. Age unfortunately often embitters us to the very things we loved most when young. Tom's love affair with IBM was not to last. The final culmination of his fulminations was his 1995 book, *The Trouble With Computers* (Landauer, 1995). Again, the cosine between the *The Trouble With Computers* book and LSA is –0.10.

Speech Instrumentation

My dissertation research on infant speech perception was done in the Kenya highlands outside of Nairobi. At the time, the only laboratory doing this work in the United States was Peter Eimas's laboratory at Brown. And at the time there was only one article on infant speech perception. Tom and I visited Eimas's lab and were stunned and somewhat disheartened by the elaborate setup to administer speech stimuli and measure and control infant sucking. It involved thousands of 1972 dollars worth of equipment, and there would be no way of replicating such a setup in a place with unplanned power outages. Tom, then working at Bell Laboratories, saw instantly how an ordinary black telephone could be commandeered into service. Speed to create the apparatus was of the essence, because we were leaving for Kenya in 2 months and there was no time to get a grant or even order the right equipment. (FedEx had not been invented yet.) The telephone microphone would act as the pressure transducer. The infant's sucks would be picked up by the microphone and transmitted to a counter, both powered by dry cell batteries. The infant sucked on a Playtex "Just Like Mother Nipple" whose hole has been plugged with a solvent that was FDA (Food and Drug Administration) safe and had been tested by a Bell Labs' chemist. This remarkable apparatus has been coined the "Suck-a-Phone" and definitely displays Edison-like ingenuity.

Plain Old Mail Service

The final invention was the one that should have made the telephone companies millions. It was called Plain Old Mail Service (or POMS), delivering e-mail without investing in a personal computer—just a small screen, small printer, and a few buttons for sending, receiving, and so on (Nachbar, 1988). There was a much bigger market for this than the Suck-a-Phone, but the marketing staff at the then Baby Bells thought that e-mail was one of those things that would never penetrate the mass market. It was for geeks. Nobody's mother or grandmother was going to want to send e-mail. And right they were.

Firsts in Cognitive Psychology

Tom's experimental and theoretical contributions to psychology are varied and significant and clearly belong in Quadrant 2 (use-inspired basic research). To name but a few:

1. Rate of implicit speech—Landauer (1962). How fast do you talk to yourself? Answer: At about the same rate as you speak. So, fast talkers really do think fast.
2. Spacing of practice—Landauer and Eldridge (1967). Items that are spaced are learned much better. In fact, an item that is spaced is twice as likely to be recalled as the same item immediately repeated. This finding has significant implications for how people should practice and study everything.
3. Semantic category size effects—Landauer and Freedman (1968). This was the first experiment to examine the effects of category size on retrieval from long-term memory. For those of you who have forgotten, it takes longer to say that a mule is an animal than a mammal. This started an entire industry within psychology of doing reaction time experiments with negative and positive exemplars of categories.
4. Memory without organization: Properties of a model with random storage and undirected retrieval (the *garbage can model*)—Landauer (1975). This was a quintessential Landauer article—rigorous iconoclasm. The homunculi and executives were left unemployed—they were not needed to account for most of the learning and memory data.
5. Word neighborhood effects—Landauer and Streeter (1973). This work found that rare words differed structurally and phonetically from common words. This was a sleeper article that came to life again with desktop computing, thereby creating work for many psychologists for years to come. This article did have a reasonably high cosine with LSA (0.31), perhaps presaging the LSA work of the late 1980s.

The next section is by Darrell Laham, a cofounder with Landauer of Knowledge Analysis Technologies LLC (K-A-T). This company was formed to explore practical applications of LSA. Laham describes some of their adventurous efforts in applying LSA to educational and other problems.

SALSA: Science and Applications of Latent Semantic Analysis

Tom Landauer's 1995 book, *The Trouble With Computers,* speaks to the lack of productivity gains attributable to the information technology revolution and suggests that the cure for the trouble is to make the design, development, and deployment of computer systems "user-centered" (Landauer, 1995). Landauer's research into improving human–computer interaction performed at Bell Labs and Bell Communications Research (Bellcore), as documented in this book, provided the genesis for LSA.

At these great industrial laboratories Landauer was charged with uncovering why people could not find what they wanted to find in the Yellow Pages. Landauer and his research group discovered a major disconnect in many information systems, both computer based and not, between the language of users and the language embedded in the systems by their developers. A series of experiments showed consistently high variability in the naming of items—ask 100 people by what one word something (e.g., a process, a computer program, a recipe) should be called and, on average, you will get 30 different answers (Furnas, Landauer, Gomez, & Dumais, 1987). Several solutions were tried, including unlimited aliasing, adaptive indexing, and latent semantic indexing.

Although LSA began as a solution for the "vocabulary problem," it has evolved into a highly regarded theory of the acquisition, induction, and representation of knowledge (Landauer & Dumais, 1997). Detailed descriptions of the LSA theory, mathematical basis, and machine learning instantiation are beyond the scope of this writing (see Landauer & Dumais, 1997; Landauer, Foltz, & Laham, 1998; also the Web sites http://www.lsa.colorado.edu and http://www.k-a-t.com). The important bit for our discussion is that through LSA computers can be automatically trained on large corpora of domain knowledge to perform tasks that require similarity judgments between texts and those judgments tend to mimic human performance.

In the LSA training process, the computer examines the patterns of word use within contexts, usually paragraphs or sections of larger texts, and determines the degree to which any known words could substitute for each other in similar contexts. LSA can determine that two words (i.e., synonyms) have the same meaning in certain contexts, even if they have never co-occurred in previous contexts. The words *car* and *automobile* are rarely seen together in natural usage—a writer tends to use one or the other for their need and audience. After LSA learns about many words as used in many contexts, it can make judgments about the similarity of any two words, even though most assessments of pair similarity, approximately 99%, are between words that never co-occurred in context in the training corpus. The inductive step in the LSA training process, traditionally solved through *singular value decomposition,* provides the concept generalization that is absent in keyword indexing. After training, every context and every term is represented as a point in a high (300–500) dimensional *semantic space.* The similarity between any term, any context, or any new context composed by combining a novel set of terms can be assessed. General applications of LSA include information retrieval (compare a query to a document set and return a list of those most conceptually similar), filtering (given a stream of contexts, identify those that are within specified limits), classification and categorization (place terms or contexts into concept groups either supervised or not), and knowledge mapping (provide a multidimensional grouping solution for a set of contexts for subsequent analysis of a domain). Another application of LSA is to identify and provide the words from the semantic space that best represent the overall meaning of a text, a type of automatic summarization.

Important to our theme of Pasteur's quadrant, LSA has been found capable of simulating a wide variety of human cognitive phenomena, ranging from developmental acquisition of recognition vocabulary to word categorization, sentence–word semantic priming, and discourse comprehension (Landauer & Dumais, 1997; Landauer et al., 1998).

In one set of experiments, we used LSA, trained "developmentally," to perform classic word sorting tasks (Anglin, 1970). Knowledge was represented at five educational stages: 3rd, 6th, 9th, and 12th graders, as well as college-level adults. LSA mimicked well the human sorting performance observed by Anglin with children and adults. In early stages LSA sorting was based primarily on concrete word relationships. As LSA "aged," it showed the same tendency as humans to move from concrete to abstract (Landauer et al., 1998).

When presented with semantic categorization tasks, LSA mimicked human performance based exclusively on language contexts as found in the training corpus without any explicit hand coding of category membership or semantic features. For example, when LSA was asked to match 140 concept names to their superordinate categories, it showed interesting differences in its performance for classification of animate natural kind categories (92% correct), inanimate natural kind categories (100%) and manmade artifacts (53%). Highly significant correlations between LSA metrics and human typicality judgments were also demonstrated (Laham, 1997).

Automated Performance Assessment of Constructed Responses

We have developed numerous educational and training applications that use LSA to assess text and provide feedback based on the assessments. The Intelligent Essay Assessor compares student writings on prescribed topics with representative writings of known quality to provide a score that accurately and reliably predicts expert reader scores. LSA is first trained on a corpus of text relevant to the domain under analysis, for example, biology or psychology, or in many cases using a large corpus of general knowledge. Representative samples of writing for a directed essay question (usually 100–200 responses are sufficient) are then placed into the space. These have been prescored for overall quality and conceptual coverage or other analytic writing traits. A new essay response is then compared by LSA for similarity to the responses. It is given a score based on its proximity to the responses of known quality—if LSA determines it is more similar to essays with high scores, it is awarded a similar high score. Scores assigned through LSA in this way, sometimes combined with concurrent statistical measures of text features, have repeatedly passed evaluations for reliability and validity (Landauer, Laham, & Foltz, 2003). In addition, the essay can be compared with learning materials segmented to represent important topics in the concept space, and the presence or absence of such concepts in the student's work can be determined. Students can then be directed to learning materials optimally chosen to remediate their specific conceptual deficiencies.

Constructing a Cake and Force-Feeding It Too

In recent years, we have been developing applications to improve user interaction with online content and online collaborators. Advocates of constructivist education, albeit without strong controlled research to back their claim, contend that the motivational and interactive qualities of discovery learning lead to deeper levels of student understanding. Cognitive load theorists suggest that the additional cognitive requirements of search-based learning are less effective than direct instruction (Sweller, 1999). LSA search techniques can be used within constructivist or discovery learning environments to optimize both the knowledge-building and collaborative processes and to reduce the associated cognitive demands.

For example, Landauer and Walter Kintsch and their team at the University of Colorado have automated the ability to select the optimum text for a learner given the learner's current state of knowledge. By assessing a piece of student writing on a topic, such as the biology of the heart, an LSA-based tool can choose from a library the text that best fits within the student's zone of proximal development (Wolfe et al., 1998). Landauer calls this the *Goldilocks principle*—the next best text introduces just the right amount of new knowledge. LSA-based assessment of the current knowledge state of the user allows optimum text assignment to proceed effectively and efficiently. In continuing research and development, LSA is being used to find the "optimum path to knowledge." Given the starting and goal states of the learner as textual descriptions turned to LSA semantic vectors, as well as a library of instructive texts, the system will guide the choice of learning material. This guided path will take the learner from start to goal while minimizing encounters with previously assimilated knowledge or material irrelevant to the desired learning outcomes.

In another case, LSA is used within a collaborative learning environment to help find converging and divergent opinions among fellow student contributions. In a collaborative workspace heavily populated with contributed notes, LSA tracks down those entries that are both conceptually most and least similar to the learner's own contributions as a means of providing directed instruction. Given a desired discussion end-state by the instructor, or at least a set of topics determined to cover the expected range of discourse, the system can also monitor the student's progress and alert both student and instructor when the discovery learning wanders far from its intended goals. These systems are currently in field trials at K-A-T in knowledge domains as diverse as science and leadership skills with learners ranging in age from middle school to adults. In one small pilot experiment, LSA ranking of student work correlated at .90 with instructor rankings of student performance.

LSA applications are now being combined with other statistical learning and natural language processing techniques to provide more effective retrieval and assessments. There are two aspects of LSA-based educational applications that are of great practical importance: First, LSA provides highly robust assessments even when given noisy data such as the output of speech recognition systems (Laham, Bennett, & Derr, 2002), and, second, its applications are considerably more economical to construct than competing methods, such as rule-based Intelligent Tutoring Systems, while providing impressively improved learning outcomes (Landauer, 2003).

By working to solve practical problems in information retrieval, and by keeping the goals and capabilities of end users in mind, Tom Landauer and his associates have developed LSA-based applications that offer important new possibilities for education and training.

The next section is by Susan Dumais, one of Landauer's colleagues at AT&T's Bell Laboratories and at Bellcore. She describes her attempts to create a computer system that can provide intelligent answers to nontrivial questions using an elaboration of approaches to text analysis that have flourished in Landauer's laboratory.

Data-Driven Question Answering in Machines (and Humans)

Most information retrieval systems operate at the level of entire documents. However, in many applications, it is useful to retrieve specific answers rather than entire documents. This section describes a question-answering system, AskMSR, that uses simple data-driven techniques applied to large volumes of texts. Despite using only very simple statistical processing, the system is successful in benchmark tests (for additional details, see Brill, Dumais, & Banko, 2002; Dumais, Banko, Brill, Lin, & Ng, 2002).

Several important themes emerge from our efforts to develop a question-answering system. First, we are working in Pasteur's quadrant, trying to solve a challenging practical problem and in the process contribute to new knowledge (see Landauer, 2003). Second, very simple statistical techniques are applied to large text collections in which redundancy can be exploited. The theme of using simple techniques with few structural assumptions harkens back to Landauer's (1975) work on memory without organization. Finally, we believe that the success of our system can inform cognitive modeling, although these links have not been fully explored in the question-answering domain.

The TREC Question Answering Track has motivated much of the recent work in the field (e.g., Voorhees & Harman, 2001). Initial research focused on developing techniques to answer short-answer, fact-based questions such as "Who killed Abraham Lincoln?" or "Where are the Rocky Mountains?" Automatic question answering from a single, small information source is extremely challenging. Consider the difficulty of finding the answer to the question "Who killed Abraham Lincoln?" from a source that contains only the text "John Wilkes Booth altered history with a bullet. He will forever be known as the man who ended Abraham Lincoln's life." Given a source that contains only a small number of formulations of the answer, a computational system is faced with the difficult task of mapping users' questions to answers by uncovering complex lexical, syntactic, or semantic relationships between questions and answer strings. When large collections are available, redundancy can be used to circumvent many of these difficult problems.

Most question-answering systems use a combination of information retrieval and natural language processing techniques. Typically, candidate passages are found using standard information retrieval techniques, and more detailed linguistic analyses of the question and passages are used to identify specific answers. A variety of linguistic and semantic resources (part-of-speech tagging, parsing, named entity extraction, semantic relations, WordNet [Miller, 1990], theorem proving, etc.) are used to extract answers in these systems. In contrast to these approaches, AskMSR attempts to solve the difficult matching and extraction problems by using simple string matching and counting techniques applied to large amounts of data. The tremendous data redundancy provided by the Web is used as a key resource in AskMSR.

The AskMSR system contains four main components.

1. *Rewrite Query*. Given a question, the system generates a number of rewrite strings, which are likely substrings of declarative answers to the question. For the query "Who killed Abraham Lincoln?" there are three rewrites: <LEFT> killed Abraham Lincoln; Abraham Lincoln was killed by <RIGHT>; and who AND killed AND Abraham AND Lincoln. The first two rewrites require that a text match an exact phrase, for example, "killed Abraham Lincoln." The last rewrite is a back-off strategy that ANDs together the query words. All query rewrites are sent to a Web search engine.

2. *Mine N-Grams*. The top k page summaries returned from each query rewrite are analyzed. All unigram, bigram, and trigram word sequences are extracted from these page summaries. The resulting n-grams are scored according to their frequency of occurrence and the weight of the query rewrite that retrieved them.

3. *Filter N-Grams*. The n-grams are filtered and reweighted according to how well each candidate matches the expected answer type. A dozen handwritten answer-type filters were developed on the basis of human knowledge about question types. These filters use surface-level string features, such as capitalization or the presence of digits. For *Who* questions, answer strings with capital letters are given added weight and those with dates are demoted.

4. *Tile N-Grams*. Finally, the n-grams are tiled together where appropriate, so that longer answers can be assembled from the unigrams, bigrams, and trigrams.

Using these four components, the best matching answer to the question is *John Wilkes Booth* because it is found in specific rewrites, it occurs often, and it contains capital letters. Answer redundancy is crucial in two steps of the analysis. First, the greater the answer redundancy in the text collection, the more likely it is that an answer occurs in a very simple relation to the question. Therefore, the need to handle difficult problems like anaphor resolution, synonymy, and alternate syntactic formulations is greatly reduced. On the Web, hundreds of pages contain transparent answer strings like "John Wilkes Booth killed Abraham Lincoln," and finding the answer in this string is easy. Second, redundancy is used in answer mining. Instead of looking at just one or two of the most likely passages, we consider hundreds of matching passages looking for consistently occurring n-grams.

The AskMSR system has been evaluated in the TREC 2001 benchmark comparisons (Voorhees & Harman, 2001). It was one of the better performing systems (top 6 out of 36 systems), correctly answering more than 300 of the 500 test questions. Most of the other systems used complex syntactic and semantic analyses. AskMSR, in contrast, succeeds because of the answer redundancy in the collection. Detailed analyses of the contributions of various system components are described in Dumais et al. (2002) and Brill et al. (2002). Two experiments that focused on redundancy are worth highlighting here. The first experiment varied the number of best-matching passages that were examined for n-gram mining. Accuracy improved from 31% to 62% as the number of passages examined increased from 1 to 200. Thus, mining partial information from many n-grams greatly improves accuracy. The second experiment compared performance using collections of different sizes. One collection contained 1 million documents (TREC), and two contained roughly 2 billion documents (Web). Accuracy improved from 35% for the small collection to 55% for the large collection. Collection size influences the ability both to find simple rewrites that match and to mine answers from results. Simple techniques operating over large amounts of data provide good performance for a challenging problem.

A more informal evaluation was conducted for the Festschrift. I posed the question "Who is Tom Landauer?" to AskMSR and the audience. The AskMSR system responded with correct, albeit somewhat sterile answers—for example, *professor of psychology, president of knowledge analysis technologies, fellow of the institute of cognitive science, former director of the cognitive science research group,* and *giving the keynote.* It took the human intelligence of his friends and colleagues to complete the picture with answers like *my husband, a great mentor, a thought-provoking colleague, a challenger of the status quo, inspiring, the best,* and *not really retiring.*

The extent to which a system like AskMSR can mimic aspects of human question-answering abilities, or the extent to which characteristics such as redundancy, co-occurrence, and information integration play key roles in human question answering, are open and interesting questions. Two aspects of AskMSR are noteworthy in their differences from systems such as Graesser and Franklin's (1990) QUEST model: rich semantic networks not used, and the accumulation of information from multiple redundant snippets. Human memory is very rich in episodic traces that could support human question answering—for example, how many times have you heard about, or read about, or visited the scene of Lincoln's assassination? One preliminary experiment would be to evaluate the extent to which questions that are difficult for people to answer are also difficult for AskMSR. A related line of research would be to explore the nature of redundancy effects in human question answering. Anderson and Schooler (1991) have drawn attention to the environment as an important source of input for rational analyses, and we hope that operational systems like AskMSR can also shed light on characteristics of human performance in complex cognitive tasks.

Coda

Landauer's accomplishments offer splendid examples of psychological research, powerful computer applications, and shrewd practical analysis, working in concert to produce both useful results and good science. His scientific quests have led him from the nurturance of rats to human growth, from the design of friendly computer systems to radically new conceptions of meaning, from educational problems to insights about learning, and from quantitative linguistics to new methods of teaching. Landauer's clear vision, his ingenuity, and his elegant style have inspired students and coworkers. The work described in this symposium is clear evidence of his beneficent influence. Pasteur's quadrant is clearly Landauer's turf. But no simple phrase can fully capture either the spirit or the substantive nature of Landauer's splendid quest. Perhaps Lynn Streeter, who is also his wife, has given us the most felicitous description—"Tom is truly *a man for all quadrants.*"

References

Anderson, J. R., & Schooler, L. J. (1991). Reflections of the environment in memory. *Psychological Science, 10,* 396–408.

Anglin, J. M. (1970). *The growth of word meaning.* Cambridge, MA: MIT Press.

Brill, E., Dumais, S. T., & Banko, M. (2002). An analysis of the AskMSR question-answering system. *Proceedings of the 2002 Conference on Empirical Methods in Natural Language Processing (EMNLP 2002),* 257–264.

Dumais, S. T., Banko, M., Brill, E., Lin, J., & Ng, A. (2002). Web question answering: Is more always better? *Proceedings of SIGIR 2002,* 291–298.

Furnas, G. W., Landauer, T. K., Gomez, L. M., & Dumais, S. T. (1987). The vocabulary problem in human–system communication. *Communications of the ACM, 30,* 964–971.

Graesser, A. C., & Franklin, S. P. (1990). QUEST: A cognitive model of question answering. *Discourse Processes, 13,* 279–303.

Kandel, E. R., Schwartz, J. H., & Jessell, T. M. (2000). *Principles of neural science.* New York: McGraw-Hill/Appleton & Lange.

Laham, D. (1997). Latent semantic analysis approaches to categorization. In M. G. Shafto & P. Langley (Eds.), *Proceedings of the 19th Annual Meeting of the Cognitive Science Society* (p. 979). Mahwah, NJ: Erlbaum.

Laham, D., Bennett, W., & Derr, M. (2002). Latent semantic analysis for career field analysis and information operations [CD-ROM]. In *Proceedings of the Interservice/Industry Simulation, Education, and Training Conference (IITSEC).* Arlington, VA: National Training Systems Association.

Landauer, T. K. (1962). Rate of implicit speech. *Perceptual and Motor Skills, 15,* 646.

Landauer, T. K. (1975). Memory without organization: Properties of a model with random storage and undirected retrieval. *Cognitive Psychology, 7,* 495–531.

Landauer, T. K. (1995). *The trouble with computers: Usefulness, usability and productivity.* Cambridge, MA: MIT Press.

Landauer, T. K. (2003). Pasteur's quadrant: Computational linguistics, LSA, and education. *Proceedings of the HLT-NAACL Workshop on Building Educational Applications Using Natural Language Processing.* Retrieved June 21, 2004, from http://acl.ldc.upenn.edu/W/W03/

Landauer, T. K., & Dumais, S. T. (1997). A solution to Plato's problem: The latent semantic analysis theory of the acquisition, induction, and representation of knowledge. *Psychological Review, 104,* 211–240.

Landauer, T. K., & Eldridge, L. (1966). Failure of Actinomycin-D to inhibit passive avoidance learning: A confirmation. *Proceedings of the Annual Conference of the Annual Psychological Association,* 123–124.

Landauer, T. K., & Eldridge, L. (1967). Effect of tests without feedback and presentation-test interval in paired-associate learning. *Journal of Experimental Psychology, 75,* 290–298.

Landauer, T. K., Foltz, P. W., & Laham, D. (1998). An introduction to latent semantic analysis. *Discourse Processes, 25,* 259–284.

Landauer, T. K., & Freedman, J. L. (1968). Information retrieval from long-term memory: Category size and recognition time. *Journal of Verbal Learning and Verbal Behavior, 7,* 291–295.

Landauer, T. K., Laham, D., & Foltz, P. W. (2003). Automated scoring and annotation of essays with the Intelligent Essay Assessor. In M. D. Shermis & J. Burstein (Eds.), *Automated essay scoring: A cross-disciplinary perspective* (pp. 87–112). Mahwah, NJ: Erlbaum.

Landauer, T. K., & Streeter, L. A. (1973). Structural differences between common and rare words: Failure of equivalence assumptions for theories of word recognition. *Journal of Verbal Learning and Verbal Behavior, 12,* 119–131.

Landauer, T. K., & Whiting, J. W. M. (1977). Correlates and consequences of stress in infancy. In R. L. Munroe & R. H. Munroe (Eds.), *Cross cultural human development* (pp. 355–375). Belmont, CA: Wadsworth.

Miller, G. A. (1990). WordNet: An on-line lexical database [Special issue]. *International Journal of Lexicography, 3*(4).

Nachbar, D. W. (1988). *POMS (plain old mail service): Electronic mail without a computer* (Bell Communications Research Technical Memorandum No. TM-ARH-011716). Morristown, NJ: Bell Communications Research.

Stokes, D. E. (1997). *Pasteur's quadrant: Basic science and technological innovation.* Washington, DC: Brookings Institution.

Streeter, L. A. (1976). Language perception of two-month-old infants shows effects of both innate mechanisms and experience. *Nature, 259,* 39–41.

Sweller, J. (1999). Instructional design in technical areas. In *Australian Education Review* (No. 43). Camberwell, Victoria, Australia: ACER Press.

Voorhees, E., & Harman, D. (Eds.). (2001). *Proceedings of the Tenth Text Retrieval Conference (TREC-2001)* (NIST Special Publication 500-250). Washington, DC: U.S. Government Printing Office.

Wolfe, M. B. W., Schreiner, M. E., Rehder, B., Laham, D., Foltz, P. W., Kintsch, W., & Landauer, T. K. (1998). Learning from text: Matching readers and text by latent semantic analysis. *Discourse Processes, 25,* 309–336.

Part II

Learning

4

How Should a Theory of Learning and Cognition Inform Instruction?

John R. Anderson, Scott Douglass, and Yulin Qin

We have developed a set of computer-based cognitive tutors (Anderson, Corbett, Koedinger, & Pelletier, 1995; Koedinger, Anderson, Hadley, & Mark, 1997) for high school mathematics that have been effective in improving learning. These tutors interact with students at the grain size of about 20 seconds during which the student might transform an equation or calculate an angle and the tutor will respond to that. The tutors are able to interact with the student at this grain size on the basis of a cognitive model that can solve these problems in the various ways students are supposed to be able to solve the problems. Compared with most computer-based instruction, this is a rather fine grain size. However, compared with current theories of human cognition, including our own Automatic Components of Thought-Rational (ACT-R; Anderson & Lebiere, 1998, 2003), this is a very gross level of interaction. Temporally, ACT-R postulates primitive acts of cognition taking under 1 second and often as little as 50 ms. Componentwise, the theory postulates separate visual, memory, imaginal, and motor components to a student action such as transforming an equation. Although our focus is on ACT-R, its grain size is typical of modern theories of cognition. This chapter examines whether there is a role for a theory of cognition at this grain size in affecting something like mastery of high school algebra. Although not offering any definitive answers to the question, we review some of our research on eye movements that has attempted to track a finer temporal grain size in mathematical problem solving, and we review some of our research on brain imaging that has attempted to track different cognitive components in mathematical problem solving.

Using Eye Movements to Instruct

Eye movements are behaviors that occur at a temporal grain size of under a second and therefore offer the opportunity of fine-grained tracking of mathematical problem solving. Gluck (1999; see also Anderson & Gluck, 2001) looked at the instructional leverage one might gain by monitoring student eye movements while interacting with an algebra tutor. The tutor Gluck developed is a simplified version of the Practical Algebra Tutor, or PAT tutor (Koedinger et al., 1997) used in schools, and its interface is illustrated in Figure 4.1. Figure 4.1a shows a screen display as it appears at the beginning of a problem. The student's task is to fill in the column labels and units, enter a variable and an expression written in terms of that variable, and then answer whatever questions are present. Figure 4.1b displays the completed problem. The first question in that problem is an example of what is called *result-unknown* problem (in which the student must in effect evaluate the expression), and the second is an example of what is called a *start-unknown* problem (in which the student must in effect solve for x). The key aspect of the problem is the expression $12 + 45x$, which the student has filled in. The principal goal of the lesson is to teach the student how to create such expressions and use them to solve problems.

Gluck (1999) found numerous points at which eye movements indicated opportunities for instructional leverage. For instance, about 40% of all tutor messages to students are not read, but current tutors proceed on the assumption that the messages have been read. Often students will quickly self-correct when they do not read the message, but if there is a long latency and the students do not read the message, the odds become high that they will make an error.

As another example, eye movements allow us to disambiguate methods of solving problems. Figure 4.2 shows two examples of students solving result-unknown problems in the tutor. In both cases the student produces the right answer, and so there are no bases in the answers they type for suspecting a difference in the solution process. However, the fixation patterns are very different. The critical difference is that in Figure 4.2a the student is fixating the algebraic expression and using it in the solution of the problem, whereas in Figure 4.2b the student is rereading the verbal statement and ignoring the expression. This reflects a difference in early mastery of algebra in which some students use algebraic expressions whereas others fall back on prealgebraic reasoning skills (Koedinger & MacLaren, 1997). Gluck (1999) showed that students solved problems more rapidly and successfully when they displayed the eye movements typified in Figure 4.2a than when they displayed the eye movements typified in Figure 4.2b.

We decided to take Gluck's (1999) research and see if we could develop instructional interventions for the tutor that were triggered by eye movements. We identified a number of occasions in which the eye movements indicated an instructional opportunity and presented brief auditory messages lasting about 2 seconds. For instance, we noted occasions when students did not read the instruction and where it seemed that the instruction was critical. One such case, discussed above, occurred when students made an error, failed to self-correct, and did not read the error message. When 10 seconds had passed without students fixating the error message for more than ¼ second, they heard "Read the help message." As another example, we identified occasions in which student eye movements indicated a deficiency in their problem-solving strategy. For instance, if the student failed to solve a start-unknown problem and failed to fixate the expression, we would direct them to use the expression. More precisely, if students made an error and had failed to fixate the expression

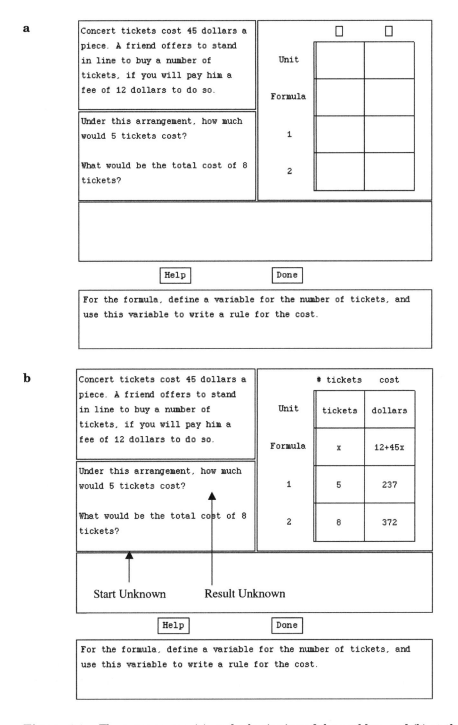

Figure 4.1. The tutor screen (a) at the beginning of the problem and (b) at the end of the problem. From "What Role Do Cognitive Architectures Play in Intelligent Tutoring Systems?" by J. R. Anderson and K. Gluck. In D. Klahr and S. M. Carver (Eds.), *Cognition and Instruction: Twenty-Five Years of Progress*, 2001, p. 244. Copyright 2001 by Lawrence Erlbaum Associates. Reprinted with permission.

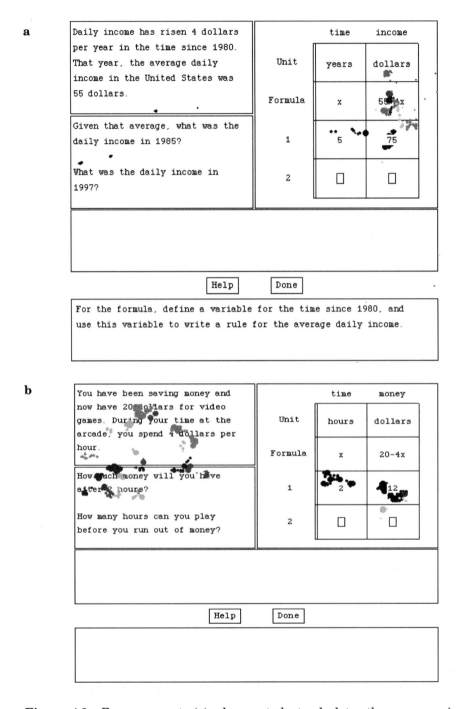

Figure 4.2. Eye movements (a) when a student calculates the answer using the expression and (b) when a student calculates the answer using the problem statement. The blotches reflect fixation points that go from dark to light with the passage of time. From "What Role Do Cognitive Architectures Play in Intelligent Tutoring Systems?" by J. R. Anderson and K. Gluck. In D. Klahr and S. M. Carver (Eds.), *Cognition and Instruction: Twenty-Five Years of Progress*, 2001, p. 250. Copyright 2001 by Lawrence Erlbaum Associates. Reprinted with permission.

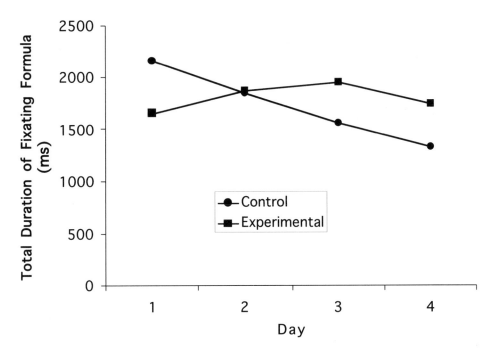

Figure 4.3. Amount of time spent fixating the formula in the control and experimental conditions as a function of the amount of practice.

for at least ¼ second, they heard the message "Try using the formula to compute your answer."

In a test in which we compared this augmented tutor with a tutor that was otherwise identical (including collection of eye movements), we found that students were able to reach the same level of mastery 20% faster with the augmented instruction. One might argue that this result does not really demonstrate that we are improving instructional effectiveness by attending to the fixation-by-fixation behavior of the student. Perhaps all the leverage simply comes from getting students to read more of the instructional messages. We would like to show that our eye-movement tutor has impact on behavior at this fine grain size. Figure 4.3 provides one example of such a refined effect. This shows how the fixation pattern of students changes over the 4 days with respect to amount of time spent encoding the formula. Figure 4.2b illustrated the curious pattern in which students would not use the formula in solving the problem. As noted, the tutor would intervene when they displayed this pattern and made an error, and it would suggest that they try to use the formula. This figure plots how much time students spent reading the formula during their first attempt to fill in the cells in the start-unknown and result-unknown cells. In the control condition students show decreased use of the formula, probably reflecting the general speedup in problem solution. However, students in the experimental condition maintained a constant rate of use of the formula. The difference in the linear trends in the two functions is significant, $t(38) = 2.12, p < .05$. This finding indicates that indeed detailed monitoring of students was having an impact on the fine-grain details of their problem-solving behavior.

So this result gives us some reason for optimism that the fine-grained temporal structure of human cognition might be relevant to achieving high-level instructional goals. However, it is important to note that this application did not actually involve the ACT-R theory or any other cognitive theory but rather was just a "commonsense" use of the eye tracking data. The ACT-R theory has been developed to address eye movement data (Salvucci, 2001). How such a fine-grained model could be used in instruction remains to be determined.

Brain Imaging and the Learning of Algebra

We (Qin, Anderson, Silk, Stenger, & Carter, 2004) have been using functional magnetic resonance imaging (fMRI) to study the learning of algebra. This work started with the use of brain imaging to study algebra equation solving in highly competent college students (Anderson, Qin, Sohn, Stenger, & Carter, 2003). That work was able to successfully relate an ACT-R model to the brain imaging data that we obtained. Figure 4.4 shows the steps that the ACT-R model goes through in solving an equation. The model involves the ACT-R components for reading the equation, imagining transformations to it, retriev-

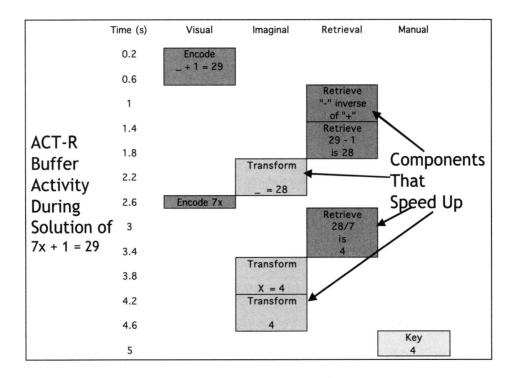

Figure 4.4. The steps ACT-R (Automatic Components of Thought-Rational) goes through in the solution of the equation $7x + 1 = 29$.

Our Modules (all left lateralized)
as 100 (5x5x4) Voxel Regions
Prefrontal/Retrieval: BA 45/46 (x = -40, y = 21, z = 21)
Motor/Manual: BA 3/4 (x = -37, y = -25, z = 47)
Parietal/Imaginal: BA 39/40 (x = -23, y = -64, z = 34)

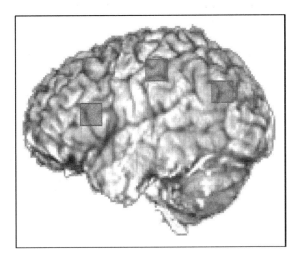

Figure 4.5. Regions of interest as identified in Anderson et al. (2003).

ing relevant facts from declarative memory, and programming the output of an answer (indicated by pressing a finger in a data glove in the magnet). Figure 4.5 illustrates three regions (all in the left cortex) that we found related to three of these components. There was a prefrontal region that seemed to reflect retrieval of relevant facts, a motor region that seemed to reflect programming of the right hand, and a parietal region that seemed to reflect the transformation of the equations.

Given this background, we decided to see if the same regions would be involved in children just learning algebra equation solving. We assessed children 11 to 14 years of age whose first instruction in equation solving was in our laboratory, and we looked at what happened to their performance over five days of an hour practice each day. We looked at their solution to equations of three levels of complexity in terms of number of steps of transformations to solve:

$$0 \text{ step: e.g., } 1x + 0 = 4$$
$$1 \text{ step: e.g., } 3x + 0 = 12, 1x + 8 = 12$$
$$2 \text{ step: e.g., } 7x + 1 = 29$$

The children were scanned in the magnet on the first and fifth day of the experiment. Figure 4.6 shows their time to solve the equations and the predictions of the ACT-R model in which all parameters were fixed (and set

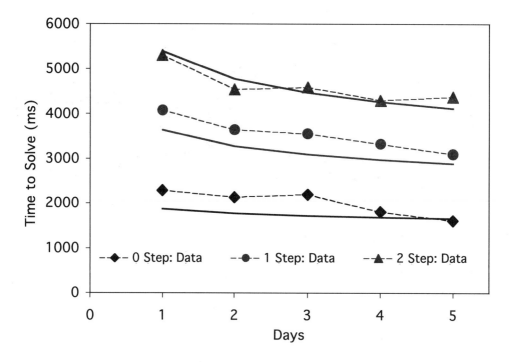

Figure 4.6. Time to solve equations of differential complexity as a function of practice.

on the basis of the adult data) except for the times for the retrieval and transformation steps in Figure 4.4, which sped up according to the following power function:

$$Time = F \bullet Days^{-a},$$

where F was estimated to be .63 seconds and a to be .28 seconds.

Figure 4.7 shows the scanning procedure for each trial in the magnet. Note that each trial is followed by a substantial intertrial interval so that the sluggish fMRI BOLD (blood oxygen level dependent) response can rise and drop before the next trial. Anderson et al. (2003) described how one can take the pattern of component activities in the different cognitive components in Figure 4.4 and

21.6 Second Structure of fMRI Trial

Prompt	Equation	ITI
+	3x+2=17	*
1.2 s 1 scan	12 s 10 scans	8.4 s 7 scans

Figure 4.7. The scanner protocol. fMRI = functional magnetic resonance imaging; ITI = intertrial interval.

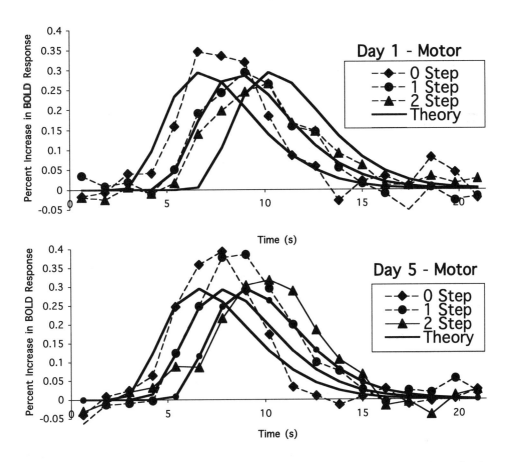

Figure 4.8. The observed and predicted BOLD (blood oxygen level dependent) responses in the motor region on Day 1 and Day 5.

convolve them with a standard gamma form for BOLD signal to predict the BOLD response in each condition. Figures 4.8, 4.9, and 4.10 show the BOLD responses obtained and predictions of the ACT-R model for the three regions of interest. In producing these BOLD functions, there are parameters estimated to reflect their magnitude and exact rise and fall times. However, there are two predictions that are parameter-free consequences of the ACT-R model in Figure 4.4.

1. The relative areas under the BOLD functions for different conditions in a brain region will be directly proportional to the time that the components are active.
2. The point at which the functions peak will reflect the difference in mean time from stimulus onset to the time when the components are active.

It is striking how well the ACT-R model predicts these BOLD functions, and this gives us reason for optimism that the brain imaging can track events

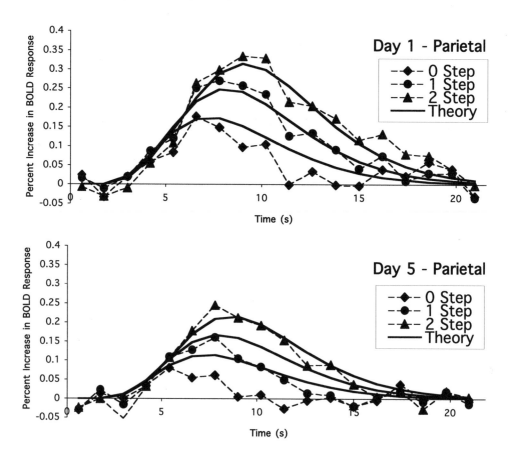

Figure 4.9. The observed and predicted BOLD (blood oxygen level dependent) responses in the parietal region on Day 1 and Day 5.

of significance with respect to the learning of mathematical cognition. It is worth noting qualitatively the different patterns predicted for the three components:

1. The size of the BOLD response in the motor area is constant across both complexity condition and practice. This is as would be expected because it is supposed to reflect the same finger press in all conditions. However, the peak of the functions is delayed as complexity increases. The effect of practice is to move the functions forward and compress the differences among them, reflecting the change in mean times with practice.

2. The size of the BOLD responses in the parietal area directly reflects the number of transformations that are occurring in the imaginal buffer. Note that there is a considerable response even in the zero-transformation condition because even in this condition it is necessary to build up a representation of the equation and extract the answer from it. With practice, the size of the BOLD responses diminishes,

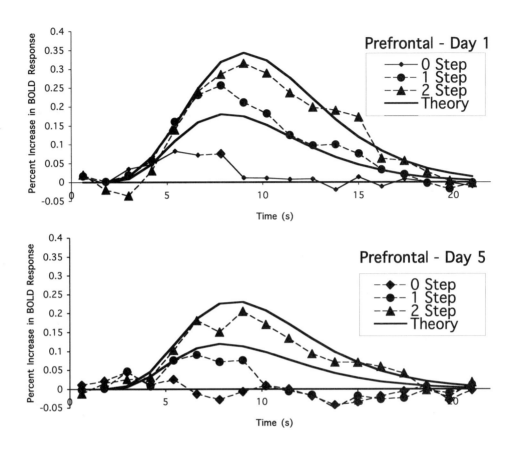

Figure 4.10. The observed and predicted BOLD (blood oxygen level dependent) responses in the prefrontal region on Day 1 and Day 5.

       reflecting the postulated speedup in the mental transformations of the equation.

3.   The BOLD functions for the prefrontal region are similar to those in the parietal region, showing differences in magnitude that reflect both number of transformations and practice. The one difference is that the response in the zero-transformation condition is predicted to be zero and nearly is so. This is because in this condition nothing has to be retrieved from long-term memory to calculate the answer.

     The pattern of data that we see in this study is very similar to the pattern of data that we have seen with our adult subjects. The one difference is that in studies of learning (not in the domain of equation solving in which our college students are already at asymptote) we find only learning-related changes in the prefrontal retrieval region and not in the parietal region that is used for problem representation. This difference suggests a greater plasticity in children's capability for learning new sorts of mental transformations.

     This study does indicate that we can find a rigorous mapping from the learning of mathematical problem solving onto brain imaging. It leaves open the issue of how one might use such brain imaging to actually improve mathematics instruction. One will never see an fMRI brain scanner in a classroom. However, we can observe brain patterns while students solve problems with our tutors in a scanner, and this information can be used to help improve the tutor instruction. There is also a promising new nonintrusive infrared technology (e.g., Strangman, Boas, & Sutton, 2002) that might someday see actual real-world use.

References

Anderson, J. R., Corbett, A. T., Koedinger, K. R., & Pelletier, R. (1995). Cognitive tutors: Lessons learned. *Journal of Learning Sciences, 4,* 167–207.

Anderson, J. R., & Gluck, K. A. (2001). What role do cognitive architectures play in intelligent tutoring systems? In D. Klahr & S. M. Carver (Eds.), *Cognition and instruction: Twenty-five years of progress* (pp. 227–262). Mahwah, NJ: Erlbaum.

Anderson, J. R., & Lebiere, C. (1998). *The atomic components of thought.* Mahwah, NJ: Erlbaum.

Anderson, J. R., & Lebiere, C. (2003). The Newell test for a theory of mind. *Behavioral and Brain Sciences, 26,* 587–637.

Anderson, J. R., Qin, Y., Sohn, M.-H., Stenger, V. A., & Carter, C. S. (2003). An information-processing model of the BOLD response in symbol manipulation tasks. *Psychonomic Bulletin & Review, 10,* 241–261.

Gluck, K. A. (1999). *Eye movements and algebra tutoring.* Unpublished doctoral dissertation, Carnegie Mellon University, Pittsburgh, PA.

Koedinger, K. R., Anderson, J. R., Hadley, W. H., & Mark, M. (1997). Intelligent tutoring goes to school in the big city. *International Journal of Artificial Intelligence in Education, 8,* 30–43.

Koedinger, K. R., & MacLaren, B. A. (1997). Implicit strategies and errors in an improved model of early algebra problem solving. In *Proceedings of the 19th Annual Conference of the Cognitive Science Society* (pp. 382–387). Hillsdale, NJ: Erlbaum.

Qin, Y., Anderson, J. R., Silk, E., Stenger, V. A., & Carter, C. S. (2004). The change of the brain activation patterns along with the children's practice in algebra equation solving. *Proceedings of the National Academy of Science, USA, 101,* 5686–5691.

Salvucci, D. D. (2001). An integrated model of eye movements and visual encoding. *Cognitive Systems Research, 1,* 201–220.

Strangman, G., Boas, D. A., & Sutton, J. P. (2002). Non-invasive neuroimaging using near-infrared light. *Biological Psychiatry, 52,* 679–693.

5

The Procedural Reinstatement Principle: Studies on Training, Retention, and Transfer

Alice F. Healy, Erica L. Wohldmann, and Lyle E. Bourne, Jr.

Much time and many resources are spent on training—in the military, in industry, in sports, and in education. This training is essential because individuals are not born with the knowledge and skills they will need to perform their jobs or other activities. But such training is also costly, so it is important to ensure that it be as efficient as possible. However, improving training efficiency should not be the only, or even the most important, consideration. If individuals have learned during training how to perform a task but then forget how to perform it sometime later, the training has not been adequate. Passing a test at the end of training does not guarantee later success on the job, in the field, or at the sports arena. Training needs to be durable as well as efficient. But even durable training will not be sufficient if the learned knowledge and skills cannot be applied to situations that are different from those encountered during training. Training can rarely capture the full set of circumstances under which tasks are subsequently encountered. It is, therefore, crucial that training be transferable as well as durable. Thus, the aim of our research program has been to develop principles that optimize all three aspects of training—its speed, durability, and transferability.

Procedural Reinstatement Principle

Our projects have involved a diverse set of knowledge and skills, ranging from simple laboratory tasks to complex military and civilian tasks such as tank gunnery (Marmie & Healy, 1995) and foreign language training (Healy &

This research was supported by Army Research Institute Contracts DASW01-96-K-0010, DASW01-99-K-0002, and DASW01-03-K-0002 and by Army Research Office Grant DAAG55-98-1-0214 to the University of Colorado. We thank Tim Curran, who served as guest editor for this chapter, for his helpful comments and suggestions.

Bourne, 1998). We describe studies from this research program illustrating how basic research in experimental cognitive psychology can provide theoretical principles with wide applicability that can lead to improvements in training effectiveness over a broad range of domains. The experiments we consider involve a variety of training tasks, including some that yielded very durable retention, with little or no loss in performance over long delay intervals, and others that yielded considerable forgetting across such delays. We were able to accommodate the full set of findings with a single theoretical principle— the procedural reinstatement principle—which builds on the procedural view of Kolers and Roediger (1984), on the distinction between procedural knowledge (knowing how to do something) and declarative knowledge (knowing that something is the case; e.g., Anderson, 1983), and on the previous theoretical principles of encoding specificity (Tulving & Thomson, 1973) and transfer-appropriate processing (Morris, Bransford, & Franks, 1977). We proposed that procedural information is well retained and if duplicated will lead to good recall of associated responses. In contrast, declarative information is quickly forgotten. Thus, long-term retention is evident to the extent that the specific procedures used during study can be reinstated during retention testing (Healy et al., 1992). We have also found that durable retention is often, and possibly always, associated with limited transferability (Healy & Bourne, 1995). The procedural reinstatement principle can explain the specificity observed by assuming that procedures are associated during learning with particular pieces of declarative information, or facts, so that durable memory depends on the reinstatement of particular fact–procedure combinations. The following are some studies providing evidence for this principle.

Experiments

Data Entry

In an early study of data entry (Fendrich, Healy, & Bourne, 1991), we found remarkable skill retention that is attributable to procedural reinstatement. Specifically, we showed subjects lists of digits to be typed using a computer keypad. In one experiment, subjects were given two days of training. Some of the lists were shown only once, and some were repeated five times across the training trials. A month later, subjects were given a retention test in which they entered some of the old lists of digits along with some new lists. Also, subjects were asked to give a recognition rating for each digit list shown at the retention test, with one group entering the digit lists before giving the recognition rating and the other group entering the digits after the recognition response. We found that subjects' typing times decreased as training progressed and changed very little over the delay. Also, response times on the retention test were shorter for the old lists repeated five times than for the new lists. The recognition test provides a direct (or explicit) measure of memory in contrast to the indirect measure of response time. Subjects had significant memory for the digit lists repeated five times one month earlier by this direct measure, as they had by the indirect response time measure, and there was better recognition performance for the digit lists repeated five times when they were entered before the recognition response than when they were entered after it. The highly durable memory found in this experiment can be understood by the procedural reinstatement principle because the testing situation guaranteed that the motoric typing procedures learned were reinstated at test, even for the recognition test when the digit lists were entered before the recognition response.

Another experiment on data entry (Fendrich, Gesi, Healy, & Bourne, 1995) provided more direct support for the importance of procedural reinstatement for long-term memory. Subjects were shown digit sequences on a computer screen. In one condition they simply read each sequence. In a second condition they entered the sequence using the numeric keypad on the computer console, and in a third condition they entered the sequence using the horizontal number row on the console. A week after training, subjects were given a retention test that required them to enter old and new sequences using, in some cases, the number row and, in other cases, the keypad. After entering each sequence, the subjects also made a recognition decision. Subjects showed highest recognition scores for the sequences entered with the same key configuration (keypad or row) at test as used at study. It is interesting that when old sequences were entered with a different key configuration at study and at test, subjects' recognition memory was no better than when they simply read the sequences at study. Entering the sequence at study aided explicit recognition only if the sequence was entered in the same way on the retention test.

Memory for Arithmetic Calculations

In a study on memory for arithmetic calculations (Crutcher & Healy, 1989), we provided a more general test of the importance to memory of mental procedures. This work was based on the *generation effect* (e.g., Slamecka & Graf, 1978), which is the finding that individuals show better retention of learned material when it is self-produced, or self-generated, than when it is simply copied, or read. We reasoned that if the generation effect is due to the activation of mental procedures, then a task requiring subjects to perform such procedures without generation may show equivalent retention to a generate task. Likewise, a task requiring generation using limited mental procedures may not result in any better retention than a read task. To test this hypothesis, we developed four tasks in which subjects saw single-digit multiplication problems and said aloud the problems and answers. In the read task, the answers were presented with the problems; thus no multiplication operations (which were the relevant mental procedures) were required by the subjects. In the generate task, the answers were absent so the multiplication operations had to be performed by the subjects. In the calculate task, the subjects also had to provide the answers to the problems, but they were told to use a calculator rather than perform the multiplication operations themselves. In the verify task, the subjects were given the problems with their answers but were required to perform the multiplication operations themselves to verify that the answers were correct. Thus, subjects performed the relevant mental procedures themselves in the generate and verify conditions, but not in the read and calculate conditions. At test, subjects were asked to recall the list of answers they had been given. Recall was poor overall but was far superior on the verify and generate tasks, in which the relevant mental procedures were performed by subjects themselves, than on the read and calculate tasks, in which the relevant mental procedures were not required by subjects. These results suggest that the standard generation effect is due to the activation of mental procedures rather than generation per se. More generally, these findings provide support for the importance of mental procedures in memory.

Memory for Course Schedules

Another task domain showing poor retention involves the recall by undergraduates of information about their course schedules. In one study (Wittman & Healy, 1995), we examined the retention of four different types of course schedule information: the actual title of the course ("what"), the instructor's name ("who"), the location of the class building on a campus map ("where"), and the class start time ("when"). We tested three groups of students on each of three different occasions, with the first test one to two years after taking the relevant courses and with six-month delays separating the three tests. Overall the level of performance was quite low, and there was a large decrease in performance on the second and third tests relative to that on the first. For example, on the third test, students remembered the name of their instructors (the "who" information) less than 40% of the time, which may be quite discouraging for teachers. On all three tests, the students' performance was best on the spatial, or "where," information. In accordance with the procedural reinstatement principle, this superiority of spatial location recall may be due to the fact that the students learned this information while using procedures that were repeated throughout the semester: They walked through the campus to the classroom each time the class was held. A similar type of procedural learning was not as readily available for the other types of information.

The objective of a follow-up experiment (Healy, King, & Sinclair, 1997) was to elucidate the role of procedural knowledge in spatial memory superiority. Students' memory for fictitious course schedules was tested within two separate situations: one in which they had previous procedural experience of the campus and one in which they were without such experience. Specifically, undergraduates from two different universities participated. All students were unfamiliar with the other campus. Different fictitious course schedules were used, each based on the directory of classes from one of the universities. Students in the familiar condition studied schedules from their own campus, and those in the unfamiliar condition studied schedules from the other campus. Recall was tested after a one-month delay. Performance was superior for the familiar condition compared with the unfamiliar condition, but only significantly on "where," or spatial, information. These results support the hypothesis that the spatial advantage is due to procedural experience, such as frequently walking through a university campus.

Memory for Driving Information

The types of information being compared in these studies of memory for course schedules differed along many dimensions, not just that relevant to the distinction between declarative and procedural information. A better test of the procedural reinstatement principle would compare memory for two types of information that differ only in the extent to which they are linked with procedures. Toward that end, Jensen and Healy (1998) sought to confirm the superiority of procedural over declarative memory using information from the *Colorado Drivers' Manual*. Two types of questions were selected. As verified by an independent group of judges, procedural questions had to do with the actual operation and driving of a vehicle (e.g., "Where parking is permitted, your vehicle must be within ____ inches of the curb"), whereas declarative questions had to do with ancillary facts (e.g., "License plates must be fastened horizontally in a manner to prevent swinging at a height of at least ____ inches from the ground"). The two types of questions were paired, both questions in a pair having the identical numerical answers (12 inches in the examples), so that the to-be-remembered information was the same for the two types. They differed only in the extent to which driving procedures were relevant. Subjects were asked to fill in the blank for each question as best as they could, giving numerical answers. We tested college students; only some of them were Colorado drivers who had previously passed the Colorado drivers' license written examination. In accordance with the procedural reinstatement principle, there was a significant advantage for the procedural questions relative to the declarative questions with the Colorado drivers and no difference between procedural and declarative questions with the other subjects, who were not Colorado drivers.

Mental Calculation

The procedural reinstatement principle provides a method for obtaining durable retention, namely by reinstating the learning procedures during subsequent testing, but the same principle predicts that those durable memories will be highly specific and lack generalizability because procedures are necessarily associated during learning with particular facts, so that durable memory depends on the reinstatement of particular fact–procedure combinations. Some evidence documenting the specificity of skills comes from the mental calculation task. In one study (Rickard, Healy, & Bourne, 1994), we trained subjects extensively to perform single-digit multiplication and division calculations. Training was limited to a subset of problems in a single operand order. Immediately following training and after a one-month delay, subjects were given four versions of each training problem. One version was the same as that used in acquisition; the three others served as tests of transfer. The manipulations used to create transfer versions were a change of operand order, a change of operation (multiplication to division or division to multiplication), and both operation and operand-order change. At both the immediate and the delayed tests on multiplication as well as division problems, response times were short-est to the no-change problems, longer to the problems changing operand order, longer still to those changing operation, and longest to those changing both operation and operand order. Because performance was worse on transfer problems than on training problems, the effects of training were highly specific for this largely cognitive mental arithmetic task.

Hand–Eye Coordination

In a more recent study (Healy, Wohldmann, & Bourne, 2002), we demonstrated specificity of training for motoric components in executing a hand–eye coordina-tion task. We used a clock face stimulus display, consisting of a start position (labeled with the letter X) surrounded by a circle of digits, 1–8. Subjects were instructed to move a cursor using a mouse onto the X to begin each trial. A digit then appeared above the X, and subjects were told to find this digit on the clock face and then move the cursor as quickly as possible from the X to the target digit represented in the circle. Our primary measure was response movement time (time to reach the target after leaving the X).

We introduced different types of stimulus–response incompatibility into the task by dissociating and putting in conflict the perceptual and motoric components of the task. We compared four conditions, in which subjects saw a standard clock face and responded using either a regular computer mouse or one of three reprogrammed mice. In the up–down condition, movements of the mouse upward produced a downward movement of the cursor, and down-ward mouse movements produced upward cursor movements, but the right–left movements were normal. In contrast, in the right–left condition, right–left movements of the mouse were reversed but the up–down movements were normal. In the combined condition, both up–down and right–left movements were reversed, and in the normal condition, no movements were reversed.

One issue in previous research of stimulus–response compatibility has been the extent to which negative effects of incompatibility persist across practice and across retention intervals (e.g., Proctor & Dutta, 1995). Our experi-ment addressed this issue to determine whether benefits of training and dura-bility of those benefits across retention intervals are equally large for different types of incompatibilities. Likewise, our experiment addressed the issue of transfer from one mouse condition to another so that we could assess the extent to which any benefits of training are generalizable across conditions of incompatibility. Specifically, subjects were trained with a given mouse condi-tion and tested for retention and transfer one week later with either the same or a different mouse condition. All four mouse conditions were used in both training and transfer sessions, with all 16 combinations examined across subjects.

We wondered whether practice with an up–down incompatibility would affect performance with a right–left incompatibility and vice versa. The two types of reversals could be independent so that learning to overcome one type would not transfer to the other type. This outcome is predicted by the specificity-of-training corollary of our procedural reinstatement principle. We were most interested in determining whether there would be any transfer from the right–left or from the up–down condition to the combined condition, which includes both types of incompatibilities. Likewise, we were interested in seeing whether there would be transfer, in the opposite direction, from the combined condition to the right–left and up–down conditions. The first of these cases could be viewed as part–whole transfer and the second as whole–part transfer. In either case, strong transfer would be expected unless the procedures do not combine additively. In fact, if additive procedures are not used, then the combined condition would not necessarily be expected to be the hardest, despite the presence of two types of reversals.

Each subject was trained in Session 1 for 400 trials, divided into five blocks of 80 trials, with each block further divided into five subblocks of 16 randomly arranged trials, two with each of the eight digits. The subjects then returned one week later for retention and transfer testing during another 400 trials in Session 2.

To evaluate the effects of training, we examined movement time as a function of the Session 1 condition for the first and last blocks of Session 1. We found much improvement during training for all three conditions involving reprogrammed mice, but only a very modest improvement for the normal condition. Also, in keeping with our predictions, performance was best in the normal condition, but, contrary to intuition, performance was no worse in the combined condition than in the right–left or up–down conditions.

To evaluate retention, we compared movement time in the last block of Session 1 with that in the first block of Session 2 for only those cases in which subjects had the same mouse conditions in both sessions. We found no forgetting across the retention interval but instead a slight, but significant improvement from Session 1 to Session 2.

To evaluate transfer, we examined movement time in only conditions involving one of the three reprogrammed mice in Session 1 and a different one of those conditions in Session 2. We considered the data from blocks at the beginning of Session 1 as well as the beginning of Session 2. Overall, we found a trend for interference rather than transfer. For example, movement times were actually slower in the first block of Session 2 of the combined/up–down condition than in the first block of Session 1 of the up–down/combined and up–down/right–left conditions. Subjects learned a lot in Session 1 of the combined/up–down condition with the combined mouse, but they transferred none of what they learned to the simpler case of the up–down mouse.

We computed an index of the amount of transfer in each of the reprogrammed mouse conditions. To derive this index, we subtracted each participant's movement time in the first block of Session 2 from the average movement time across subjects in the same mouse condition in the first block of Session 1. By this index, there was no transfer, with two exceptions (see Figure 5.1). Small part–whole transfer was evident in the right–left/combined and up–down/combined cases, when the combined task occurred in Session 2. However, there was no whole–part transfer, so that performance in Session 2 was quite poor in the opposite combined/right–left and combined/up–down cases, when the combined task occurred in Session 1.

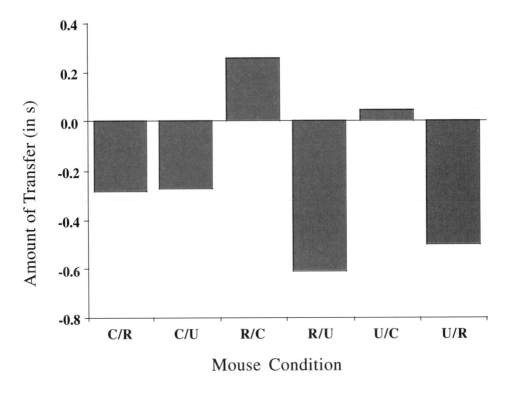

Figure 5.1. Transfer index as a function of condition in hand–eye coordination experiment. C = combined; U = up–down; R = right–left.

We, thus, found that practice with a given form of incompatibility led to large improvements during training and high durability across a one-week delay but minimal transfer from one type of incompatibility to another. These findings suggest that there is more than one skill involved in learning to deal with hand–eye incompatibility. Up–down, right–left, and combined movement reversals all require different skills that are independent in the sense that there is essentially no transfer from one to another. These results are, therefore, consistent with the specificity-of-training corollary of the procedural reinstatement principle. They also suggest that the processes used to overcome different types of incompatibilities do not combine additively, so that there is no whole–part transfer and only little part–whole transfer. Further in support of this conclusion, the combined condition did not show response times that were longer than the average of those in the separate reversal conditions.

Duration Estimation

Recently, we addressed the procedural reinstatement principle with a new task, namely the estimation of short intervals of time (Healy, Wohldmann, Parker, & Bourne, 2004). Because of subjects' prior experience estimating time in seconds or minutes, we used a new fundamental time unit to obtain a purer evaluation of the effects of training duration estimation, with 1 unit equal to 783 milliseconds.

In the prospective production estimation task we used, subjects practiced estimating six different time intervals given in these arbitrary units. Subjects were not told the length of a unit; however, they were able to learn this information through training because feedback was provided on every trial.

The aim of our experiment was to evaluate the effects of a secondary task on the primary task of duration estimation and to examine the long-term retention and transfer of the duration estimation skill. There were two sessions, training and retraining, with a one-week delay between them. In both sessions, subjects were given six blocks of trials, with each block including six different intervals to be estimated, all of which were less than one minute. There were two conditions, no switch and switch, which depended on whether subjects performed the same task during training and retraining. In both sessions, half of the subjects in each condition performed no secondary task, and the other half performed a difficult secondary task in which they recited aloud the alphabet backward by every third letter beginning from a random letter given to them at the start of each trial.

We examined the proportional absolute error, which is the absolute (i.e., unsigned) difference between the participant's actual estimate and the interval to be estimated divided by the interval to be estimated. For this measure, we found significant improvement across training blocks, primarily across the first two training blocks, reflecting practice with the task, and there was more improvement in Session 1 than in Session 2. We were most interested in the changes in performance between the end of Session 1 and the beginning of Session 2 a week later when the switch in tasks occurred for half of the subjects. We compared performance on the last block of Session 1 with that on the first block of Session 2 and found that subjects in the no-switch condition showed no forgetting between sessions even though there was a one-week delay separating them. This finding supports the procedural reinstatement principle, providing clear evidence of skill durability. Also in line with the procedural reinstatement principle is the large increase in error between sessions found for subjects in the switch condition, providing clear evidence of skill specificity. The decline in performance between sessions for those subjects in the switch condition was found for both switching directions, although it was greater for subjects who switched from the no-alphabet to the alphabet task.

Again, we computed an index of transfer by subtracting performance on the first block of Session 2 for each subject from the average performance for subjects given the same task on the first block of Session 1. We found no significant transfer in either switch group. In contrast, large transfer was evident for both no-switch groups by this measure (see Figure 5.2).

This experiment, thus, provided a clear demonstration that improvement in estimating intervals during training was specific to the presence or absence of a secondary task used during training. Both subjects who were trained with the secondary alphabet task and those who were not trained with the secondary task showed substantial improvement during training. When subjects from both of those training groups returned after a one-week delay, they showed no forgetting for the estimation skill that they had acquired if they did not switch

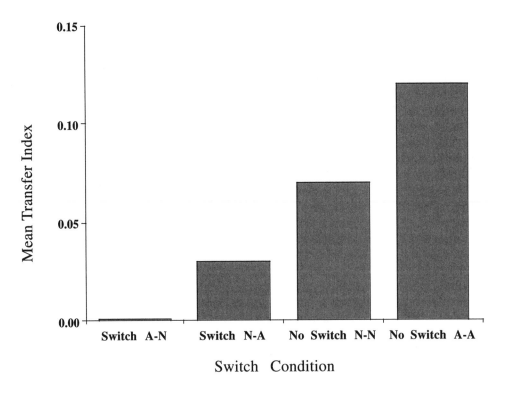

Figure 5.2. Transfer index as a function of condition in duration estimation experiment. A = alphabet; N = no alphabet.

tasks between the two sessions. However, when subjects did switch tasks between Session 1 and Session 2, then they showed an increase in error, which was large when Session 1 involved the easier no-alphabet task and Session 2 involved the harder alphabet task, but was also evident when Session 1 involved the harder alphabet task and Session 2 involved the easier no-alphabet task. In fact, in both cases subjects' performance at the start of Session 2 was equal to that for the same task at the start of Session 1. Thus, there was no forgetting between the two sessions in the no-switch condition and no transfer between the two sessions in the switch condition.

In this experiment, we found that performance was specific to the presence or absence of the secondary task. The question arises whether performance on the primary task is also influenced by the specific nature of the secondary task. To explore this issue, in a new study (Wohldmann, Healy, & Bourne, 2003), we examined the transfer of training under one specific secondary task to subsequent performance under the same secondary task, the same type of secondary task, or a different type of secondary task. Specifically, we compared four different secondary task conditions, each of which was coupled with the primary task of time estimation. The secondary tasks differed both in domain and in difficulty. We used two different alphabet secondary tasks: a relatively simple task involving repeating the alphabet forward by ones and the relatively difficult task we used earlier involving repeating the alphabet backward by threes. We also used two new tone-counting secondary tasks: a simple task requiring subjects to count silently a single regularly paced tone and a more difficult task requiring subjects to count separately two irregularly paced tones, one high in pitch and the other low in pitch. Because the most preferred strategy for estimating time is by means of rhythmic counting, the simple secondary tasks were intended to promote a rhythmic counting strategy, whereas the difficult secondary tasks were intended to inhibit such a strategy.

As in the last experiment, subjects were trained for six blocks of trials with six intervals, and then they returned one week later for retraining with six more blocks of trials using the same six intervals. The secondary task used during training was varied independently of the secondary task used during retraining in a factorial between-subjects design. All 16 combinations of training task and retraining task were used. Thus, the secondary tasks used during training and retraining were either the same, different but from the same domain, different but of the same difficulty, or different in both domain and difficulty.

As in the last experiment, to examine retention and transfer, we focused on the two blocks surrounding the one-week retention interval: the last block of Session 1 and the first block of Session 2. Also, as previously, we examined the proportional absolute error for the estimated interval. We found that when subjects performed the exact same task in both sessions, they showed relatively little forgetting across the one-week delay, although the small increase in error across the retention interval was significant. When subjects switched secondary tasks, however, they showed a dramatic increase in error from the first to the second session, when they switched only between levels of difficulty, switched only between domains, or switched between both difficulty levels and domains. Thus, there was little forgetting across the retention interval when the secondary tasks were the same during training and retraining, but performance at the start of retraining was substantially worse than at the end of training when the secondary task used during retraining did not match the secondary task used during training in either domain or difficulty. These findings strongly suggest that the strategies subjects acquired for performing the duration estimation task during training were specific to the secondary task. For example, even though subjects could perform each of the simple secondary tasks using a rhythmic counting strategy, there was no transfer between the simple tone task and the simple alphabet task.

Theoretical and Practical Implications

In terms of theory, the results from this study are consistent with the procedural reinstatement principle, on the assumption that the procedures used for the primary task of duration estimation are different when the secondary tasks differ because duration estimation is integrated with the demands of the secondary task. Subjects may use a counting strategy with every secondary task, but that strategy is likely to involve number counting with no secondary task, letter counting with an alphabet task, and tone counting with a tone-counting task. For example, in the difficult alphabet task, the requirement to recite the alphabet backward by threes becomes integrated with the requirement to estimate time. Our findings, therefore, demonstrate that the procedural reinstatement principle applies to the procedures involved in an irrelevant but concurrent secondary task, not just to the primary task. In fact, our findings suggest that for experienced subjects the primary task may functionally merge with the secondary task so that the two are not performed independently. For this reason, we distinguish between the nominal tasks defined by the experimenter (i.e., separate primary and secondary tasks) and the functional task learned by the subject (i.e., an integrated combination of the primary and secondary tasks; Healy et al., 2004).

In terms of applications, these findings demonstrate that it is important to train individuals on the full set of task operations that will be used in future performance, including apparently irrelevant secondary task operations, not just primary task operations. If the required operations change after training, then the individuals' performance may revert to the initial level, so that their training would be essentially useless. Therefore, an effective training regime must incorporate, as much as possible, all future task requirements. It may seem that this recommendation coincides with what is frequently done in applied settings. However, there are many real-world situations that are inconsistent with this advice. For example, in athletics, swimmers often use different suits in training and in competition, and baseball players often practice batting with weighted bats. Likewise, in military and industrial settings, simplified simulators, which do not include all task components, are often used for training. Our research challenges any training regime in which the practice conditions and the subsequent testing conditions are not the same. More specifically, our findings imply that for a training simulator to be effective, it must incorporate all eventual task requirements.

References

Anderson, J. R. (1983). *The architecture of cognition.* Cambridge, MA: Harvard University Press.

Crutcher, R. J., & Healy, A. F. (1989). Cognitive operations and the generation effect. *Journal of Experimental Psychology: Learning, Memory, and Cognition, 15,* 669–675.

Fendrich, D. W., Gesi, A. T., Healy, A. F., & Bourne, L. E., Jr. (1995). The contribution of procedural reinstatement to implicit and explicit memory effects in a motor task. In A. F. Healy & L. E. Bourne, Jr. (Eds.), *Learning and memory of knowledge and skills: Durability and specificity* (pp. 66–94). Thousand Oaks, CA: Sage.

Fendrich, D. W., Healy, A. F., & Bourne, L. E., Jr. (1991). Long-term repetition effects for motoric and perceptual procedures. *Journal of Experimental Psychology: Learning, Memory, and Cognition, 17,* 137–151.

Healy, A. F., & Bourne, L. E., Jr. (Eds.). (1995). *Learning and memory of knowledge and skills: Durability and specificity.* Thousand Oaks, CA: Sage.

Healy, A. F., & Bourne, L. E., Jr. (Eds.). (1998). *Foreign language learning: Psycholinguistic studies on training and retention.* Mahwah, NJ: Erlbaum.

Healy, A. F., Fendrich, D. W., Crutcher, R. J., Wittman, W. T., Gesi, A. T., Ericsson, K. A., & Bourne, L. E., Jr. (1992). The long-term retention of skills. In A. F. Healy, S. M. Kosslyn, & R. M. Shiffrin (Eds.), *From learning processes to cognitive processes: Vol. 2. Essays in honor of William K. Estes* (pp. 87–118). Hillsdale, NJ: Erlbaum.

Healy, A. F., King, C. L., & Sinclair, G. P. (1997). Maintenance of knowledge about temporal, spatial, and item information: Memory for course schedules and word lists. In D. G. Payne & F. G. Conrad (Eds.), *Intersections in basic and applied memory research* (pp. 215–230). Mahwah, NJ: Erlbaum.

Healy, A. F., Wohldmann, E. L., & Bourne, L. E., Jr. (2002, November). *Specificity of hand–eye coordination: Training and transfer effects.* Paper presented at the 43rd Annual Meeting of the Psychonomic Society, Kansas City, MO.

Healy, A. F., Wohldmann, E. L., Parker, J. T., & Bourne, L. E., Jr. (2004). *Training, retention, and transfer in duration estimation: The procedural reinstatement framework.* Manuscript submitted for publication.

Jensen, M. B., & Healy, A. F. (1998). Retention of procedural and declarative information from the *Colorado Drivers' Manual.* In M. J. Intons-Peterson & D. Best (Eds.), *Memory distortions and their prevention* (pp. 113–124). Mahwah, NJ: Erlbaum.

Kolers, P. A., & Roediger, H. L., III. (1984). Procedures of mind. *Journal of Verbal Learning and Verbal Behavior, 23,* 425–449.

Marmie, W. R., & Healy, A. F. (1995). The long-term retention of a complex skill. In A. F. Healy & L. E. Bourne, Jr. (Eds.), *Learning and memory of knowledge and skills: Durability and specificity* (pp. 30–65). Thousand Oaks, CA: Sage.

Morris, C. D., Bransford, J. D., & Franks, J. J. (1977). Levels of processing versus transfer appropriate processing. *Journal of Verbal Learning and Verbal Behavior, 16,* 519–533.

Proctor, R. W., & Dutta, A. (1995). Acquisition and transfer of response selection skill. In A. F. Healy & L. E. Bourne, Jr. (Eds.), *Learning and memory of knowledge and skills: Durability and specificity* (pp. 300–319). Thousand Oaks, CA: Sage.

Rickard, T. C., Healy, A. F., & Bourne, L. E., Jr. (1994). On the cognitive structure of basic arithmetic skills: Operation, order, and symbol transfer effects. *Journal of Experimental Psychology: Learning, Memory, and Cognition, 20,* 1139–1153.

Slamecka, N. J., & Graf, P. (1978). The generation effect: Delineation of a phenomenon. *Journal of Experimental Psychology: Human Learning and Memory, 4,* 592–604.

Tulving, E., & Thomson, D. M. (1973). Encoding specificity and retrieval processes in episodic memory. *Psychological Review, 80,* 352–373.

Wittman, W. T., & Healy, A. F. (1995). A long-term retention advantage for spatial information learned naturally and in the laboratory. In A. F. Healy & L. E. Bourne, Jr. (Eds.), *Learning and memory of knowledge and skills: Durability and specificity* (pp. 170–205). Thousand Oaks, CA: Sage.

Wohldmann, E. L., Healy, A. F., & Bourne, L. E., Jr. (2003, April). *Training and transfer on the skill of time estimation using a dual-task methodology.* Paper presented at the 73rd Annual Convention of the Rocky Mountain Psychological Association, Denver, CO.

6

Material Appropriate Difficulty: A Framework for Determining When Difficulty Is Desirable for Improving Learning

Mark A. McDaniel and Gilles O. Einstein

An exciting and provocative application of cognitive psychology to education rests on basic findings showing that introducing difficulty into learning improves long-term performance and transfer. Many of these basic findings are related to the work of the researchers honored by this volume, as well as their colleagues' work. For instance, building on Bill Battig's (1972, 1979) theme that producing contextual interference during learning promotes long-term retention, Mannes and Kintsch (1987) found that presenting an outline that was inconsistent with the organization of a technical article enhanced performance on inference-level and problem-solving tests compared with presenting a noninterfering outline. Along similar lines, Schneider, Healy, and Bourne (2002) reported that intermixed training regimens for foreign vocabulary led to better long-term performance than easier-blocked training regimens. McNamara and Healy (1995), among others (e.g., McDaniel, Waddill, & Einstein, 1988), have shown that generating answers to problems produces better retention than reading answers. Landauer and Bjork (1978) focused on testing difficulty and found that a succession of increasingly difficult recall tests improved long-term recall compared with a succession of easier tests.

From this diverse range of work, Bjork (1994) has synthesized the general notion that difficulties and challenges for the learner are desirable and should be introduced into instructional practice. Bjork has specifically suggested that the kinds of difficulties just mentioned, as well as others, be considered "desirable difficulties" that merit investigation and introduction into educational settings.

Inspired in part by the theories and research of the august group of scholars honored by this volume as well as our own basic memory research, we embrace the idea that some types of difficulty are desirable for learning and some are not. An important theme we develop is that prescriptions based on broad classes of desirable difficulty, such as generation, may not always be entirely fruitful.

To gain predictive power for effective prescription of desirable difficulty, we describe a contextualistic framework that focuses on the processing stimulated by difficulty, the materials to be learned, and brief consideration of characteristics of the learner. We then apply the framework to the educationally relevant task of remembering text-based information and show that a particular difficulty manipulation will benefit retention under Condition A but not Condition B, whereas an alternative difficulty manipulation will fail under Condition A but not Condition B. We turn first to basic experimental findings that provide the foundation for our framework.

Basic Experimental Findings With Word Lists

Research over the last several decades has convincingly demonstrated that the type or quality of processing is more important for determining learning and memory performance than the amount of time spent studying the material. There is now abundant evidence that good relational or organizational processing and extensive individual-item processing (resulting in distinctive encodings) enhance memory. Einstein and Hunt (1980; Hunt & Einstein, 1981) argued that relational and individual-item processing lead to the encoding of qualitatively different kinds of information and that both are important for optimal free recall. It is critical, for the purpose of this chapter, to note they also argued that the materials as well as the orienting activities induce certain kinds of processing and thus that the mnemonic benefits of each type of processing depend on the nature of the material.

As a concrete example of these ideas, consider Einstein and Hunt's (1980) research in the context of word lists. They presented subjects with either an obviously related list of items (six items from each of six taxonomic categories) or an ostensively unrelated list that actually contained six items from each of six ad hoc categories (e.g., things that fly, things that are green). Their assumption was that the related list normally encourages the encoding of relational information and the unrelated list normally encourages the encoding of individual-item or distinctive information. Einstein and Hunt also varied whether subjects performed an individual-item or relational orienting task. They assumed that a pleasantness-rating task would focus attention on the meaning of the individual items and a task of sorting items into categories would focus attention on the relations among the items. Consistent with the view that optimal recall results when both relational and individual-item information are encoded, the effectiveness of the individual-item and relational orienting tasks depended on the nature of the materials. Specifically, individual-item processing improved recall (compared with relational processing) with the related list, whereas relational processing improved recall (compared with individual-item processing) with the unrelated list. They (see also Hunt & Einstein, 1981) also found that clustering (a measure of relational encoding) was high whenever subjects received a related list or performed the relational task. In contrast, recognition performance on a test that required discrimination among similar category items (a measure of individual-item encoding) was high whenever subjects received an unrelated list or performed the individual-item task. This research clearly indicates that the ideal condition for encoding both individual-item and relational information is when the processing that is performed is complementary (i.e., not redundant) with the processing afforded by the to-be-learned materials (for more detailed analyses, see Engelkamp, Biegelmann, & McDaniel, 1998).

The Material Appropriate Difficulty Framework

Expanding on the above theoretical and empirical work, we suggest that the desirability of difficulty for enhancing learning and retention will depend on three fundamental components. First, one must distinguish the type of processing stimulated by the particular difficulty that is embedded into the learning task. We suggest that a useful heuristic is to consider the degree to which particular kinds of difficulty stimulate relational versus individual-item processing. Second, the cognitive engineer (educator) must be sensitive to the type of processing afforded by the to-be-learned material. Again, we suggest that distinguishing between relational and individual-item processing provides a generally fruitful level of analysis (Hunt & McDaniel, 1993; McDaniel & Einstein, 1989). Third, the overlap between the type of processing stimulated by difficulty and that encouraged by the material will determine the desirability of the difficulty. When the type of processing stimulated by difficulty and the processing encouraged by the material are redundant, then difficulty is not expected to significantly enhance retention. In this case, additional time on task is not productive, and thus difficulty is not desirable. Difficulty is desirable when it stimulates types of processing that are not encouraged by the materials themselves. That is, the material appropriate difficulty (MAD) framework identifies desirable difficulty as that which requires processing that is complementary to the processing afforded by the learning material.

Note that a fundamental and central outcome of this view is that desirable difficulty is a relative construct based on the interaction of the difficulty and the to-be-learned material. The provocative idea here is that a particular type of difficulty can be desirable when applied to one type of material and undesirable when applied to another type of material. Thus, we suggest that the desirability of difficulty is more accurately determined in a contextualistic sense rather than in terms of an absolute taxonomy of difficulties that are prescribed to be desirable for enhancing learning.

As a concrete example of these constructs in the basic experimental research, consider an experiment by McDaniel, Einstein, and Lollis (1988). Building on Einstein and Hunt's (1980) work described earlier, McDaniel et al. modified the pleasantness rating (individual-item processing) and the sorting (relational processing) tasks to make them more difficult to complete than the standard versions of these orienting tasks. Notable increases in processing time confirmed that regardless of the type of word list (related or unrelated), the modified tasks created difficulty compared with the standard versions. The mnemonic benefits of difficulty, however, were dependent on the degree to which the processing stimulated by the difficulty task was complementary to the processing afforded by the particular word list. Increasing difficulty for pleasantness rating (individual-item processing) significantly increased recall of the related list (affording relational processing) compared with recall displayed by the standard pleasantness rating task (mean increase of 5 words); increasing the difficulty of sorting (relational processing) was not desirable for the related list, as there was no increase in recall compared with standard sorting (mean loss of 1.5 words). The opposite pattern was obtained for the unrelated list (affording individual-item processing). Now difficult sorting improved recall substantially compared with standard sorting (mean increase of 7.3 words), whereas difficult pleasantness rating produced much less improvement compared with standard pleasantness rating (mean increase of 2.7 words).

To illustrate the potency of these ideas for educationally relevant materials and with a general class of difficulty that has earned the mantle of "desirable," we next apply the MAD framework to text materials and generation tasks.

Material Appropriate Difficulty Applied to Generation as Desirable Difficulty: Now You See It, Now You Don't

Basic research has demonstrated that generating words rather than reading words generally improves memory for those words (e.g., McDaniel, Waddill, & Einstein, 1988; Slamecka & Graf, 1978; among others). On the basis of these findings, some have reasonably suggested that generation can be viewed as a way to create desirable difficulty to enhance student learning in educational contexts (deWinstanley & Bjork, 2001). For purposes of exposition, we term this the *standard difficulty* view. Though such a view follows from the basic experimental cognitive literature, note that it is counter to most educational practice, which we term the *standard educational* view. As but one illustration of this, a recent winner of teacher of the year award at one of our universities expressed his educational philosophy as transforming complex material into simple constructs. Our MAD framework suggests important refinements to both of these approaches.

Consider learning from text material. There are several ways to implement text presentation so that the information has to be generated rather than read. Borrowing directly from the word-list literature, letters can be removed from words so that the words in the text are presented in fragmented form (e.g., deWinstanley & Bjork, 2001; McDaniel, Ryan, & Cunningham, 1989). Another variant is to require generation of words from scrambled letters. Extending this to text, sentences can be presented in a random order (e.g., Schwarz & Flammer, 1981), and the learner must generate a coherent text from the scrambled sentences.

What should we expect in terms of learning when the text is purposefully designed to create difficulty for the learner? On the standard education view, this should lessen learners' comprehension of the material compared with reading, and recall should suffer. On the standard difficulty view that generation is desirable difficulty, the expectation is that presenting text composed of fragmented words or randomly ordered sentences should increase memory for the information in the text compared with simply reading the text. (Note that the assumption throughout is that the learner can complete the generation task; if the learner cannot generate the information, then memory would not be expected to benefit.)

The MAD view underscores the need to analyze the type of processing stimulated by the particular generation task, with a focus on distinguishing between relational and individual-item processing. Generating a text by unscrambling sentences presumably produces extensive organizational processing, processing devoted to considering and figuring out relationships among the sentences. In contrast, generating fragmented words in the text presumably encourages more extended processing of the individual concepts that compose the text (termed *atomic propositions* in van Dijk & Kintsch's, 1983, text theory) and processing of how these concepts combine to form an idea (termed *complex propositions* in van Dijk & Kinstch's theory). Support for these assumptions was reported in a study that applied these two generation tasks to a narrative about a half-inning of a baseball game, with recall tested by questions that targeted the three major plays described in the passage (relational questions) and questions that targeted six specific details in the text (individual-item questions). Sentence-unscrambling generation produced the best performance for the relational questions, whereas word-fragment generation produced the best performance for the individual-item questions (McDaniel, Hines, Waddill, & Einstein, 1994, Experiment 1).

Now, suppose that these two generation tasks are applied to various types of text. The central tenet in MAD is that the processing afforded by the particular target texts, as well as the overlap between this processing and that stimulated by generation, is critical for whether generation (and difficulty in general) is in fact desirable. For present purposes let us assume the texts are folktales and didactic expositions. Inspired in part by Walter Kintsch and colleagues' seminal work in discourse and text comprehension (van Dijk & Kintsch, 1983), it is plausible that folktales invite sufficient relational processing during casual reading. This relational processing might be supported by readers' prior knowledge of conventional frames and scripts about episodes that are activated for comprehension, by readers' knowledge of canonical structures of folktales that provide organization (van Dijk & Kintsch, 1983), or by causal chains inherent in folktales that relate initial events in the tale to the final outcome (Fletcher & Bloom, 1988; Trabasso & van den Broek, 1985). Thus for folktales, extensive and controlled relational processing stimulated by difficult sentence unscrambling is functionally redundant with the relational processing afforded by reading and comprehending the text. However, extensive processing of individual propositions stimulated by the difficult fragmented-word generation task is complementary to the relational processing engaged during reading. Accordingly, for folktales MAD anticipates that sentence-unscrambling generation will produce modest, if any, significant increases in recall, whereas word-fragment generation will produce significant increases in recall compared with reading and sentence unscrambling.

MAD anticipates the reverse for expository texts. Expository text appears to invite processing that focuses on individual propositions (see McDaniel & Einstein, 1989). Thus, relational processing stimulated by sentence unscrambling should now significantly improve recall. In contrast, extensive processing of individual propositions stimulated by word-fragment generation would now be redundant with the item-specific processing invited by the expository texts. Accordingly, word-fragment generation will not increase recall for expository texts.

The MAD predictions have been borne out in several experiments as shown in Table 6.1. It is noteworthy that learners were relatively successful at completing both generation tasks. Accordingly, an absence of positive benefits for generation is not because subjects failed to do the generation task. Further, variations in the degree to which learners were successful at completing the generation tasks across texts could not account for the MAD pattern in free recall.

Examination of the processing times in Table 6.1 indicates that both generation tasks always produced substantial difficulty. The recall scores, however, indicate that these tasks did not consistently improve recall. In light of the extensive effort produced by generation without concomitant enhancement in recall, it would be inaccurate to categorically propose that generation reflects desirable difficulty. More troublesome for the standard difficulty view, even a particular generation task cannot be assumed to produce desirable difficulty. Positive effects of a particular generation task can be obtained with one type of text but not another type of text. These results support the idea that determination of desirable difficulty for enhancing educational practice needs to include in part considerations of material appropriateness.

We turn now to applying MAD to anticipating the value of more traditional educational study adjuncts. Working from a standard view that additional semantic processing benefits memory, one would anticipate that reading adjuncts that orient students to the meaning of the reading material should generally enhance learning. It is interesting to note, however, that research on reading adjuncts indicates that their effects on learning tend to be inconsistent. For example, asking subjects to use advance organizers sometimes improves memory for the materials and sometimes does not (see Mayer, 1979, for a review). Similar inconsistent effects have been obtained with adjunct questions (see Hamilton, 1985, for a review). According to the MAD framework, these adjuncts should be effective to the extent that they encourage the encoding of information that is not typically afforded by the materials.

To test this idea, we (Einstein, McDaniel, Owen, & Cote, 1990) varied the type of reading adjunct that subjects used while reading either the folktale or the expository texts described earlier. Specifically, some subjects answered adjunct questions designed to encourage individual-item processing. These questions were presented after each paragraph in the text, and they queried information specific to the immediately preceding paragraph. Other subjects were asked to develop an outline as they read; our assumption was that this encouraged encoding of relational or macro structure information. Consistent with expectations, for the folktale, answering adjunct questions improved recall compared with the read-only control condition, whereas outlining did not. Conversely, for the expository passage, outlining improved memory, whereas answering individual-item adjunct questions did not. Thus, research with educationally relevant adjuncts is completely consistent with the MAD framework and suggests that reading adjuncts will be effective to the extent that they

Table 6.1. Comparison of Relational and Individual-Item Generation Tasks With Folktales and Expositions

Dependent measure	Experiment (Exp.)	Passage type	Read only	Generation task	
				Sentence unscrambling	Word fragments
Time (in minutes)	McDaniel et al. (1986)[a] Exp. 1	Folktale	1.2	5.9	12.1
		Expository	2.1	16.7	17.5
	McDaniel et al. Exp. 2	Folktale	1.9	8.6	7.8
		Expository	1.8	12.3	8.9
	Einstein et al. (1990)[b] Exp. 1	Folktale	1.5	7.8	8.2
		Expository	1.9	13.4	12.6
	Einstein et al. Exp. 3	Folktale	1.7		
		Expository	2.0	13.4	7.3
Proportion of propositions recalled	McDaniel et al. Exp. 1	Folktale	.43	.43	.49
		Expository	.15	.28	.14
	McDaniel et al. Exp. 2	Folktale	.36	.47	.62
		Expository	.22	.40	.19
	Einstein et al. Exp. 1	Folktale	.45	.52	.56
		Expository	.28	.43	.19
	Einstein et al. Exp. 3	Folktale	.41		.56
		Expository	.22	.32	

[a]McDaniel, Einstein, Dunay, and Cobb (1986).
[b]Einstein, McDaniel, Owen, and Cote (1990).

encourage the type of processing that is complementary to that encouraged by the reading materials.

Extensions to Material Appropriate Difficulty

Our approach encourages a contextualistic view for determining desirable difficulty in educational applications. As such, not only the target materials but also characteristics of the learner (see Jenkins, 1979) would be expected to modulate the desirability of particular types of difficulty for enhancing learning. To illustrate this theme, we continue to focus on generation and text memory. We have so far assumed that certain types of text will tend to afford extraction of relational information and other types of text to afford processing of item-specific information. A further refinement of this assumption is that the reader's ability will also influence which type of information is gained from reading.

A particularly interesting aspect of analyzing desirable difficulty from the perspective of individual differences in reading ability concerns poor readers. If educators are reluctant to increase difficulty for skilled students, then proposing that less-skilled students be presented with more difficult learning formats would surely elicit strong skepticism (to put it mildly). Indeed, basic work by McNamara and Kintsch (1996) has shown that increasing text difficulty (by reducing referential coherence) enhances learning for high-knowledge readers but not low-knowledge readers. In contrast, the contextualistic approach to desirable difficulty that we have outlined makes the provocative claim that certain combinations of text type and difficulty will enhance text recall for certain types of less-skilled readers. In fact, our framework allows the counter-intuitive possibility that less-skilled, but not skilled readers, will be aided by difficulty.

Consider readers who are poor at forming coherent, organized representations of the content of the text (poor "structure builders"; Gernsbacher, 1990). For these readers, even well-structured texts with causal chains (like folktales) may not promote effective relational processing during reading. Thus, for this type of less-skilled comprehender and folktale discourse, the sentence-unscrambling generation task requiring controlled and extensive processing of relational connections would not necessarily be redundant (as it is for most readers for folktales; see Table 6.1). Accordingly, were these less-skilled comprehenders able to successfully unscramble the random sentences into a coherent tale, then recall should improve compared with reading the tale.

McDaniel, Hines, and Guynn (2002) tested these ideas using the sentence-unscrambling generation task and the folktales described previously in this chapter. Using the Gernsbacher (1990) multimedia comprehension battery (the picture-story version), subjects were separated into groups of less-skilled and more-skilled readers and assigned to read-only or sentence-unscrambling conditions. First, note that the less-skilled readers were able to reorder the sentences into a text that approximated the canonical version of the tale (1.7 mean deviation in sentence order from the canonical passage compared with a 1.1 mean deviation for more-skilled readers). Turning to the recall results, consistent with findings reported above, the sentence-unscrambling generation task did not enhance recall compared with reading (Ms = 0.41 proportion of propositions recalled for both tasks) for the more-skilled comprehenders. Again, this generation task did not serve as desirable difficulty for this type of material. It is important to note, however, that this very same generation task produced significant improvements in recall of folktales compared with reading (Ms = 0.34 and 0.25, respectively) for the less-than-average comprehenders.

So, counterintuitive to prevailing views, a particular generation task can be desirable for poor readers but not for good readers. We suggest that the improvement in recall (and by extension comprehension) reported by McDaniel et al. (2002) reflects that the generation task forced relational processing that these less-skilled comprehenders did not engage spontaneously even for well-structured texts like folktales. To reinforce that desirability of difficulty (e.g., generation) hinges fundamentally on the overlap of processing stimulated by the difficulty task with the processing ordinarily engaged by the learner and afforded by the material, we also tested readers who were identified as less skilled by the Nelson–Denny Reading Test (Brown, Nelson, & Denny, 1973). Though reading skill and its assessment are complex, generally performance on the Nelson–Denny Reading Test is thought to reflect in part word-decoding skills—skills not involved in the picture story battery we used to identify those comprehenders less skilled at forming coherent representations. Indeed, less-skilled Nelson–Denny readers have been found to rely on higher-order information in the text to compensate for poor decoding skills (Petros, Bentz, Hammes, & Zehr, 1990). For these less-skilled readers, sentence unscrambling with folktales would not be desirable difficulty because these readers are presumably not deficient in relational processing ability and the folktale itself encourages relational processing. The free-recall results bear out this expectation (McDaniel et al., 2002, Experiment 1a). In contrast to less-skilled structure-building comprehenders, sentence-unscrambling generation did not significantly enhance recall of the folktales for the poor Nelson–Denny readers (M = 0.45 for the generation group and M = 0.41 for the read group).

Conclusions and Extensions for Educational Application

The theoretical framework and pattern of findings described herein underscore the point that prescribing desirable difficulty for educational purposes (or even for laboratory outcomes) is not straightforward because the desirability of a particular difficulty task depends on fundamental contextual aspects of the learning environment. We suggest that the MAD framework provides a fruitful start toward understanding the complex interplay of learning materials, learner characteristics, and the desirability of difficulty for enhancing learning and retention. A central tenet of this framework is that gauging the desirability of a particular processing task involves an appreciation that the materials themselves afford a particular type of processing. In our view, difficulty is most desirable and effective when it stimulates processing that complements that afforded by the material.

Regarding educational practice, one might assume the target materials, especially didactic text materials, can be assumed to regularly afford a certain type of processing (perhaps proposition specific) so that certain classes of desirable difficulty (organizational) can be generally prescribed. Unfortunately, even this analysis may be too simplistic. McDaniel, Waddill, Finstad, and Bourg (2000) found that within a particular text genre (narratives), the rated interest of the target text appeared to modify the processing invited by the text, which in turn influenced the desirability of the different types of generation tasks. The narratives that readers rated as more interesting were recalled significantly better when generated from word fragments (proposition-specific processing) compared with reading but not when generated from scrambled sentences. In contrast, the narratives that readers rated as less interesting were recalled significantly better when generated from scrambled sentences but not when generated from word fragments.

Textbooks probably also vary in "text-based" interest. For example, a current 11th-grade history text focuses one section on the interesting content from the book *Galileo's Daughter* (Sobel, 1999). To the extent that use of interesting material in textbooks can change the dynamics of reading (see Hidi, 1990; McDaniel et al., 2000), determination of MAD for educational text may need to extend beyond text-genre analyses stimulated by van Dijk and Kintsch's (1983) work that have been so fruitful in applying MAD to text materials.

Another feature of the learning context that we believe will be important in determining desirable difficulty, and one that the MAD framework does not touch on, are aspects of the testing environment, like retention interval and type of test. Very little work has examined how retention intervals influence the desirability of difficulty. Most of the basic work tests memory after short retention intervals. The sparse work that has focused on both short and long retention intervals suggests further interesting interactions. For example, Einstein et al. (1990), working with the text materials (folktales and expository passages) and processing tasks (letter deletion and sentence reordering) described earlier, tested recall for those passages one week after learning. As expected, the benefits of performing an appropriate difficulty manipulation (i.e., letter deletion with a folktale and sentence reordering with an expository passage) persisted after a one-week delay (compared with a read-only control condition). It is surprising, however, that the sentence-reordering task produced benefits (compared with the read-only control condition) with the folktale after the one-week delay even though there were no benefits of this task on immediate recall. This finding is in line with suggestions in the literature that relational information (McDaniel & Masson, 1977) and macrostructure information (Kintsch & van Dijk, 1978) are relatively more important for memory after a delay. This research suggests that difficulty manipulations (and materials) that produce good memory over the long term may be different from those that produce good immediate memory and more generally suggests the need for additional research examining memory of text after long retention intervals.

Finally, following the extensive work on transfer appropriate processing (McDaniel, Friedman, & Bourne, 1978; Morris, Bransford, & Franks, 1977; Roediger, Weldon, & Challis, 1989), we know that the type of test task will influence the desirability of difficulty (see McDaniel & Einstein, 1989). Kintsch's work cited earlier provides several clear examples. In McNamara and Kintsch (1996), the less coherent text facilitated performance of high-knowledge readers for a conceptual organization task but not for recall and multiple choice. Mannes and Kintsch (1987) found that the interfering (inconsistent) outlines facilitated performance on inference questions but actually reduced performance on recall and recognition of the text content. In a similar vein, McDaniel and Donnelly (1996) reported that requiring learners to generate explanations for scientific principles produced gains on inference questions but not for recall of the material (compared with a control text).

In conclusion, we echo the sage advice of Jenkins (1979) to keep in mind the components of his contextually oriented tetrahedral framework. Indeed, his warnings that memory is not simple and that processing manipulations "cannot lead to general conclusions" (p. 444) reverberate throughout this chapter. According to Jenkins, interactions are the rule rather than the exception, and the mnemonic benefits of different orienting tasks will depend on the nature of the materials, characteristics of the learner, and type of criterial task. We offer the MAD framework as a beginning but powerful theoretical perspective for specifying the kinds of difficulty manipulations that will be effective in different situations.

References

Battig, W. F. (1972). Intratask interference as a source of facilitation in transfer and retention. In R. F. Thompson & J. F. Voss (Eds.), *Topics in learning and performance* (pp. 131–159). New York: Academic Press.

Battig, W. F. (1979). The flexibility of human memory. In L. S. Cermak & F. I. M. Craik (Eds.), *Levels of processing in human memory* (pp. 23–44). Hillsdale, NJ: Erlbaum.

Bjork, R. A. (1994). Memory and metamemory considerations in the training of human beings. In J. Metcalfe & A. Shimamura (Eds.), *Metacognition: Knowing about knowing* (pp. 185–205). Cambridge, MA: MIT Press.

Brown, J. I., Nelson, M. J. B., & Denny, E. C. (1973). *The Nelson–Denny reading test*. Boston: Houghton Mifflin.

deWinstanley, P., & Bjork, E. L. (2001, November). *Processing strategies and the generation effect: Implications for how to make a better reader*. Paper presented at the 42nd Annual Meeting of the Psychonomic Society, Orlando, FL.

Einstein, G. O., & Hunt, R. R. (1980). Levels of processing and organization: Additive effects of individual-item and relational processing. *Journal of Experimental Psychology: Human Learning and Memory, 6*, 588–598.

Einstein, G. O., McDaniel, M. A., Owen, P. D., & Coté, N. C. (1990). Encoding and recall of texts: The importance of material appropriate processing. *Journal of Memory and Language, 29*, 566–581.

Engelkamp, J., Biegelmann, U., & McDaniel, M. A. (1998). Relational and item-specific information: Trade-off and redundancy. *Memory, 6*, 307–333.

Fletcher, C. R., & Bloom, C. P. (1988). Causal reasoning in the comprehension of simple narrative texts. *Journal of Memory and Language, 27*, 235–244.

Gernsbacher, M. A. (1990). *Language comprehension as structure building*. Hillsdale, NJ: Erlbaum.

Hamilton, R. J. (1985). A framework for the evaluation of the effectiveness of adjunct questions and objectives. *Review of Educational Research. 55*, 47–85.

Hidi, S. (1990). Interest and its contribution as a mental resource for learning. *Review of Educational Research, 60*, 549–571.

Hunt, R. R., & Einstein, G. O. (1981). Relational and item-specific information in memory. *Journal of Verbal Learning and Verbal Behavior, 20*, 497–514.

Hunt, R. R., & McDaniel, M. A. (1993). The enigma of organization and distinctiveness. *Journal of Memory and Language, 32*, 421–445.

Jenkins, J. J. (1979). Four points to remember: A tetrahedral model of memory explanations. In L. S. Cermak & F. I. M. Craik (Eds.), *Levels of processing in human memory* (pp. 429–446). Hillsdale, NJ: Erlbaum.

Kintsch, W., & van Dijk, T. A. (1978). Toward a model of text comprehension and production. *Psychological Review, 85,* 363–394.

Landauer, T. K., & Bjork, R. A. (1978). Optimal rehearsal patterns and name learning. In M. M. Gruneberg, P. E. Morris, & R. N. Sykes (Eds.), *Practical aspects of memory* (pp. 625–632).New York: Academic Press.

Mannes, S. M., & Kintsch, W. (1987). Knowledge organization and text organization. *Cognition and Instruction, 4*, 91–115.

Mayer, R. E. (1979). Can advance organizers influence meaningful learning? *Review of Educational Research, 49*, 371–383.

McDaniel, M. A., & Donnelly, C. M. (1996). Learning with analogy and elaborative interrogation. *Journal of Educational Psychology, 88*, 508–519.

McDaniel, M. A., & Einstein, G. O. (1989). Material appropriate processing: A contextualistic approach to reading and studying strategies. *Educational Psychology Review, 1*, 113–145.

McDaniel, M. A., Einstein, G. O., Dunay, P. K., & Cobb, R. E. (1986). Encoding difficulty and memory: Toward a unifying theory. *Journal of Memory and Language, 25*, 545–656.

McDaniel, M. A., Einstein, G. O., & Lollis, T. (1988). Qualitative and quantitative considerations in encoding difficulty effects. *Memory and Cognition, 16*, 8–14.

McDaniel, M. A., Friedman, A., & Bourne, L. E., Jr. (1978). Remembering the levels of information in words. *Memory and Cognition, 6*, 156–164.

McDaniel, M. A., Hines, R. J., & Guynn, M. J. (2002). When text difficulty benefits less-skilled readers. *Journal of Memory and Language, 46*, 544–561.

McDaniel, M. A., Hines, R. J., Waddill, P. J., & Einstein, G. O. (1994). What makes folk tales unique: Content familiarity, causal structure, scripts, or superstructures? *Journal of Experimental Psychology: Learning, Memory, and Cognition, 16*, 789–798.

McDaniel, M. A., & Masson, M. E. (1977). Long-term retention: When incidental semantic processing fails. *Journal of Experimental Psychology: Human Learning and Memory, 3*, 270–281.

McDaniel, M. A., Ryan, E. B., & Cunningham, C. J. (1989). Encoding difficulty and memory enhancement for young and old readers. *Psychology and Aging, 4*, 333–338.

McDaniel, M. A., Waddill, P. J., & Einstein, G. O. (1988). A contextual account of the generation effect: A three-factor theory. *Journal of Memory and Language, 27*, 521–536.

McDaniel, M. A., Waddill, P. J., Finstad, K., & Bourg, T. (2000). The effects of text-based interest on attention and recall. *Journal of Educational Psychology, 92*, 492–502.

McNamara, D. S., & Healy, A. F. (1995). A procedural explanation of the generation effect: The use of an operand retrieval strategy for multiplication and addition problems. *Journal of Memory and Language, 34*, 399–416.

McNamara, D. S., & Kintsch, W. (1996). Learning from texts: Effects of prior knowledge and text coherence. *Discourse Processes, 22*, 247–288.

Morris, C. D., Bransford, J. D., & Franks, J. J. (1977). Levels of processing versus transfer appropriate processing. *Journal of Verbal Learning and Verbal Behavior, 16*, 519–533.

Petros, T. V., Bentz, B., Hammes, K., & Zehr, H. D. (1990). The components of text that influence reading times and recall in skilled and less skilled college readers. *Discourse Processes, 13*, 387–400.

Roediger, H. L., III, Weldon, M. S., & Challis, B. H. (1989). Explaining dissociations between implicit and explicit measures of retention: A processing account. In H. L. Roediger III & F. I. M. Craik (Eds.), *Varieties of memory and consciousness: Essays in honour of Endel Tulving* (pp. 3–41). Hillsdale, NJ: Erlbaum.

Schneider, V. I., Healy, A. F., & Bourne, L. E., Jr. (2002). What is learned under difficult conditions is hard to forget: Contextual interference effects in foreign vocabulary acquisition, retention, and transfer. *Journal of Memory and Language, 46*, 419–440.

Schwarz, M. N. K., & Flammer, A. (1981). Text structure and title: Effects on comprehension and recall. *Journal of Verbal Learning and Verbal Behavior, 20*, 61–66.

Slamecka, N. J., & Graf, P. (1978). The generation effect: Delineation of a phenomenon. *Journal of Experimental Psychology: Human Learning and Memory, 4,* 582–604.

Sobel, D. (1999). *Galileo's daughter: A historical memoir of science, faith, and love.* New York: Walker.

Trabasso, T., & van den Broek, P. (1985). Casual thinking and the representation of narrative events. *Journal of Memory and Language, 24,* 612–630.

van Dijk, T. A., & Kintsch, W. (1983). *Strategies of discourse comprehension.* New York: Academic Press.

Part III

Memory

7

The Long-Term Neglect
of Long-Term Memory:
Reasons and Remedies

Harry P. Bahrick

One hundred and twenty years of psychological memory research have had scarcely any impact on education. The value of education depends heavily on the life span of acquired knowledge, and it is surprising and disappointing that memory research has not yielded benefits to this important domain of society. This failure is not due to the intransigence of educators. In contrast to memory research, psychological research on learning, human development, individual differences, test construction, and textbook writing has profoundly influenced educational practice, including pedagogy as well as the curriculum. The failure of memory research to affect educational practice is due primarily to our research focus on short-time retention of episodic memory content. Walter Kintsch (1974, p. 4) stated the issue clearly over 30 years ago:

> Most of the experimental research concerning memory has never really dealt with problems of the acquisition and retention of knowledge, but with episodic memory which is not at all the problem of interest in education. . . . An educational technology squarely based upon psychological research needs research concerned with problems of knowledge.

Neisser (1978) labeled the failure of memory research to address the retention of academic content a scandal.

I believe the reasons memory scholars have failed to investigate the retention of knowledge programmatically lie in the history and sociology of our discipline. Our historical commitment to the experimental paradigm played an important role. The experimental paradigm requires laboratory manipulation of independent variables and a focus on processes that transpire within a time frame laboratory observations can accommodate (Bahrick, 1989, 1994). Many of the conditions that affect the maintenance of knowledge are not readily manipulated, however, and their long-term effects may not be observable within

---

This work was supported by Grant RO1AGO19803 from the National Institutes of Health.

short time periods. Learner motivation, for example, is not easily manipulated in experiments, and the long-term effects of conditions of acquisition and rehearsal of knowledge may extend over periods of many years and may differ categorically from their more immediate effects (Bahrick, 2000; Bjork, 1994).

Control is the essence of the scientific method, and experiments generally afford the best opportunities of control. It therefore makes sense that experiments remain the method of choice in science. However, topics that are of great significance to society should not be ignored or neglected simply because the relevant phenomena are not amenable to manipulation or control. Instead, we must develop alternative research strategies appropriate for exploring memory functions and other phenomena that cannot be investigated experimentally.

During the past 30 years a handful of investigations have dealt with long-term retention of educational content, but the overwhelming body of psychological memory research continues to be irrelevant to this important societal concern. In this chapter I first discuss the historical and sociological reasons for this continuing neglect, and then review some methods and results of the Ohio Wesleyan University (OWU) research program concerned with the long-term maintenance of knowledge.

Historical Background

The experimental paradigm was first adopted by psychologists to demonstrate that psychological phenomena lend themselves to scientific inquiry. The experimental method was the predominant method of physics, the most prestigious field of science during the 19th century. When pioneer psychologists demonstrated this method could be used effectively to establish psychophysical principles and to investigate sensory processes, reaction time, and rote memory, they helped to persuade academic authorities to establish psychology as a scientific discipline distinct from philosophy. In this context it is historically clear why Ebbinghaus (1885) and his followers adopted the experimental method in their pioneering investigations. What is less clear are the reasons memory scholars failed for nearly 90 years to enlarge their methodological repertoire to explore memory performance that did not focus on short-term retention of associative content.

The natural sciences were not so constrained. They developed appropriate nonexperimental research strategies to explore phenomena that are not readily subjected to control or experimentation. Investigations in astronomy, seismology, geology, and meteorology are among the many examples that come to mind. Alternative research strategies were also adopted early on in other domains of psychology, such as tests and measurements, developmental psychology, social psychology, and abnormal psychology. These disciplines focused on individual differences, following the Darwinian model, and they made use of correlation and regression analyses. In contrast, research in learning, memory, and perception remained committed to experimentation, and individual differences were generally relegated to the function of estimating experimental error. The premier journals of these fields continue to be labeled "experimental," and that emphasis remains evident in editorial decisions and in decisions regarding research support by the largest granting agencies. The dichotomy between experimental and correlational approaches to psychological research was discussed and deplored long ago by others, such as Cronbach (1957), but the past half century has seen only limited evidence of the convergence Cronbach advocated.

I believe that at least two additional historical legacies played a role in our reluctance to consider alternatives to memory experiments: our philosophical heritage of analytic associationism and a legacy of German scholarship that valued pure science more highly than the applications of science. Associationism, an outgrowth of empiricist philosophy, dominated learning and memory research from 1885 to about 1970. Associationists assumed that memory content can be reduced to a mosaic of individual associations and that the phenomena of learning and memory could be understood by exploring the conditions under which individual associations are strengthened and weakened. On the basis of these assumptions, pioneer memory researchers focused on experimental methods to infer the strength of associative connections. These methods included the Ebbinghaus (1885) technology as well as classical and instrumental conditioning. My teachers, whom I hold in high esteem, would not have considered a dissertation an acceptable contribution to memory scholarship unless it was based on the associationist paradigm. That paradigm, however, does not easily encompass the retention of knowledge systems (Bahrick, 1985), and Bartlett's (1932) pioneering work on organizational aspects of memory had little impact until the cognitive revolution of the 1970s legitimized the study of more complex memory functions.

Academic psychologists were also influenced by a tradition of German scholarship that assigned greater value and prestige to pure than to applied science. This tradition was fostered in 19th-century German universities, and it was rooted in the impressive series of discoveries in the physical sciences that ultimately yielded many technological benefits. On the basis of this record of success, the pursuit of general scientific principles came to be valued more highly than the pursuit of specific technological goals. In the Humboldtian university, scientists were protected against societal pressures for immediately useful applications of their work. Applied sciences such as engineering or industrial psychology are rarely represented on the faculty of German universities; they are more likely to be housed in separate institutions of technology.

Whereas the elitist status of pure versus applied science influenced American psychologists through the legacy of Titchener and other students of Wundt, the pragmatic zeitgeist of America challenged this heritage. American society took great pride in practical inventions and paid high tribute to Edison, Bell, Whitney, and the Wright brothers, among others. Our homegrown philosophy of pragmatism epitomized this ethos and profoundly influenced education and psychology. America led the world in replacing the classical curriculum with more functional content, and the related pedagogical reforms were strongly influenced by psychological research. Functional psychologists pioneered research on individual differences; tests and measurements; the technology of learning; and industrial, forensic, clinical, and other applications of psychology, and the applied sciences remained an integral part of the university curriculum. Most of the contributions of applied psychology were based on correlational data obtained in a variety of naturalistic settings. However, nonlaboratory approaches to memory research remained controversial and were viewed critically as recently as 1989 (Banaji & Crowder, 1989); in 1991 a whole issue of the *American Psychologist* was devoted to a dialogue concerning the alleged "bankruptcy of ecological memory research." The advances of naturalistic memory research over the past two decades, including research in autobiographical memory (Rubin, Wetzler, & Nebes, 1986), the effects of emotion and trauma on memory (Bahrick, Parker, Fivush, & Levitt, 1998), work on eyewitness identification (Wells & Bradfield, 1999), as well as memory pathology have helped preempt much of this dialogue.

It is important in this context to differentiate nonexperimental, naturalistic investigations from applied memory research. The goal of the former is to promote understanding of memory functions that are not suitable for laboratory exploration, and the goal of the latter is to improve memory performance. Although the immediate objectives are distinct, they are not mutually exclusive. Applied memory research may of course lead to enhanced understanding of memory functions in addition to promoting performance in a given context, and naturalistic investigations often lead to improved performance. This is true because naturalistic investigations typically focus on tasks and situations in which the memory system is engaged on a day-to-day basis.

Cognitive memory research is no longer dominated by analytic associationism, and the past 30 years have brought much progress in understanding complex memory processes. What has changed much less, however, is the focus on time-compressed investigations of short-term retention, with the corresponding neglect of memory processes that occur over long periods.

Memory scholars must continue to defend basic research regardless of whether the research shows promise of applied benefits. There is ample proof in our history that the benefits of scientific findings can be serendipitous and unpredictable. At the same time, I believe scientists have an obligation to address phenomena of societal concern relevant to their domain of expertise, even when those phenomena do not lend themselves easily to traditionally accepted research paradigms. Accordingly, we should reconsider policies that virtually preclude such benefits. In the long run, failure to be responsive to societal needs will damage our credibility and may ultimately lead to diminished public support. Programmatic investigations of the retention of academic content would strongly enhance the relevance of memory research to education. We can achieve this goal by continuing to develop research strategies appropriate for investigating the long-term maintenance of knowledge.

Two Methods for Investigating Long-Term Retention

I now review two of the methods we developed in the OWU research program on knowledge maintenance. I focus on methods because I believe that methods are critical to opening unexplored research domains. The experiential content of most cognitive processes is private, and likely to remain private. But each time we develop a new research method or procedure, some aspects of cognition that were private become subject to public observation, or at least to logical inference. We started with psychophysical methods. These methods yielded insights about the limitations of our sense modalities. Conditioning procedures gave us insights into how associations are formed and retained, REM techniques allowed us to infer when people dream, and lie detector techniques yielded inferences about when people are not telling the truth. The limits of our science are set by the available methods, and the available methods were not well suited to investigate acquisition or maintenance of knowledge because these processes typically involve long time periods.

The First Method

The original purpose of the OWU knowledge maintenance research was pragmatic and simplistic. We conceived maintenance of a knowledge domain to be analogous to maintaining a motor skill or a level of aerobic capacity. Accordingly, we thought that maintaining a level of knowledge would require a certain amount, type, and frequency of rehearsal activity. For example, if someone had acquired a vocabulary of several thousand words in a foreign language, we wanted to find the frequency and duration of rehearsals needed to maintain access to that vocabulary.

Much of the educational content acquired in elementary schools, such as knowledge of arithmetic, reading, and writing skills, is maintained throughout adult life because that content is rehearsed with high frequency. Such content therefore did not lend itself to our inquiry. In contrast, content acquired in high school or college courses may be infrequently rehearsed, and a large part of the knowledge of algebra, foreign languages, history, and so on is forgotten soon after it is acquired (Bahrick, 1984b; Bahrick & Hall, 1991a). To obtain information about rehearsal levels needed to maintain various amounts of such knowledge, we used a method that involved multiple regression analyses of data obtained from a large number of individuals who had acquired knowledge that was infrequently rehearsed. Some of the individuals we tested had completed training as recently as a few weeks prior to testing, others as many as 50 years ago. We obtained estimates of their level of original knowledge, the time elapsed since they had completed acquisition training, the frequency and type of rehearsal of the knowledge during the retention interval, and their current level of knowledge. For example, in the case of a foreign language acquired in school, we estimated original knowledge on the basis of the number of courses taken in high school or college and the grades received in these courses. To assess rehearsal levels, individuals estimated the frequency and recency of speaking, listening, reading, or writing in that language. To assess current level of knowledge, we administered a test that yielded separate scores on 10 subtests of vocabulary recall and recognition, reading comprehension, grammar, and so on. All data were then subjected to regression analyses in which the level of original knowledge, the retention interval, and the estimates of rehearsal activities were predictor variables and performance on various retention subtests were the predicted variables. Higher order terms for predictor variables and interaction terms were maintained in the regression program if they significantly reduced unaccounted-for variance. By evaluating the

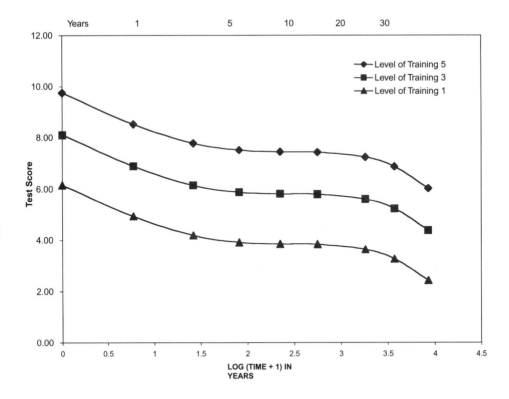

Figure 7.1. The projected effect of level of training on the retention of English–Spanish recognition vocabulary. From "Semantic Memory Content in Permastore: 50 Years of Memory for Spanish Learned in School," by H. P. Bahrick, 1984, *Journal of Experimental Psychology: General, 113,* p. 17. Copyright 1984 by the American Psychological Association. Reprinted with permission.

regression equations for successive retention intervals, the equations yielded projected retention functions for performance on each subtest for periods of up to 50 years. Notwithstanding the various sources of error and unreliability, the regression equations yielded correlations ranging from .67 to .77 with performance on the various subtests of retention. The regression analysis also enabled us to project families of retention functions to predict retention for various levels of original training, as shown in Figure 7.1.

Multiple regression technology had, of course, been available for many years, but it had not been used previously to project retention functions. The sociology and traditions of our discipline discouraged nonexperimental explorations of retention, as previously discussed, and the necessary calculations for large samples were prohibitive, prior to the advent of computers.

We were unable to achieve our original goal of projecting families of retention functions on the basis of the amount, frequency, and recency of rehearsal activities. The reason for this failure was that rehearsal levels for the vast majority of our subjects were so low that they had no significant effect on retention. Although this was a disappointing finding, it led to the discovery of the phenomenon observed in Figure 7.1. The projected functions show a retention plateau of approximately 30 years duration. The minimal effects of rehearsal have been removed statistically, and the functions indicate that losses of retention cease 3 to 5 years after acquisition terminates and do not resume for about 30 years. This finding was observed for all language subtests except for those measuring retention of grammar and of idioms, and it has been confirmed in several other investigations dealing with various types of content, for example, memory for names and faces (Bahrick, Bahrick, & Wittlinger, 1975), knowledge of a city (Schmidt, Peeck, Paas, & van Breukelen, 2000), retention of high school algebra (Bahrick & Hall, 1991a), cognitive psychology (Conway, Cohen, & Stanhope, 1991, 1992), and skills (Healy et al., 1992). We named the content exhibiting this degree of stability *permastore content*, and because of the obvious theoretical and applied significance of the phenomenon, we focused much of our subsequent research on exploring the conditions that yield such stability.

Before describing these efforts I review our theoretical interpretation of the *permastore phenomenon*. First, we showed how retention functions can be transformed readily into frequency distributions of the life span of the acquired content (Bahrick, 1984b). The percentage of content lost during the intervals between successive data points on a retention plot corresponds to the percentage of content with a life span defined by the limits of that interval. For example, if retention diminishes from 80% to 60% between tests administered 1 hour and 10 hours after learning terminates, then 20% of the content has a life span of between 1 and 10 hours. When percentages are computed on this basis for successive testing intervals, they yield a frequency distribution for the life span of the acquired content. For the retention function shown in Figure 7.1, the life span frequency distribution is dichotomous rather than continuous. The life span of content is either shorter than 5 years or longer than 30 years, because virtually no content is lost during the interval from 5 to 30 years. From this dichotomous distribution, we inferred that a discrete increment in the life span of content must occur during acquisition. The fact that no content had life spans of 10, 15, or 20 years suggests that increments in life spans from less than 5 years to 30+ years occurred discretely rather than gradually during acquisition.

Second, to pursue our original goal of estimating rehearsal levels needed to maintain particular levels of acquired knowledge, we had to find domains in which individuals rehearsed content more frequently than foreign language content acquired in schools. We succeeded in two subsequent investigations (Bahrick, 1983; Bahrick, Hall, Goggin, Bahrick, & Berger, 1994). In the first (Bahrick et al., 1994), bilingual Hispanic immigrants who came to the United States between the ages of 12 and 20 and used English an average of 14% of the time maintained their English language recognition vocabulary during 30+ years of residence in the United States, as shown in Figure 7.2. Figure 7.2 also shows that higher percentages of English usage (82%) yield continuing growth in the size of the original vocabulary. In that study the amount of rehearsal needed to maintain the original level of knowledge was readily established

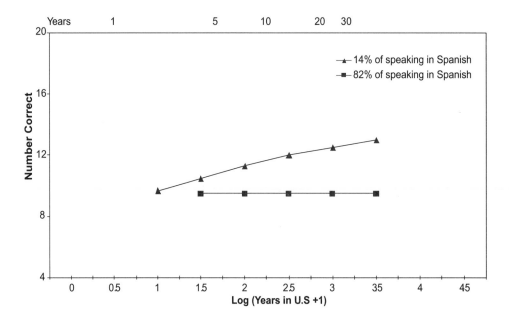

Figure 7.2. Projected scores on English vocabulary recognition as a function of time spent speaking Spanish. From "Fifty Years of Language Maintenance and Language Dominance in Bilingual Hispanic Immigrants," by H. P. Bahrick, L. K. Hall, J. P. Goggin, L. E. Bahrick, and S. A. Berger, 1994, *Journal of Experimental Psychology: General, 123,* p. 281. Copyright 1994 by the American Psychological Association. Reprinted with permission.

because a single rehearsal variable (the percentage of time the subjects used the English language) was responsible for most of the variance in the predicted variable.

When several rehearsal variables codetermine maintenance of knowledge, evaluation of the required rehearsal levels is a function of trade-offs among the variables. This situation is exemplified in the second study (Bahrick, 1983) that involved an investigation of memory for landmarks and streets of Delaware, Ohio, and that study illustrates a more general method of answering questions about required rehearsals. We tested 851 students and alumni of OWU located in Delaware, Ohio, for their knowledge of the city. Some alumni were tested at the time of their graduation and others as long as 50 years later. We estimated rehearsals of knowledge on the basis of the reported frequency, duration, and recency of visits to Delaware during the time since graduation. Estimates of original knowledge were based on test results obtained from the most recent graduates. Variables such as the number of years of college attendance, use of a car or bicycle during college attendance and on later visits, and the location of residence in Delaware were also included in the regression. A hierarchical regression program comparable with the one described earlier yielded an equation that predicted retention of spatial and verbal aspects of knowledge as a function of the retention interval, as well as the frequency,

Table 7.1. Number of Visits per Year Needed to Maintain Free Recall of Street Names at the Graduation Level

Most recent visit (months)	Duration of each visit (days)				
	1	2	3	4	5
0	12.57	8.11	5.98	4.74	3.93
0.5	12.93	8.34	6.16	4.88	4.04
1.00	13.19	8.51	6.28	4.98	4.12
1.50	13.39	8.64	6.37	5.05	4.18
2.00	13.55	8.74	6.45	5.11	4.23

Note. From "Maintenance of Knowledge: Questions About Memory We Forgot to Ask," by H. P. Bahrick, 1979, *Journal of Experimental Psychology: General, 108,* p. 307. Copyright 1979 by the American Psychological Association. Reprinted with permission.

duration, and recency of visits during that interval. By specifying a retention level corresponding to performance at graduation and assuming various values for the most recent visit and for the duration of each visit, we evaluated the regression equation for the number of visits per year that would yield the specified level of retention. Table 7.1 (Bahrick, 1979) gives the trade-off values that are projected to maintain the level of knowledge achieved at graduation. The assumed rehearsal values must of course fall within the range of values represented in the data set; that is, the trade-off values must not depend on extrapolations.

A number of limitations apply to these methods and to the interpretation of results. In most of our investigations the effects of the retention interval per se are confounded with the effects of aging of the individual. This confound does not cloud the interpretation of the permastore phenomenon because the potential confounding of two sources of forgetting is not a problem for periods during which no forgetting is observed. Moreover, although this confound exists for all memory investigations, in theory, the effects of aging on memory can be assumed to be trivial for short retention intervals. The confound becomes problematic when the retention interval extends over several years, but it can be avoided by comparing retention for several groups that acquire the same content at different ages. Although our investigations involved mostly academic content acquired when subjects were of approximately the same age, we were able to test subjects of different ages at acquisition in two investigations (Bahrick, 1984a; Bahrick, Bahrick, Bahrick, & Bahrick, 1993) and found that retention of content over an 8-year period did not differ significantly for subjects who were between the ages of 30 and 65 years at acquisition (Bahrick, 1984a).

The Second Method

We developed a second, semiexperimental method to examine the impact of interventions designed to maintain or prolong access to knowledge of long standing. For this purpose, we focused on what we call *marginal knowledge*, defined as knowledge reliably documented on tests of recognition but unreliably recalled. The successful recall of marginal content depends on the momentary external and internal retrieval context. Most knowledge domains of long standing include large portions of marginal content. Thus, vocabulary correctly identified on recognition tests exceeds by far the vocabulary accessible on tests of recall (Bahrick, 1984b; Herrmann, Buschke, & Gall, 1987). The same is true for knowledge of algebra tested in recall or recognition format (Bahrick & Hall, 1991a). Marginal knowledge is uniquely suited for investigating the impact of interventions on stabilizing access to semantic memory content because changes of access probability can be observed within relatively short periods. In contrast, recall of nonmarginal knowledge of long standing is so stable that it is far more difficult to observe the impact of interventions designed to improve it.

We distinguish between two types of maintenance interventions that we label *corrective* and *preventive* (Bahrick & Hall, 1991b). Corrective interventions restore access to marginal memory targets following a recall failure, and their effect is assessed by estimating the half-life or other indicants of effect duration. Preventive interventions involve successful retrievals of a marginal memory target, and their effect on prolonging access is assessed by a method we labeled the *method of asymmetrical fluctuations*. This method is based on the following rationale: Knowledge systems of long standing are characterized by long periods of overall retention stability (Bahrick, 1984b). Such stability implies that recall fluctuations of individual target items on successive retention tests be symmetrical. That is, the number of targets that change from a recall success to a recall failure between tests n and $n + 1$ must equal the number of targets that change in the opposite direction for the overall level of recall to remain constant. In fact, this does not happen. When retention tests over the same targets are readministered to the same subjects within hours, days, or weeks, fluctuations are asymmetrical. A much greater number of positive (previous recall failures that become successes) than negative fluctuations are observed (Bahrick & Hall, 1991b; Herrmann et al., 1987). The resulting "hypermnesia," or overall improvement in retention of an otherwise stable knowledge system, reflects the testing effect and is limited to items that are retested. No difference in recall probability is observed for control targets that are tested only once on either the first or the second test (Bahrick & Hall, 1991b).

We inferred that the asymmetry of upward over downward fluctuations of recall reflects the effect of having successfully retrieved some of the marginal targets. The act of retrieval of a marginal target prevents failures of access that would have occurred for some targets on Test 2, absent the preventive retrieval on Test 1. We further assumed that symmetry of upward and downward fluctuations between Tests 1 and 2 is restored when the preventive intervention effect has dissipated. Thus the magnitude and duration of asymmetry of fluctuations become indicants of the magnitude and duration of preventive maintenance interventions. Our results (Bahrick & Hall, 1991b; Bahrick & Phelps, 1988) show that the half-life of the effect of a single preventive maintenance retrieval is longer than one month. This finding suggests that successive, preventive maintenance interventions are capable of stabilizing access to marginal knowledge for very long periods.

In most naturalistic situations individuals maintain knowledge by deciding when, how, and how often to rehearse. Accordingly, we have focused our recent efforts on how individuals monitor their memory to control their long-term access to knowledge. Feedback from successful and unsuccessful attempts at retrieval provides the critical information. By allowing individuals to use this feedback to control their encoding and rehearsal strategies in quasi-experimental investigations, we learn about the effectiveness of these strategies, and ultimately about the way in which knowledge is best maintained in naturalistic settings.

Progress of psychological research depends on developing methods appropriate to investigate the phenomena of interest. Traditional memory experiments are not well suited for exploring long-term access to knowledge, and therefore the findings of traditional experiments have had no impact on education. Programmatic research based on the development of appropriate methods is needed to make memory research responsive to this important societal need.

References

Bahrick, H. P. (1979). Maintenance of knowledge: Questions about memory we forgot to ask. *Journal of Experimental Psychology: General, 108,* 296–308.

Bahrick, H. P. (1983). The cognitive map of a city: 50 years of learning and memory. In G. Bower (Ed.), *The psychology of learning and motivation: Advances in research and theory* (Vol. 17, pp. 125–163). New York: Academic Press.

Bahrick, H. P. (1984a). Memory for people. In J. E. Harris & P. E. Morris (Eds.), *Everyday memory, actions and absent mindedness* (pp. 19–34). London: Academic Press.

Bahrick, H. P. (1984b). Semantic memory content in permastore: 50 years of memory for Spanish learned in school. *Journal of Experimental Psychology: General, 113,* 1–29.

Bahrick, H. P. (1985). Associationism and the Ebbinghaus legacy. *Journal of Experimental Psychology: Learning, Memory, and Cognition, 11,* 439–443.

Bahrick, H. P. (1989). The laboratory and the ecology: Supplementary sources of data for memory research. In L. Poon, D. Rubin, & B. Wilson (Eds.), *Everyday cognition in adulthood and late life* (pp. 73–83). Hillsdale, NJ: Erlbaum.

Bahrick, H. P. (1994). Extending the life-span of knowledge. In L. Penner, H. Knoff, G. Batsche, & D. Nelson (Eds.), *The challenge in mathematics and science education: Psychology's response* (pp. 61–82). Washington, DC: American Psychological Association.

Bahrick, H. P. (2000). Long-term maintenance of knowledge. In E. Tulving & F. I. C. Craig (Eds.), *The Oxford handbook of memory* (pp. 347–362). New York: Oxford University Press.

Bahrick, H. P., Bahrick, L. E., Bahrick, A. S., & Bahrick, P. E. (1993). Maintenance of foreign language vocabulary and the spacing effect. *Psychological Science, 4,* 316–321.

Bahrick, H. P., Bahrick, P. O., & Wittlinger, R. P. (1975). Fifty years of memories for names and faces: A cross-sectional approach. *Journal of Experimental Psychology: General, 104,* 54–75.

Bahrick, H. P., & Hall, L. K. (1991a). Lifetime maintenance of high school mathematics content. *Journal of Experimental Psychology: General, 120,* 20–33.

Bahrick, H. P., & Hall, L. K. (1991b). Preventive and corrective maintenance of access to knowledge. *Applied Cognitive Psychology, 5,* 1–18.

Bahrick, H. P., Hall, L. K., Goggin, J. P., Bahrick, L. E., & Berger, S. A. (1994). Fifty years of language maintenance and language dominance in bilingual Hispanic immigrants. *Journal of Experimental Psychology: General, 123,* 264–283.

Bahrick, H. P., & Phelps, E. (1988). The maintenance of marginal knowledge. In U. Neisser & E. Winograd (Eds.), *Remembering reconsidered: Ecological and traditional approaches to the study of memory* (pp. 178–192). New York: Cambridge University Press.

Bahrick, L. E., Parker, J. F., Fivush, R., & Levitt, M. (1998). The effects of stress on young children's memory for a natural disaster. *Journal of Experimental Psychology: Applied, 4,* 308–331.

Banaji, M. R., & Crowder, R. G. (1989). The bankruptcy of everyday memory. *American Psychologist, 44,* 1185–1193.

Bartlett, F. C. (1932). *Remembering: A study in experimental and social psychology.* Cambridge, England: Cambridge University Press.

Bjork, R. A. (1994). Memory and metamemory considerations in the training of human beings. In J. Mettcalfe & A. Shimamura (Eds.), *Metacognition: Knowing about knowing* (pp. 185–205). Cambridge, MA: MIT Press.

Conway, M. A., Cohen, G., & Stanhope, N. (1991). On the very long-term retention of knowledge acquired through formal education: Twelve years of cognitive psychology. *Journal of Experimental Psychology: General, 120,* 358–372.

Conway, M. A., Cohen, G., & Stanhope, N. (1992). Very long-term knowledge acquired at school and university. *Applied Cognitive Psychology, 6,* 467–482.

Cronbach, L. J. (1957). The two disciplines of scientific psychology. *American Psychologist, 12,* 671–684.

Ebbinghaus, H. (1885). *Über das Gedächtnis* [Memory]. Leipzig, Germany: Dunker & Humbolt.

Healy, A. F., Fendrich, D. W., Crutcher, R. J., Wittman, W. T., Gesi, A. T., Ericsson, K. A., & Bourne, L. E., Jr. (1992). The long-term retention of skills. In A. F. Healy, S. M. Kosslyn, & R. M. Shiffrin (Eds.), *From learning process to cognitive processes: Essays in honor of William K. Estes* (Vol. 2, pp. 87–118). Hillsdale, NJ: Erlbaum.

Herrmann, D. J., Buschke, H., & Gall, M. B. (1987). Improving retrieval. *Applied Cognitive Psychology, 1,* 27–33.

Kintsch, W. (1974). *The representation of meaning in memory.* New York: Wiley.

Neisser, U. (1978). Memory: What are the important questions? In M. M. Gruneberg, P. E. Morris, & H. N. Sykes (Eds.), *Practical aspects of memory* (pp. 3–24). London: Academic Press.

Rubin, D. C., Wetzler, S. E., & Nebes, R. D. (1986). Autobiographical memory across the lifespan. In D. Rubin (Ed.), *Autobiographical memory across the lifespan* (pp. 202–221). New York: Cambridge University Press.

Schmidt, H. G., Peeck, V. H., Paas, F., & van Breukelen, G. P. (2000). Remembering the street names of one's childhood neighbourhood: A study of very long-term retention. *Memory, 8,* 37–49.

Wells, G. L., & Bradfield, A. L. (1999). Distortions in eyewitnesses' recollections: Can the postidentification-feedback effect be moderated? *Psychological Science 10,* 138–144.

8

Rich False Memories: The Royal Road to Success

Elizabeth F. Loftus and Daniel M. Bernstein

One does not have to look far to find compelling cases in which individuals have held distorted memories about events from their past. Neisser and Harsch (1992) reported on numerous cases in which people mistakenly remembered first hearing the news about the *Challenger* explosion from television, when actually they had first heard about it from a friend or other source. More tragic are the many cases of wrongful conviction caused by faulty memory, where in some instances individuals spent years in prison. Here, the crimes occurred, but the wrong person was "remembered," and DNA testing ultimately uncovered the error. An entire issue of *Judicature*, the journal of the American Judicature Society, was devoted to this issue of wrongful convictions (see Radelet, 2002). There some of the leading scholars in the world talked about the DNA-discovered errors and their causes. Faulty eyewitness memory is continually thought to be the leading cause.

Look a little further and you will find wholly false memories about the past, or what we call *rich false memories*. By this we mean the subjective feeling that one is experiencing a genuine recollection, replete with sensory details, and even expressed with confidence and emotion, even though the event never happened. Mack (1994) reported on a number of individuals who believed and remembered that they had been abducted by aliens, taken to distant spaceships, sexually experimented on, and finally returned to their beds on earth. Although we do not have the DNA hammer, many scientists would be willing to declare that these are absolutely false memories based on other grounds.

From Misinformation to Rich False Memory

The wrongful conviction cases seem to parallel a process that has been studied under the rubric of the *misinformation effect*. In the wrongful conviction case, an event (the crime) occurs. Next, some activity occurs that distorts memory for the event (e.g., a leading question, a biased lineup). Finally, the victim or witness testifies erroneously in court, misidentifying the person who committed the crime. Analogously, in the misinformation studies, an event occurs (e.g., a simulated accident). Next, some activity occurs that distorts memory for the event (e.g., a leading question, exposure to misleading information). Finally, the participant's memory is tested. A common result is that the participant falls sway to the misinformation, rendering the memory less accurate. Hundreds, perhaps thousands of misinformation studies have established the power of these manipulations to distort or contaminate memory (for a review, see Ayers & Reder, 1998). People have been led to believe in simple distortions, such as that a stop sign was a yield sign or that a fellow with straight hair had curly hair. More dramatic, they have been led to believe that they saw a wounded animal (that was not there) near the scene of a tragic terrorist bombing that actually had occurred (Nourkova, Bernstein, & Loftus, 2004).

The alien abduction and satanic ritual abuse cases seem to parallel a process that has been studied under the rubric of what might be called *memory planting*. The late Carl Sagan talked about the alien abduction "memories" and drew parallels to those involving satanic ritual abuse (Sagan, 1995, p. 165). In both cases, there are specialists—alien abduction specialists, satanic ritual abuse specialists. In both cases, the specialist (a therapist or therapist-like individual) hears of the individual's complaint. In both, the specialist is "profoundly moved by the unmistakably genuine agony" of the individual. Some specialists then ask leading questions and use other methods that can lead suggestible individuals to produce memory reports. Analogously, in the memory-planting studies, some activity occurs that tries to create a wholly false memory (e.g., conveying false information that allegedly came from a family informant). Finally, subjects are asked whether they remember various events occurring to them in the past. A common result is that the subjects fall sway to the suggestion and claim to have experienced the fabricated events. Many of these memory-planting techniques lead to what we are calling rich false memories.

Creating Rich False Memories

One of the earliest attempts to plant a rich false memory involved a procedure whereby subjects were given short narrative descriptions of childhood events and encouraged to try to remember those events. Although subjects believed that all of the descriptions were true and had been provided by family members, actually one was a pseudo-event that had not occurred. In this study, approximately 25% of subjects were led to believe, wholly or partially, that at age 5 or 6 they had been lost in a shopping mall for an extended time, were highly upset, and were ultimately rescued by an elderly person and reunited with their family (Loftus & Pickrell, 1995). In later studies using a similar procedure, subjects were led to believe that they had been hospitalized overnight or that they had an accident at a family wedding (Hyman, Husband, & Billings, 1995). Even more traumatic, in yet other studies, subjects were convinced that they had been the victim of a vicious animal attack (Porter, Yuille, & Lehman, 1999) or had nearly drowned and had to be rescued by a lifeguard (Heaps & Nash, 2001).

Reviewing the body of work using what they call the *familial informant false narrative procedure*, Lindsay, Hagen, Read, Wade, and Garry (2004) noted that across eight studies, an average of 31% of subjects produced false memories. Sometimes the various investigators distinguished between a partial false memory and a complete false memory. Although the distinction is fuzzy, at least one definition of "complete" is that the subjects demonstrate that they genuinely believe they are remembering the event. In studies that made this distinction, still 20% of the subjects were classified as having a complete false memory, rather than merely accepting that the pseudo-event occurred or speculating about it. The notion of a complete false memory is akin to what we are calling a rich false memory, namely, an experience about which a person can feel confident, provide details, even express emotion about an event that never happened.

Even With Bizarre Pseudo-Events?

Many of the scenarios in the various false narrative studies involve purported events that are either common or plausible. It has been argued that it would be enormously difficult, if not impossible, to create false memories about events that are rare, bizarre, or implausible. For instance, Pezdek, Finger, and Hodge (1997) were unable to plant a false memory of having received a rectal enema as a child. Yet, one response to this claim is to point to studies in which people have indeed been led to believe in rather implausible experiences. Mazzoni, Loftus, and Kirsch (2001) increased belief in subjects that, as young children, they had witnessed a person being demonically possessed. They accomplished this feat by first having subjects rate the plausibility of various events, including the event of witnessing demonic possession. They also rated the likelihood of having personally experienced these events in childhood. Subsequently, subjects read short articles describing possession, including a testimony from a prestigious person who reported experiencing such witnessing. Finally, subjects repeated the plausibility and life event ratings. A major finding was that those who received the articles–testimonial about demonic possession not only found the idea more plausible but also increased their confidence that it had personally happened.

The possession manipulation varied across the studies. When it included a review of the articles–testimonial plus some false feedback to the participant, it was particularly effective. The false feedback involved giving subjects a *fear profile* in which their level of fear toward various objects (e.g., spiders, animals) was analyzed. Whatever their responses on the profile, they were told that the profile indicated that they had probably witnessed demonic possession as a child, and this was the cause of their fears. Even without the fear profile, when subjects merely reviewed the articles, they rated demonic possession as more plausible and increased their confidence that it had happened to them. The addition of the false feedback enhanced the false memory effect. What is particularly striking about these results is that the manipulation was effective even with people who entered the study with a belief that demonic possession was rather implausible.

Mazzoni et al. (2001) discussed these findings in conjunction with a model of false memory formation. According to the model, one first needs to be led to the belief that the pseudo-event is plausible. Later, one is led to the belief that the pseudo-event personally occurred. Finally, one is led to experience the pseudo-event as if it were a genuine memory. The distinction between belief and memory (Stages 2 and 3 in the model) is well illustrated by the example of "had my umbilical cord cut after birth." People can believe that this occurred to them, even quite confidently, but they presumably have no actual "memory" for the experience. Likewise with pseudo-events, people can believe that they occurred, even if they have no subjective feeling of memory. In the demonic possession studies, the manipulation does appear to have inflated plausibility (Stage 1 of the model). Subsequently, the subjects also demonstrated increased confidence that the event had happened to them (Stage 2 of the model). The subjects in this study were not pressed to determine whether the beliefs were also accompanied by rich sensory detail, so that we could characterize them as being rich false memories. But such work has been done with other false memories studies and could be done with this unusual item.

Accessing True Memories Versus Planting False Ones?

In this line of research, a question repeatedly arises. Is the suggestive manipulation leading people to uncover a true memory or is it leading to the creation of a false one? So the "lost in the mall" suggestion could conceivably be leading people to dredge up a genuine experience of being lost, even if they had temporarily forgotten about it. Although in the "familial informant false narrative procedure" the family members insist that the pseudo-event never occurred, it is conceivable that the family member informants are wrong. To gather evidence bearing on whether suggestive manipulations are truly planting false memories, researchers have adopted several techniques. One such technique involves attempting to plant not merely implausible memories but events that would be impossible.

In a series of studies designed to plant impossible memories, subjects evaluated advertising copy for a Disney resort. Some saw a generic ad that mentioned no cartoon characters. Others saw a fake ad for Disney that featured Bugs Bunny. Later on, subjects were asked about any personal trips to Disney that they had taken as a child. In one study, exposure to the fake ad led 16% of subjects to claim that they had met Bugs Bunny at Disney (Braun, Ellis, & Loftus, 2002). This scenario is, of course, impossible because Bugs Bunny is a Warner Bros. cartoon character and would not be featured at a Disney resort. Or, as the *Los Angeles Times* put it: "the wascally Warner Bros. wabbit would be awwested on sight" at Disney ("You Must Remember This," 2003). Multiple exposure to the fake Bugs ad led to even higher false memory rates, boosting the rate to 25% in one study and 36% in a second study (Grinley, 2002). In one of these studies, subjects were asked explicitly what they remembered about meeting Bugs. A quarter of subjects fell sway to the suggestion. Of those who recalled the encounter with Bugs, 62% recalled that they shook his hand, 46% recalled hugging him. Moreover, over 25% remembered touching his ear, touching his tail, and hearing him say "What's up doc?" One participant even remembered that Bugs was holding a carrot. Thus, subjects imbued their false memory with sensory detail, a finding that is important because people sometimes use the presence of sensory detail as a cue to distinguish their true from false memories.

Another attempt to plant an impossible memory suggested to subjects that they remember "Having a nurse remove a skin sample from my little finger" when they were under age 6. A check of government records revealed no evidence that this medical procedure had ever taken place in the United Kingdom where the subjects were tested. And yet after imagination, subjects became more confident that the false event happened to them. Many of them expressed a rich false memory, for example, "There was a nurse and the place smelled horrible" (Mazzoni & Memon, 2003, p. 187).

Other clever attempts to plant at least highly improbable memories have achieved decent success. In one case, subjects were given photographs of themselves as young children and encouraged to recall the events depicted in the photographs. Although most of the photos were genuine, one photo was fake. It was created by digitally introducing a real childhood image into the basket of a hot-air balloon (Wade, Garry, Read, & Lindsay, 2002). Family informants insisted the event never happened to the participant, and yet after reviewing the fake photos, 50% of subjects reported having memories of the experience. For example, one participant remembered the following: "I'm pretty certain it occurred when I was in form one [6th grade] at um the local school there . . . basically for $10 or something you could go up in a hot air balloon and go up about 20 odd meters . . . I'm pretty certain that mum is down on the ground taking a photo" (p. 600).

A variant of this procedure tried to plant a false memory of putting Slime in the teacher's desk in Grade 1 or 2. (Slime is a bright-colored gooey substance sold as a child's toy.) The specific suggestion ostensibly came from a family informant and included the information that the prank was done with a friend, that the teacher was unhappy, and that the students were forced to sit in the corner facing the wall for a half hour as punishment. Subjects frequently claimed to remember this event, and the false memory rate was boosted when subjects viewed their school class group photo from the same time period. In the photo condition, 65% of subjects were judged to have memories of the pseudo-event. These false memories appear to be quite rich:

> These findings are particularly dramatic in that subjects judged as having false memories gave quite high ratings of the extent to which they felt they were remembering the event, of the extent to which remembering the event was like reliving it, and of their confidence that the event had actually occurred. (Lindsay et al., 2004, p. 153)

Lindsay et al. (2004) advanced a number of possible explanations for why the class photo (which did not depict the Slime prank) worked so well. It may have added to the memory's authenticity, it enabled subjects to speculate about the event, and it provided some perceptual details that were subsequently blended with products of imagination to produce images of the pseudo-event.

Consequences of False Memories

In virtually all of the memory-planting studies, the ultimate question asked of subjects is whether they believe that the pseudo-event happened in their past. Sometimes they are then probed to determine whether the event is "remembered." Occasionally, there are attempts to determine whether the event is held with confidence, whether it is accompanied by sensory detail, or whether it is associated with emotion. But even after determining that a rich false memory has been created, little is known about whether holding such a false memory is associated with any consequences later on. Does the false memory affect the thoughts or behaviors of the individual in some further way? For example, if a false memory is planted that the participant met Bugs Bunny at Disney, would the participant later think about Bugs whenever Disney is mentioned? Or, if a false memory is planted that a participant experienced a vicious attack by a dog as a child, would the participant show fear of dogs later on?

Grinley (2002) explored the consequences of the Bugs Bunny manipulation. Recall that in one of her thesis experiments, she convinced approximately 36% of subjects that they had met Bugs Bunny at a Disney resort. In this study she also explored the impact of the manipulation on semantic associations. Subjects viewed pairs of cartoon characters and indicated the extent to which the characters were related to one another. For example, how related are Mickey Mouse and Minnie Mouse, Donald Duck and Sleeping Beauty, Mickey Mouse and Bugs Bunny? Naturally, people find Mickey and Minnie to be closely related, and they find Donald and Sleeping Beauty to be relatively unrelated. But after the Bugs manipulation, people find Mickey and Bugs to be more closely related than control subjects do. Thus, the false memory manipulation influenced the thought processes of the exposed subjects, and in that sense created a consequence. Whether subjects would act differently as a result of their altered thought processes is a matter for future research.

A more compelling example of a false memory having consequences for an individual comes from preliminary work conducted by Heather Collins as part of her honors thesis conducted in our lab (Collins, 2001, reviewed in Pickrell, Bernstein, & Loftus, in press). Collins asked whether people who were led to believe that they had been attacked by a small dog as children would later show inclinations to avoid that type of animal. In her study, subjects were first asked whether various events had happened to them as children. The key item, buried in a long list, was whether they "were unexpectedly attacked by a small dog." Sometime later, some of these subjects were given bogus feedback, based on previously completed questionnaires, that they had likely been attacked by a small dog. When subsequently asked about the key experience, these subjects were more confident that they had been attacked in this way as children. In terms of consequences, those individuals also later indicated that they were less interested in owning a dog as a pet, compared with controls who had not received the false feedback manipulation. So the memory-altering manipulation appears to be able to influence one's later interests, preferences, attitudes, or whatever this report is measuring. Whatever they are, what we have here is a demonstration that our suggestive false memory manipulations can have consequences beyond a simple report of belief or memory. Although Collins showed an influence on reported preferences in her study, it still is an empirical question whether her manipulation would also affect actual behavior (e.g., would people be less likely to actually purchase or obtain a dog as pet?). Of course, we do know that a primary determinant of a person's behavior is the intention the person has to perform that behavior (Cappella, Yzer, & Fishbein, 2003). And intention itself is a function of the attitude that the person has toward performing the behavior, so it seems reasonable to speculate that the manipulations might affect actual behavior.

We have recently conducted pilot work addressing this question. Subjects completed a questionnaire about childhood experiences pertaining to food, for example, "Slipped on a banana peel and fell down" or "Ate freshly picked vegetables." Embedded within this list of events was a critical item. For one group of subjects (egg group), this item was "Got sick after eating too many hard boiled eggs." For another group of subjects (pickle group), this item was "Felt ill after eating a dill pickle." Subjects returned to the lab a week later and were given false feedback allegedly coming from a sophisticated computer program. They were told that their answers to previous questionnaires indicated that they had either gotten sick from eating hard boiled eggs (egg group) or that they had gotten sick after eating a dill pickle (pickle group). Next, subjects completed the same food questionnaire that they had completed 1 week prior. Our first question was whether the bogus feedback increased people's beliefs about the critical item. As predicted, the egg group was now more likely to believe that they had, in fact, become ill after eating hard-boiled eggs as children. And those given the false feedback about getting sick on a dill pickle showed increased confidence that that had occurred in their childhood.

Our main question, though, was whether this increase in autobiographical belief would translate into subsequent observable behavior. Would subjects who thought that they had gotten sick after eating hard-boiled eggs or eating pickles as children now be more likely to avoid such foods? To test this, we asked subjects to imagine themselves at a barbeque with 100 guests. We then asked them to rate how likely they would be to eat certain foods. Embedded within this list of foods were the critical items: hard-boiled eggs and dill pickle spears. As we had predicted, subjects in the egg group rated themselves as less likely to want to eat hard-boiled eggs, and those in the pickle group said that they were less likely to want to eat dill pickles.

We realize that it is one thing to say that "I wouldn't want to eat dill pickles at a barbeque" and another thing altogether to actually avoid dill pickles at a barbeque. However, as we mentioned above, intentions are excellent predictors of actions. In future work, we hope to test this idea by giving subjects the real choice of eating foods that they falsely believe that they got sick eating as children and other foods with which they have no bad experience—either imagined or real. For example, we might suggest to subjects that they got sick after eating chocolate as children and then present them with the real option of eating chocolates or other nonchocolate candies. Based on our egg/pickle results, we hope to show that subjects will more often choose the other candies, because they now believe (falsely) that they had had a bad experience with chocolate as children. If we obtain this effect, we might even have a new dieting technique! These experiments indicate that people can be led to believe past events that never happened, and that such beliefs can change not only the way in which people think about the present but also the way in which they now behave.

Distinguishing True and False Memories

Many of the false memory studies have explored whether true and false memories differ. Most studies find that when comparing groups of false memories with groups of true ones, there are statistical differences. For example, Loftus and Pickrell (1995) compared the false memories of being lost with reports of true memories, and they found that subjects used fewer words in describing their false memories and rated the clarity of their false memories as lower than the true ones. They were also less confident in the false memories. Hyman and Pentland (1996) investigated the role of mental imagery in the formation of false memory and reported that false memories differ from some true memories. However, true memories that were not recalled at first and then recalled up to 3 weeks later were similar to false memories in terms of emotional strength, image clarity, and the confidence with which subjects held such memories. Hyman and Pentland pointed out that true memories, like false ones, are constructed (Bartlett, 1932), underscoring the difficulty in discerning true from false memories (for further evidence supporting this conclusion, see Heaps & Nash, 2001; Porter et al., 1999).

Recent work using neuroimaging has attempted to locate differences in the brain that might reveal something about true and false memories. The goal of much of this work is to demonstrate that true and false memories have different neural signatures (Curran, Schacter, Johnson, & Spinks, 2001; Fabiani, Stadler, & Wessels, 2000; Miller, Baratta, Wynveen, & Rosenfeld, 2001). The allure of such work has not been ignored, and there is likely to be considerable effort expended in the future on the neurophysiology of false memory. However, as we have argued elsewhere, this work tells the memory researcher little about the veracity of particular memories (Bernstein & Loftus, 2002). The reason for this is that findings are based on group averages. Unfortunately, group averages do not allow us to focus on an individual memory and to reliably discern whether it is true or false. Another potential problem with neuroimaging work on false memory is that such studies typically involve memory for words recently learned, and the few studies that have been done using this procedure have yielded inconsistent results. The methodological constraints of neuroimaging tools such as functional magnetic resonance imaging (fMRI) and event-related potentials (ERPs) make it difficult to study the types of rich false memories that we have been discussing. False memories of recently learned words are bound to be far more pallid than the rich false memories we are discussing.

Individuals who have rich (probably false) memories of alien abduction have been recently studied by Richard McNally and his collaborators (McNally, 2003). One study explored whether people who believe they have been abducted exhibit heightened physiologic reactivity (heart rate, skin conductance) that is common to patients with posttraumatic stress disorder (PTSD) when they think about their true traumas. The abductees studied had experienced apparent sleep paralysis and hypnopompic hallucinations (such as seeing figures hovering near their beds). Most had recovered memories with techniques such as guided imagery and hypnosis. Some recovered memories involved sexual intercourse with aliens, or having sperm extracted for breeding purposes. They listened to prerecorded audiotaped scripts about their experiences. Their physiological reactions were similar to those shown by people with PTSD who listen to audiotaped scripts of their true traumas. McNally (2003) noted that these findings underscore "the power of belief to drive a physiology consistent with actual traumatic experience" (p. 273).

One further concern in the true versus false memory distinction department is this: In many of the real-world cases, there are numerous attempts to get people to remember, to discuss their memories, to imagine the details, and more. These very techniques can serve to make the false memories be experienced as more detailed and vivid, and can make them even more indistinguishable from true memories.

Implications

Theoretical

False memories can be created using a variety of means. The process by which this occurs, though, is still unclear. As we described above, Mazzoni et al. (2001) have proposed a three-stage model by which false memories arise. Briefly, one must be led to believe that the event is plausible. Next, one must come to believe that the event personally occurred. Finally, one must experience the event as if it were a real memory. We recently demonstrated that surprising fluency accounts for the first two steps of this model (Bernstein, Godfrey, Davison, & Loftus, in press). *Surprising fluency* is defined as an unexpected rush of meaning that accompanies one's information-processing experience. Bernstein et al. presented subjects with life events that either were intact (e.g., "broke a window playing ball") or contained a key word that was scrambled (e.g., "broke a nwidwo playing ball"). In one experiment, subjects were asked to rate the events in terms of the likelihood that they occurred before the age of 10 in the average North American child's life. In other experiments, subjects were asked to rate the life events in terms of the likelihood that they occurred personally before the age of 10. In both cases, unscrambling a word was sufficient to increase one's belief that the event occurred in the average North American child's life as well as one's own childhood.

The process by which solving an anagram can lead one to believe that the event is generally plausible and that it likely occurred in one's own childhood is as follows: When subjects first encounter the anagram, they expect their processing to be slow and laborious. However, they quickly solve the anagram and experience a rush of meaning, akin to an "aha." This sudden rush of meaning is experienced as surprising fluency that the participant, in turn, experiences as familiarity (see Whittlesea & Williams, 2001). The participant then seeks to attribute this familiarity to a source, and in so doing, mistakenly attributes it to childhood experience rather than to the fact that he or she just unscrambled an anagram (see also Bernstein, Whittlesea, & Loftus, 2002). In a series of experiments, we demonstrated that fluency per se is insufficient to explain the increase in confidence. Instead, surprising fluency seems to account better for the way in which an event can be seen as plausible and likely to have occurred in one's own life. We argued that the same process may help explain how pseudo-events can be experienced as real, rich memories that subtly become part of one's autobiography.

Much of the work that we have described in this chapter can be explained using this familiarity misattribution model. To create rich false memories, investigators have used a variety of techniques. They may ask subjects to imagine themselves experiencing certain events such as breaking a window. The act of imagination makes this event feel more familiar when it is subsequently encountered on a list of possible childhood events, because the event is processed surprisingly well. This familiarity is then misattributed to childhood experience rather than being correctly attributed to the act of imagination. Similarly, asking subjects to try to remember a fictitious event causes them to imbue the experience with sensory detail and even emotion. When subjects later are asked whether the event in question is a real memory, their previous attempt at recollection causes the event to feel highly familiar now. Subjects may find it difficult to discern the memory's origin and mistakenly accept it as real (see Johnson, Hashtroudi, & Lindsay, 1993). Thus, familiarity misattribution may explain how events come to be seen as both generally plausible and personally experienced as real memories.

Applied

It should be clear by now that there are many ways to lead people to falsely believe that something happened in their past that did not, and in some cases to lead them to develop rich false memories. As we have noted before, this is not simply a nuisance for the individual, but it also represents a serious social problem contributing to miscarriages of justice in the legal system, to mistreatments of patients in clinical settings, and to consumer gullibility to manipulative advertising (van de Wetering, Bernstein, & Loftus, 2002). When innocent people are jailed, when therapy patients are made sicker, we have a societal problem worth worrying about.

It might sound rather trite, but perhaps one of the best remedies for these problems is widespread education. If people were made more aware of the problem of false memories, they might become less susceptible. Encouraging people to think hard about the potential source of the memories or the source of particular details in a memory has been shown to reduce the false memory problem, although it does not eliminate it (Chambers & Zaragoza, 2001). People might profitably be trained to examine these sources autonomously and routinely.

In addition to raising awareness on the part of the rememberer, it would be useful to educate those who are in a position to influence the memories of others. Police and other investigators need to be aware of their power to influence, and to avoid inadvertent contamination of memory. A question as seemingly innocent as "Mrs. Jones said it happened this way, what did you see?" is just the kind of manipulation that our studies have shown can lead people to misremember the past.

Clinicians too need to be wary. When they take a client who has no memories of sexual abuse and use leading questions, guided imagery, dream interpretation, and other techniques to plumb the past, they may be inadvertently creating a past. More than a few clients have been led to develop some of the richest false memories that we have ever seen (Loftus & Ketcham, 1994).

Concluding Remarks

We have tried to show how people can be led to believe in details and events in their past that never occurred. Our focus has been on what we call rich false memories, or wholly false memories about the past. Evidence is growing that memory is highly malleable and that it can both aid us and lead us astray. Most of the time, memory serves us very well. At times, though, memory misleads us. Sometimes the error is inconsequential; other times, it can be disastrous. We have reviewed some of our own work and that of others showing how false memories arise and how they can influence the way we think about the world and the way we behave. We have also discussed some of the difficulties inherent in trying to differentiate true and false memories. Finally, we offered a theoretical account of false memory formation and discussed some real-world applications of false memory research. Future work on false memory will undoubtedly answer some of the many questions that remain. For the present, the major hurdle for individuals, juries, and clinicians is to remain cognizant of the fact that rich false memories can appear and feel just as real and true as true memories. Just because the memory report is detailed, just because the person expresses confidence, just because the individual is highly emotional when reporting, does not mean it really happened.

References

Ayers, M. S., & Reder, L. M. (1998). A theoretical review of the misinformation effect: Predictions from an activation-based memory model. *Psychonomic Bulletin & Review, 5,* 1–21.

Bartlett, F. C. (1932). *Remembering: A study in experimental and social psychology.* Cambridge, England: Cambridge University Press.

Bernstein, D. M., Godfrey, R., Davison, A., & Loftus, E. F. (in press). *Memory's free radicals: When familiarity alters autobiography.* Memory & Cognition.

Bernstein, D. M., & Loftus, E. F. (2002). Lingering difficulties distinguishing true and false memories: A comment on Shevrin's psychoanalytic view of memory. *Neuro-Psychoanalysis, 4,* 129–141.

Bernstein, D. M., Whittlesea, B. W. A., & Loftus, E. F. (2002). Increasing confidence in remote autobiographical memory and general knowledge: Extensions of the revelation effect. *Memory & Cognition, 30,* 432–438.

Braun, K. A., Ellis, R., & Loftus, E. F. (2002). Make my memory: How advertising can change our memories of the past. *Psychology and Marketing, 19,* 1–23.

Cappella, J. N., Yzer, M., & Fishbein, M. (2003). Using beliefs about positive and negative consequences as the basis for designing message interventions for lowering risky behavior. In D. Romer (Ed.), *Reducing adolescent risk* (pp. 210–219). Thousand Oaks, CA: Sage.

Chambers, K. L., & Zaragoza, M. S. (2001). Intended and unintended effects of explicit warnings on eyewitness suggestibility: Evidence from source identification tests. *Memory & Cognition, 29,* 1120–1129.

Collins, H. R. (2001). *Another reason to dislike Chihuahuas and other small dogs: Behavioral consequences of false memories.* Unpublished honors thesis, University of Washington, Seattle.

Curran, T., Schacter, D. L., Johnson, M. K., & Spinks, R. (2001). Brain potentials reflect behavioral differences in true and false recognition. *Journal of Cognitive Neuroscience, 13,* 201–216.

Fabiani, M., Stadler, M. A., & Wessels, P. M. (2000). True but not false memories produce a sensory signature in human lateralized brain potentials. *Journal of Cognitive Neuroscience, 12,* 941–949.

Grinley, M. J. (2002). *Effects of advertising on semantic and episodic memory.* Unpublished master's thesis, University of Washington, Seattle.

Heaps, C. M., & Nash, M. (2001). Comparing recollective experience in true and false autobiographical memories. *Journal of Experimental Psychology: Learning, Memory, and Cognition, 27,* 920–930.

Hyman, I. E., Jr., Husband, T. H., & Billings, F. J. (1995). False memories of childhood experiences. *Applied Cognitive Psychology, 9,* 181–197.

Hyman, I. E., Jr., & Pentland, J. (1996). The role of mental imagery in the creation of false childhood memories. *Journal of Memory and Language, 35,* 101–117.

Johnson, M. K., Hashtroudi, S., & Lindsay, D. S. (1993). Source monitoring. *Psychological Bulletin, 114,* 3–28.

Lindsay, D. S., Hagen, L., Read, J. D., Wade, K. A., & Garry, M. (2004). True photographs and false memories. *Psychological Science, 15,* 149–154.

Loftus, E. F., & Ketcham, K. (1994). *The myth of repressed memory.* New York: St. Martin's Press.

Loftus, E. F., & Pickrell, J. E. (1995). The formation of false memories. *Psychiatric Annals, 25,* 720–725.

Mack, J. E. (1994). *Abduction: Human encounters with aliens* (Rev. ed.). New York: Ballantine Books.

Mazzoni, G. A. L., Loftus, E. F., & Kirsch, I. (2001). Changing beliefs about implausible autobiographical events: A little plausibility goes a long way. *Journal of Experimental Psychology: Applied, 7,* 51–59.

Mazzoni, G. A. L., & Memon, A. (2003). Imagination can create false autobiographical memories. *Psychological Science, 14,* 186–188.

McNally, R. J. (2003). *Remembering trauma.* Cambridge, MA: Harvard University Press.

Miller, A. R, Baratta, C., Wynveen, C., & Rosenfeld, J. P. (2001). P300 latency, but not amplitude or topography, distinguishes between true and false recognition. *Journal of Experimental Psychology: Learning, Memory, and Cognition, 27,* 254–361.

Neisser, U., & Harsch, N. (1992). Phantom flashbulbs: False recollections of hearing the news about *Challenger.* In E. Winograd & U. Neisser (Eds.), *Affect and accuracy in recall: Studies of "flashbulb" memories* (pp. 9–31). New York: Cambridge University Press.

Nourkova, V., Bernstein, D. M., & Loftus, E. F. (2004). Altering traumatic memory. *Cognition & Emotion, 18,* 575–585.

Pezdek, K., Finger, K., & Hodge, D. (1997). Planting false childhood memories: The role of event plausibility. *Psychological Science, 8,* 437–441.

Pickrell, J. E., Bernstein, D. M., & Loftus, E. F. (in press). The misinformation effect. In R. Pohl (Ed.), *Cognitive illusions: A handbook on fallacies and biases in thinking, judgment and memory.* Hove, England: Psychology Press.

Porter, S., Yuille, J. C., & Lehman, D. R. (1999). The nature of real, implanted, and fabricated memories for emotional childhood events: Implications for the recovered memory debate. *Law and Human Behavior, 23,* 517–537.

Radelet, M. L. (2002). Introduction: Wrongful convictions of the innocent. *Judicature, 86,* 67–68.

Sagan, C. (1995). *The demon-haunted world.* New York: Random House.

van de Wetering, S., Bernstein, D. M., & Loftus, E. F. (2002). Public education against false memories: A modest proposal. *Cognitive Technology, 2,* 4–7.

Wade, K. A., Garry, M., Read, J. D., & Lindsay, D. S. (2002). A picture is worth a thousand lies: Using false photographs to create false childhood memories. *Psychonomic Bulletin & Review, 9,* 597–603.

Whittlesea, B. W. A., & Williams, L. D. (2001). The discrepancy-attribution hypothesis: I. The heuristic basis of feelings of familiarity. *Journal of Experimental Psychology: Learning, Memory, and Cognition, 27,* 3–13.

You must remember this [Editorial]. (2003, February 24). *Los Angeles Times,* p. 10, Part 2.

9

The Functionalist Agenda in Memory Research

James S. Nairne

One of the benefits of working in applied settings is that problems tend to be well defined. It is relatively easy to measure progress, and analytical techniques can be objectively evaluated. If the charge is to help a banker remember the vault code, it is not difficult to tell whether the intervention is working—the vault either opens or remains closed. For the laboratory researcher, however, problems are often ill defined. There can be no clear starting point, well-stated goal, or simple way of evaluating or marking progress.

Consider the study of pure memory, an enterprise widely pursued by researchers in cognitive psychology. Most memory researchers focus on a particular memory system or process, such as episodic, semantic, or implicit memory, and they conduct experiments to (a) isolate its underlying mechanisms and (b) determine its parameters of operation. The goal is to analyze the system's structure and its component parts in much the same way that a chemist might analyze a chemical compound by breaking it down into simpler elements. Attention is rarely given to the system's function at this point, largely because understanding function is presumed to depend on understanding structure. After all, how can we determine the function of a system unless we first understand the system itself? It is necessary to isolate the critical components, along with some rules for their interaction, and then—perhaps—the adaptive role that the system plays in cognition can be specified.

In this chapter, I discuss some of the implications of this widely practiced structuralist, or nonfunctional, approach to the analysis of memory. To begin, as noted above, problems crafted within a structuralist framework tend to be ill defined. When we set out to study *implicit memory*, it is difficult to gauge progress, or measure success, because the objective is unclear. The components of an implicit memory system are unknown; consequently, there is no way of determining when, or if, the system has been fully described. Researchers often end up studying tasks as a result, such as paired-associate learning or word-fragment completion, because task performance is easy to evaluate objectively. The trouble with this focus, however, is that the link between the studied tasks and the true memory system of interest can be tenuous or, more likely, inadequately specified.

Second, there are compelling reasons to believe that our memory systems are functionally designed. Our capacity to access and use the past did not develop in a vacuum; instead, our memory systems evolved to help us solve particular problems, adaptive problems that arose in our ancestral past. Without a functional perspective, as a result, it will be extremely difficult to determine how any mnemonic system works (or we can easily be led astray). As a starting point, we should assume that the structural components of the system exist, and work the way they do, because they are design features—that is, they contribute to solving a problem that is regularly faced by the organism (Klein, Cosmides, Tooby, & Chance, 2002; Tooby & Cosmides, 1992). Note that structure from this perspective is a by-product of function rather than the other way around: Nature designs, or selects, particular structural features because they aid in solving a problem faced by the species (Dennett, 1995).[1]

Finally, as I discuss in the main body of the chapter, ignoring the primacy of function in our analyses can lead to principles, or theoretical positions, that are misleading or wrong. Two such widely held principles are considered here: (a) Memory, especially short-term memory, depends directly on the activation of a trace, which, in turn, decays over time; and (b) memory, especially long-term memory, depends directly on the similarity or match between retrieval cues and traces, as encoded. Note that neither of these principles is placed in any kind of functional context; there is no consideration given to a central problem that the memory system might be attempting to solve, other than a vague reference to "memory." As a consequence, we are left with principles that generate equivocal predictions and, in fact, violate general dictums of memory theory in some cases (see Nairne, 2001, 2002a, 2002b). Before developing these points in detail, I begin by addressing the question that sits at the heart of any functional analysis: What is memory for?

What Is Memory For?

Everyone agrees that the ability to store, recover, and use the past serves an adaptive role. But did our memory systems evolve primarily to solve the problem of reproducing the past or to solve other problems? Some have argued that memory's primary function is to help us use the past, in combination with the present, to decide on an appropriate plan of action (e.g., N. H. Anderson, 1996; Glenberg, 1997). In some respects, designing a system literally to reproduce the past makes little adaptive sense. A past event can never occur in exactly the same way again, nor can it be perceived in a like manner. In the words of

---

[1]Not all structural components are necessarily adaptations, that is, components that have been sculpted by the mechanisms of natural selection. It is still reasonable to assume, however, that their role in remembering is functionally designed, regardless of whether they are adaptations, exaptations (i.e., co-opted components that evolved for different reasons), or even spandrels (i.e., components that by themselves are not adaptations but are linked in some way to other evolved traits; e.g., Gould & Vrba, 1982). Moreover, my use of the term *designed* is not meant to imply the existence of a preexisting plan but rather refers to the process through which components conform to prevailing environmental demands.

William James, identical experiences require "an unmodified brain. The organ, after intervening states, cannot react as it did before" (James, 1884, p. 11).

In addition, granted that our memory systems are functionally designed, the stored components might well have little meaning outside of a particular goal context. For example, stored experiences could simply feed into an inferential "whole" that renders the experiences themselves unimportant, or changes them in such a way that they become unrecognizable as specific experiences. Trait judgments are easily remembered and applied—for example, whether we think an individual is likable—but they seem not to depend on recovery of the specific episodes on which they are based (N. H. Anderson, 1996; Klein et al., 2002). Scripts and schemas regularly guide remembering, such as when we attempt to recall our latest visit to a fast-food restaurant, but our memories often bear little resemblance to any particular episode or experience (Bower, Black, & Turner, 1979).

One can even imagine conceptualizations of memory in which the individual components are never actually stored. Experience might merely change affordances, or the range of possible interactions that we can have with the environment (Glenberg, 1997). Cutting off the leg of a chair changes how we can interact with it in the future, regardless of how or when the original removal took place. Similarly, experience might alter our perceptions, or the likelihood of certain responses, without reference to the situations that produced the change. The original events need not be reproduced, or remembered accurately, to exert lasting effects on our cognitions or behaviors. Present behavior can reflect the past, a true function of memory, without a lasting record of the event that precipitated the change.

At the same time, reproduction is not completely useless. We need to remember to take medication at a particular time, call to mind the name of a colleague, and remember necessary telephone numbers or passwords. Our ancestors in the Pleistocene era certainly needed to remember the specific locations of food, water, and competing groups. Nothing inferential would be appropriate in these situations; it is the literal location or sequence of numbers that is needed to accomplish the goal. Reproduction thus becomes an adaptive outcome, and we can assume that our memory systems contain functionally designed mechanisms appropriate to this end. (This is a comforting conclusion given that the vast majority of laboratory research over the past century has been directed at studying literal reproduction [Koriat, Goldsmith, & Pansky, 2000].)

It is important, however, to note that any functional design for reproduction needs to contain mechanisms for ensuring that the act of reproduction is context dependent. Passwords and telephone numbers are appropriately remembered only within specific environments, and there are costs associated with inappropriate retrievals (J. R. Anderson & Milson, 1989). Reproduction thus becomes a matter of discriminating where and when to produce a response based on information available in the present. At any given moment, a wide range of responses is available (e.g., each of us must now remember multiple user IDs and passwords)—the task is to select the response that is most appropriate for that context. Recognizing the context-dependent nature of reproduction is crucial because it implies that our theories of remembering cannot simply focus on the characteristics of a response, or a memory trace; instead, the focus should be on conditional response selection: For a given environment, how is the most appropriate response, or memory, selected? The outcome of the selection process will depend on the features present in the situation (the retrieval cues) as well as on the characteristics of any stored information (e.g., Toth & Hunt, 1999; Tulving, 1983).

Activation, Decay, and Remembering

With this functional analysis of reproduction in mind, I turn now to the oft-argued proposal that memory, particularly short-term memory, depends on the activation of a memory trace, which, in turn, decays over time. Note that reproduction is tied directly to a property of the trace in this case—activation—and no reference is made to context, or to any kind of response selection process. Activation alone determines retention and, although there may be situations that increase or decrease activation levels, reproduction itself is assumed to be context independent.

It is interesting to note that short-term memory may be one instance in which reproduction is not context dependent; that is, information sits at the focus of awareness and, as such, is instantly available. In William James's original conception of primary memory, items did not need to be retrieved because they were, in effect, already in a state of retrieval: "an object of primary memory is not thus brought back; it was never lost; its date was never cut off in consciousness from that of the immediately present moment" (James, 1890/1983, p. 608). The Jamesian view maps easily onto the concepts of activation and decay. One can conceive of information receding slowly into the past, hastened along by a decay process, until it drops below a threshold of awareness and instant availability.

Modern conceptions of working memory adopt the Jamesian idea but package it in a more modularized architecture. For example, Cowan (2001) distinguished between activated information in memory and a smaller, more restricted, subset of information that sits at the focus of awareness. The latter suffers from capacity limitations (roughly four chunks), and its contents can be immediately accessed—that is, the items reside in a "retrieval-free" zone. As Kintsch and others have noted, it is common for working memory theorists to assume "that information 'in' working memory is directly and effortlessly retrievable" and that retrieval from working memory, unlike long-term memory, is "not cue dependent" (Kintsch, Healy, Hegarty, Pennington, & Salthouse, 1999, p. 414). Consider Cowan's (2001) commentary on the finding that proactive interference (PI) sometimes fails to occur in immediate recall contexts: "This presumably occurs because four or fewer items are, in a sense, already retrieved; they reside in a limited-capacity store, eliminating the retrieval step in which PI occurs" (p. 103).

Baddeley's popular working memory model (Baddeley, 2000; Baddeley & Hitch, 1974) has a similar flavor, although in Baddeley's conception capacity limitations arise from trade-offs between decay and processes devoted to maintaining above-threshold activation levels (e.g., rehearsal). Active traces are maintained in loops and stores and are forgotten whenever reactivation fails to counteract the relentless ravages of decay. Juggling is an apt metaphor: Items can be maintained aloft to the extent that each can be caught and retossed before gravity drives them into the ground. Here, capacity limitations are not a property of air (e.g., a store or a resource) but rather are determined by the balance between retossing (activation) and the downward pull of gravity (decay). Unlike Cowan, Baddeley avoids strong claims about the immediate availability of stored items—that is, items may need to be retrieved—but retention in his model remains closely tied to activation and forgetting is closely tied to decay.

From a functional perspective, it seems adaptive to possess a system that keeps subsets of information immediately available, perhaps as a necessary ingredient for language processing or online problem solving. In the working memory system, an articulatory rehearsal process might have developed to help us prolong or maintain information in a form suitable for producing and comprehending spoken language. However, to link an item's mnemonic status solely to its activation level, or to the simple passage of time, makes virtually no adaptive sense. Records of the recent past have value in some situations and not others, regardless of their activation status. When asked to remember a just-presented telephone number, it is important to maintain a literal record of the immediate past. However, one can easily imagine situations, perhaps even the majority of situations, in which such a maintenance process would lead to considerable clutter. Functional memory is a matter of target selection, picking and choosing the most appropriate response given the current task requirements. Relying on activation alone, or a subset of items maintained at the focus of awareness, is a poor mechanism for adaptive decision making or for ensuring skilled performance (Ericsson & Kintsch, 1995).

Following Cowan (2001), one might argue that activation itself, or residence in the focus of awareness, accrues from some kind of context-dependent selection process (i.e., items are "already retrieved"). Under such a scenario, memory records are selected for maintenance, or for residence at the focus of awareness, on the basis of an analysis of the appropriateness of the record in that situation. As I have argued elsewhere (Nairne, 2002b, 2003), it makes sense to conceptualize the continuous record of immediate experience as a pattern of retrieval cues, to be interpreted and selected, rather than as available items "sitting" in some limited-capacity work space. Maintenance activities such as rehearsal are then more appropriately viewed as multiple acts of *recall*, which, in turn, generate additional records for subsequent interpretation.[2] In this conception, however, item recall is not determined by activation per se, but rather by the outcome of a cue-driven retrieval process. We interpret the remnants of immediate experience, selecting responses that are appropriate for the current situation (see Nairne, 1990).

Once we acknowledge that reproduction is cue driven rather than retrieval free, then trace-based concepts such as decay and activation start to lose their

---

[2] It remains an open question as to how many items can be considered part of an "act of recall." Practically, of course, people can only recall one item at a time.

meaning and power of prediction. Consider decay: It is conceivable that immediate experience leaves behind a record of activity (e.g., a residual pattern of phonological information from language-based processing), and these features, in turn, might decay spontaneously over time. However, the remaining features, by themselves, cannot predict recall; they are merely cues whose predictive value will depend on the discrimination problem facing the organism. One can easily imagine scenarios in which interpreting the activity record will be helped by the loss of features. For example, suppose a certain proportion of trace features is shared by many other possible targets or interpretations (e.g., cue overload). Losing features over time might help solve the discrimination problem in this case, assuming that the shared features are lost and features that uniquely specify a particular target response remain.[3] The fact that memory over the short term can decrease, stay the same, or even improve over time is consistent with this type of reasoning and inconsistent with the simpleminded activation view (see Nairne, 2002b, 2003, for reviews).

If we conceptualize remembering over the short term from a functional perspective, as an active process of response selection based on residual cues, then it makes little adaptive sense to tie reproduction to activation, or forgetting to decay. Some activation of retrieval cues may be necessary for memory, but activation alone is certainly not sufficient for generating an appropriate response. Performance will depend on the particular cues that are active, as well as on the set of possible responses that could be produced. A given activated feature, or set of features, will help or hinder this interpretation process, depending on the context. Stated more generally, the success of remembering cannot be determined by the characteristics of a cue (its strength or activation) or by the characteristics of a single target response, but only through consideration of the cue to target(s) interaction (see Tulving, 1983).

The Encoding-Retrieval Match

Essentially, the same case applies to the proposal that memory, especially long-term memory, depends directly on the similarity, or match, between retrieval cues and traces, as encoded. This is another widely held view, one that has been touted as an important principle by many in the memory field. Toth and Hunt (1999) suggested that the direct relationship between match and retention represents "one of the most important principles ever articulated about memory" (p. 254). Textbooks and review articles regularly proclaim as well, without reservation, that "memory is best when the retrieval environment matches the environment present during encoding" (Haberlandt, 1999, p. 309).

Appeals to similarity, or the cue–target match, once again ignore the functional context of remembering. Just as activation considers only the proper-

---

[3]One can also imagine that the composition of the target set, or the range of possible trace interpretations, might change on a moment-by-moment basis; thus, it would not be possible to predict until the exact moment of recall which features are helpful or not.

ties of a trace, the encoding-retrieval match focuses on the relationship between a cue and one target response and fails to consider the discrimination problem in effect. From a functional perspective, it is more reasonable to assume that cue–target similarity will help target selection in some circumstances and hurt it in others. Match may be generally correlated with retention, but it is unlikely to be the underlying cause of retention. Instead, it is the ability of the retrieval cue to help us discriminate an appropriate response from an inappropriate response that drives retention, not cue–target similarity per se (see Nairne, 2002a, for an extended discussion of this point).

To illustrate, consider the following thought experiment: Subjects are asked to read aloud a list of homophones presented visually on a computer screen (e.g., *pair, pare, pear, pare, pair*, etc.). At test, we ask everyone to write down the homophone that occurred in the third serial position (*pear*). In one condition, we provide no cues, only the retrieval query; in a second condition, we supply an additional cue—the sound of the target word. Note that we have improved the functional cue–target match in this second condition; there are more overlapping features between the retrieval cue and the encoded trace (we will assume that the auditory information is encoded). However, performance is unlikely to improve. All of the items on the list sound alike, so the sound provides no discriminative information about the appropriate response. We may have improved the encoding-retrieval match, but retention in all likelihood will not follow suit.

One can also easily imagine situations in which improving the cue–target match will hurt the retention of a particular target response. Suppose we bolster the encoding-retrieval match by adding cue–target features that are shared by other competitor responses. There may be an increase in the number of overlapping features between the cue and the target, but the discrimination problem itself (picking the correct target response) suffers. Edward DeLosh and I conducted an experiment several years ago to demonstrate this point (DeLosh & Nairne, 1996): Subjects learned to associate nonwords (e.g., *PAVIS*) with three simultaneously presented word cues (e.g., *ROUND, RED, SOFT*). Two of the words were uniquely associated with a nonword (*ROUND* and *RED* were paired only with *PAVIS*); the third cue (*SOFT*) received additional pairings with other nonwords on the list. At test, subjects attempted to recall each nonword in the presence of (a) one unique cue (*ROUND*), (b) two unique cues (*ROUND + RED*), or (c) one unique cue and the shared cue (*ROUND + SOFT*). The results are shown in Figure 9.1.

In terms of the encoding-retrieval match, moving from one unique cue to two unique cues increases the similarity between the encoding and retrieval environments. Each nonword was learned in the presence of three word cues, and providing two of those words at test more closely reinstates the context of original encoding than merely providing one. It is not surprising that performance improved in the two-unique-cue condition compared with the one-unique-cue condition. However, quite different results were obtained in the condition using one unique and one shared cue. Cue–target similarity also improved in this condition, compared with the single-cue condition—in fact, nominally by the same amount as in the two-unique-cue condition—but overall

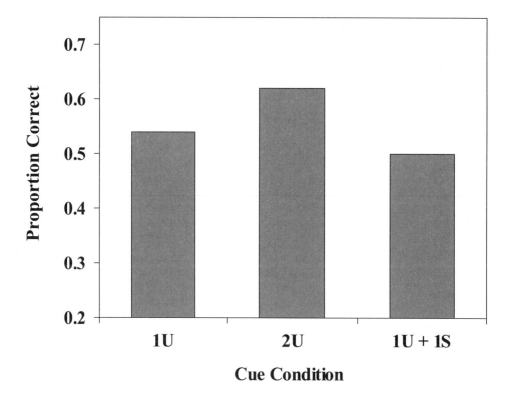

Figure 9.1. Proportion correct target recall for the one-unique-cue (1U), two-unique-cues (2U), and one-unique- and one-shared-cue (1U + 1S) conditions.

performance declined. The reason is simple: The shared cue was predictive of a number of other target responses rather than specifying only one target response, which increased the net difficulty of the target discrimination problem.

I am not suggesting that the match between a cue and a target response is irrelevant in all situations. On the contrary, as the similarity between a cue and an encoded target increases, correct recall of the associated target will usually improve as well. Yet, it is not really the match that is controlling performance; empirically, increasing the match can increase, have no effect, or even decrease target recall performance depending on the circumstance. What matters instead is the presence of distinctive cues—cues that uniquely specify the correct response. In many situations, increasing the cue–target match will increase the chances that distinctive cue features will be present, but, as the examples discussed previously demonstrate, the relationship between the match and retention is essentially correlational rather than causal.

From a functional perspective, the appropriateness of a cue, or the value of a cue–target match, will depend on the particular problem that happens to be in play. If the task is to pick a response from among a set of highly similar competitors, such as remembering the position of a particular item in a sequence, then adding shared features is likely to compound the discrimination problem. If the task is to choose from among a wide variety of responses, such as in a free-recall context in which the recall of any list response is appropriate, then adding shared features is apt to be beneficial. Knowing the match between a cue and the target, by itself, will not be sufficient to predict performance. The mnemonic value of the cue–target match, or the predictive value of an item's general activation level, can only be assessed within a particular functional context.

The Value of Reverse Engineering

In a functional analysis, recognition of the goal—the adaptive problem that the mnemonic system is solving—occurs first, followed by an analysis akin to reverse engineering (e.g., Dennett, 1995). Such a strategy is widely used in applied fields (see Gillan & Schvaneveldt, 1999) and is beneficial for many reasons: First, as noted earlier, it is reasonable to assume that our cognitive systems are functionally designed. Our memory systems follow particular operating rules and interact in predictable ways because those systems are designed to solve specific adaptive problems. As a consequence, the components are likely to be design features: They are engineered to solve specific problems and cannot be adequately understood outside of the problem context.

Second, from a practical standpoint, reverse engineering enables the problem-solver to isolate important from unimportant features of a design. Klein et al. (2002) offered the example of a three-hole punch. Imagine your task is to understand such a mechanism (which, of course, punches holes in paper sheets for inclusion in a binder). From a structuralist perspective, you could measure the dimensions of the device, note the spacing of the sharpened cutting pegs, analyze the spring-controlled handpress, and identify the paper confetti that falls out when the device is shaken. However, without knowledge of the device's function—what the device is designed to accomplish—it will be exceedingly difficult to understand why these components exist, or how and why they work together. As Klein et al. (2002) noted, one can imagine clever theorists concocting models that focus on how the device makes confetti, or on how to use slender metal devices as paperweights.

As argued earlier, memory researchers often set out to study memory systems, such as implicit or explicit memory, without a clear understanding of the adaptive context. In many cases, what appear to be critical components have been isolated and parameters of operation marked and catalogued. However, the findings are usually noted in isolation, without specification of their functional role. Consider the current fascination with false memory, the finding that people will falsely recall and recognize words after studying associatively related word lists (e.g., Roediger & McDermott, 1995). Dozens of empirical studies have been conducted on this phenomenon, and a number of clever hypotheses have been generated and tested, but virtually all of this research has occurred in a functional vacuum. It is the phenomenon itself that research-ers are attempting to understand, not the role that the implicit generation of associates, or the breakdown in source monitoring, plays in helping us solve a vexing adaptive problem. As a result, it is difficult to know whether we are isolating design features that are critical to an important memory system or simply generating hypotheses about mnemonic confetti.

Third, it is easy to show that adopting a functionalist perspective can lead to predictions or hypotheses that would not otherwise have been generated. For example, in their functional analysis of retention, J. R. Anderson and Schooler (1991) suggested that people's memory systems evolved primarily to capture the way events naturally occur and co-occur in the environment; that is, memory systems are designed to reflect salient informational properties of the environment. Laboratory research has long revealed that retention im-proves as a power function of practice and generally declines as a power function of retention interval. J. R. Anderson and Schooler have shown that these functions approximate the likelihood that information actually occurs, and hence is needed, in nature. For example, if an event occurs at Time N, it is much more likely to occur again at Time $N + 1$ than it is at Time $N + 2$, and the form of the relationship between occurrence and time closely resembles a power function.

Other insights have come from the adaptive analysis of skilled and expert performance. Ericsson and Kintsch (1995) have shown, for example, that skilled performers acquire the ability to encode information in a way that successfully anticipates when that information will be needed. It is neither sufficient nor adaptive simply to keep online information "active" in working memory during skilled performance; skilled performers can resume a task when interrupted and show flexibility as the task demands change. This led to the proposal of *long-term working memory*, a specific design feature that allows information to be stored directly in long-term memory but in a fashion that maintains its immediate accessibility (through cue-driven retrieval). In providing a general commentary about the analysis of working memory, Ericsson and Delaney (1999) noted the following: "It is no longer possible to isolate the critical compo-nents of working memory without first considering their functional context in the corresponding skilled activities" (p. 269).

Finally, as I discussed in the main body of this chapter, structuralist thinking can lead to the generation of principles and proposals that make little sense in a functional context. Concepts such as activation, decay, or the encoding-retrieval match have little meaning outside of particular memory environments, although each could potentially serve as a design feature in an adaptive memory system. It might be appropriate, for example, to build decay into a system (e.g., to reduce clutter), but its true impact on remembering can only be assessed in the context of a specific discrimination problem. To paraphrase William James, a strong proponent of the functionalist agenda, we cannot expect to understand a house by focusing on its bricks and mortar. It is important to have a clear idea of what the structure is for, what the house is designed to do, before things such as bricks and mortar will begin to make sense.

References

Anderson, J. R., & Milson, R. (1989). Human memory: An adaptive perspective. *Psychological Review, 96*, 703–719.

Anderson, J. R., & Schooler, L. J. (1991). Reflections of the environment in memory. *Psychological Science, 2*, 396–408.

Anderson, N. H. (1996). *A functional theory of cognition.* Mahwah, NJ: Erlbaum.

Baddeley, A. D. (2000). The episodic buffer: A new component of working memory? *Trends in Cognitive Sciences, 4*, 417–423.

Baddeley, A. D., & Hitch. G. (1974). Working memory. In G. H. Bower (Ed.), *The psychology of learning and motivation* (Vol. 8, pp. 47–89). New York: Academic Press.

Bower, G. H., Black, J. B., & Turner, T. J. (1979). Scripts in memory for text. *Cognitive Psychology, 11*, 177–220.

Cowan, N. (2001). The magical number 4 in short-term memory: A reconsideration of mental storage capacity. *Behavioral and Brain Sciences, 24*, 87–185.

DeLosh, E. L., & Nairne, J. S. (1996, May). *Similarity or discriminability? An evaluation of the fundamental assumption of the encoding specificity principle.* Paper presented at the 68th Annual Meeting of Midwestern Psychological Association, Chicago, IL.

Dennett, D. C. (1995). *Darwin's dangerous idea: Evolution and the meanings of life.* New York: Simon & Schuster.

Ericsson, K. A., & Delaney, P. F. (1999). Long-term working memory as an alternative to capacity models of working memory in everyday skilled performance. In A. Miyake & P. Shah (Eds.), *Models of working memory* (pp. 257–297). Cambridge, England: Cambridge University Press.

Ericsson, K. A., & Kintsch, W. (1995). Long-term working memory. *Psychological Review, 102*, 211–245.

Gillan, D. J., & Schvaneveldt, R. W. (1999). Applying cognitive psychology: Bridging the gap between basic research and cognitive artifacts. In F. T. Durso (Ed.), *Handbook of applied cognition* (pp. 3–31). New York: Wiley.

Glenberg, A. M. (1997). What is memory for? *Behavioral and Brain Sciences, 20*, 1–55.

Gould, S. J., & Vrba, E. S. (1982). Exaptation: A missing term in the science of form. *Paleobiology, 8*, 4–15.

Haberlandt, K. (1999). *Human memory: Exploration and application.* Needham Heights, MA: Allyn & Bacon.

James, W. (1884). Some omissions of introspective psychology. *Mind, 9*, 1–26.

James, W. (1983). *The principles of psychology.* Cambridge, MA: Harvard University Press. (Original work published 1890)

Kintsch, W., Healy, A. F., Hegarty, N., Pennington, B. F., & Salthouse, T. A. (1999). Models of working memory: Eight questions and some general issues. In A. Miyake & P. Shah (Eds.), *Models of working memory* (pp. 412–441). Cambridge, England: Cambridge University Press.

Klein, S. B., Cosmides, L., Tooby, J., & Chance, S. (2002). Decisions and the evolution of memory: Multiple systems, multiple functions. *Psychological Review, 109*, 306–329.

Koriat, A., Goldsmith, M., & Pansky, A. (2000). Toward a psychology of memory accuracy. *Annual Review of Psychology, 51*, 481–537.

Nairne, J. S. (1990). A feature model of immediate memory. *Memory & Cognition, 18*, 251–269.

Nairne, J. S. (2001). A functional analysis of primary memory. In H. L. Roediger III, J. S. Nairne, I. Neath, & A. M. Surprenant (Eds.), *The nature of remembering: Essays in honor of Robert G. Crowder* (pp. 282–296). Washington, DC: American Psychological Association.

Nairne, J. S. (2002a). The myth of the encoding-retrieval match. *Memory, 10*, 389–395.

Nairne, J. S. (2002b). Remembering over the short-term: The case against the standard model. *Annual Review of Psychology, 53*, 53–81.

Nairne, J. S. (2003). Sensory and working memory. In A. F. Healy & R. W. Proctor (Eds.), *Comprehensive handbook of psychology: Vol. 4. Experimental psychology* (pp. 423–444). Hoboken, NJ: Wiley.

Roediger, H. L., III, & McDermott, K. B. (1995). Creating false memories: Remembering words not presented in lists. *Journal of Experimental Psychology: Learning, Memory, and Cognition, 21,* 803–814.

Tooby, J., & Cosmides, L. (1992). Psychological foundations of culture. In J. Barkow, L. Cosmides, & J. Tooby (Eds.), *The adapted mind* (pp. 19–136). New York: Oxford University Press.

Toth, J. P., & Hunt, R. R. (1999). Not one versus many, but zero versus any: Structure and function in the context of the multiple memory systems debate. In J. K. Foster & M. Jelicic (Eds.), *Memory: Systems, process, or function? Debates in psychology* (pp. 232–272). New York: Oxford University Press.

Tulving, E. (1983). *Elements of episodic memory.* New York: Oxford University Press.

Part IV

Information Processing

10

Attention, Automaticity, and Executive Control

Gordon D. Logan

Throughout my career, my work has been concerned with cognitive control. I have carried out two parallel lines of research, one on automatic processing, which might be viewed as the abdication of control, and one on executive processing, which is the exercise of control. From the beginning, my work has had a Colorado flavor. Inspired by Lyle Bourne's work on rules in categorization (Bourne, 1966; Haygood & Bourne, 1965), I have always thought of rules and algorithms as the means by which executive processing controls thought and action, although more recently I have come to think that this rule-based processing occurs most often early in practice (e.g., Logan, 1988). Inspired by Walter Kintsch's work on propositional representations (Kintsch, 1974, 1988; Kintsch & van Dijk, 1978), I have thought of propositions as the representations that control performance (e.g., Logan, 1995; Logan & Gordon, 2001; Logan & Zbrodoff, 1999). Inspired by Tom Landauer's work on memory (Landauer, 1975; Landauer & Dumais, 1995), I came to think of memory representations as exemplars or instances and to think of memory as a record of the trajectory of attention through a problem space (e.g., Logan, 1990; Logan & Etherton, 1994). These seminal ideas shaped my early career and set the stage for my recent work. In the pages that follow, I describe the stage that was set around 1990 and the play that has unfolded on it since.

The Instance Theory of Automaticity

Automaticity and Resource Theory

When I was in graduate school, resource theories of attention dominated the field (e.g., Kahneman, 1973; Posner & Boies, 1971). From this perspective, different tasks demanded different amounts of resources. It was natural to

This research was supported by Grants BCS 0133202 and 0218507 from the National Science Foundation.

think that some processes would demand no resources at all—these were automatic processes. The resource metaphor gave substance to the idea of *automaticity*, explaining why automatic processes had the properties they had (Logan, 1978, 1979). Automatic processes were fast because they were not limited by the availability of attentional capacity. Automatic processes were obligatory—beyond control—because control was exerted through the allocation of capacity, and processes that did not require capacity could not be controlled—turned on or off—by the allocation of capacity. Automatic processes were not subject to interference from concurrent tasks because dual-task interference occurred only between processes that competed for capacity. A process that demanded no capacity suffered no interference from concurrent capacity-demanding processes.

Around 1980, resource theories were attacked strenuously and in my view, they never recovered. Theorists such as Neisser (1976), Allport (1980), and Navon (1984) challenged the idea that performance was limited by a central source of processing capacity, suggesting structural limits, incompatibilities, and inexperience as alternative explanations of performance deficits. A multitude of data suggested that there were several sources of dual-task interference, which led resource theorists to propose multiple-resource theories as alternatives to the dominant, single-resource theory (Navon & Gopher, 1979; Wickens, 1980). According to multiple-resource theories, tasks that rely on the same resources interfere with each other, but tasks that rely on different resources do not. So two spatial tasks interfere with each other and two verbal tasks interfere with each other, but a spatial task does not interfere with a verbal task or vice versa. Critics argued that multiple-resource theories provided post hoc explanations of dual-task interference but not a priori predictions (e.g., Navon, 1984). These attacks on resource theory challenged the resource-theoretic conception of automaticity, weakening its ability to account for the properties of automaticity. Something else was needed to take its place.

Automaticity as Memory

Throughout the 1980s, the focus of research on automaticity shifted from documenting the properties of automatic processes to understanding how automaticity might be acquired (e.g., Anderson, 1982; Newell & Rosenbloom, 1981; Schneider, 1985). At the same time, a "new look" was emerging in memory research. Investigators were discovering (or rediscovering) implicit memory—the performance benefits of prior exposure—that differed in important ways from standard explicit memory measures of recall and recognition (e.g., Jacoby, 1983; Jacoby & Dallas, 1981; Tulving, Schacter, & Stark, 1982). It was a small step to see that automaticity might be another example of implicit memory: The benefits of a single exposure might be compounded over hundreds and thousands of exposures.

It was a bigger step to see how the idea of compounded implicit memory could account for the quantitative properties of *automatization*, namely, the power-function speedup in reaction time that seemed to describe all learning curves (Newell & Rosenbloom, 1981; but see Heathcote, Brown, & Mewhort,

2000). It turned out that Landauer had solved the problem in his classic 1975 article on an exemplar approach to semantic memory. He proved that a random parallel search of an unstructured memory would produce retrieval times that decreased as a power function of the number of examples. I was able to show that the same conclusion followed from a parallel race between instances in memory, using standard findings in the statistics of extreme values. I generalized the prediction from means to standard deviations and to entire distributions of reaction times (Logan, 1988, 1992; also see Cousineau, Goodman, & Shiffrin, 2002).

The idea of automaticity as memory provided an alternative to resource theory that explained why automatic processing had the properties it had (see Logan, 1988). Automatic processing was fast because fluent memory retrieval is fast, particularly when there are many instances racing to be retrieved. Automaticity is obligatory because retrieval is an obligatory consequence of attending to an object or event. Automatic processing is not subject to dual-task interference because fluent memory retrieval takes little time and provides a smaller "temporal target" to be subject to interference from concurrent tasks.

The instance theory of automaticity was based on three assumptions: *obligatory encoding,* which said that attention to an object or event was sufficient to cause it to be encoded into memory; *obligatory retrieval,* which said that attention to an object or event was sufficient to cause things associated with it to be retrieved from memory; and *instance representation,* which said that objects and events were encoded, stored, and retrieved separately—as exemplars or instances (Logan, 1988). Together, these assumptions implied a learning mechanism. Obligatory encoding causes a task-relevant database to build up in memory with repeated experience. Obligatory retrieval causes that database to become available when familiar stimuli are encountered again. And instance representation would allow for the race between exemplars that predicts the power function speedup. Following Bourne (1966; Haygood & Bourne, 1965), I assumed that initial performance was governed by rules or algorithms, and automatization reflected a transition from rules and algorithms to memory retrieval as the task-relevant database built up in memory (also see Johansen & Palmeri, 2002).

The assumptions of obligatory encoding and obligatory retrieval placed a heavy burden on the concept of attention, which was unspecified in the theory. Attention caused encoding and attention caused retrieval, but the theory said nothing about what attention was. A large part of my work since 1990 has been devoted to cashing in this intellectual debt, testing the assumptions that attention causes encoding and retrieval, and providing a theory of attention that can do the work implied in these assumptions.

The Attention Hypothesis

The tests of the obligatory-encoding and obligatory-retrieval assumptions can be described as tests of an attention hypothesis, which asks whether attention is necessary or sufficient (or both) for encoding and retrieval. The logic of the tests is to manipulate the focus of attention and determine whether that affects what is acquired during automatization (encoding) and what is expressed during automatic performance (retrieval). The manipulations of attention were organized around a distinction between different kinds of selection that were proposed by Treisman (1969): *input selection*, which reflects a choice of stimuli to analyze, and *analyzer selection*, which reflects a choice of analysis to perform on the stimuli.

Input Selection

Logan and Etherton (1994) presented subjects with pairs of words and had them search through each pair for a member of a target category (e.g., metals). Targets and distractors were paired consistently throughout training and the pairing changed in a transfer block (e.g., *STEEL* was paired with *CANADA* throughout training and paired with *FRANCE* in transfer). If subjects divided attention between the words, they were sensitive to the pairing, showing large costs in reaction time when the pairing changed at transfer. If subjects focused attention on one of the words (e.g., by responding to a cue that indicated the target's location), they were insensitive to the pairing, showing no cost when pairing changed at transfer. These results suggest that input selection determines what gets encoded into memory. Subjects who attended both words learned how the words were paired; subjects who attended only one word did not learn the pairing.

Logan and Etherton's (1994) results could reflect the effects of attention at training or at transfer. Boronat and Logan (1997) manipulated the focus of attention in both phases. Subjects showed cost of changing pairing only if they attended both words in training and in transfer. Subjects who attended both words in training but only one word at transfer may have learned the relations between the words, but focusing attention on one word at transfer blocked retrieval of associations with the other word. Subjects who attended one word in training never learned the associations. When given the opportunity to express that learning by dividing their attention between the words at transfer, they showed no sensitivity to changes in pairing.

Logan, Taylor, and Etherton (1996) focused subjects' attention on target words by coloring them red or green (distractor words were white). Specific target words were consistently colored throughout training and the color changed at transfer (e.g., *BRASS* was green and *STEEL* was red throughout training). Subjects showed no sensitivity to changes in pairing. In subsequent experiments, subjects had to report the color of the targets, and in these conditions, they were sensitive to changes in pairing. Logan, Taylor, and Etherton (1999) performed similar experiments manipulating the consistency with which words appeared in locations (e.g., *STEEL* appeared in the top position throughout training, and *BRASS* appeared in the bottom position). Again, changing the location at transfer had little effect on performance unless subjects were instructed to explicitly report the target's location. These experiments suggest that the properties that direct attention to an object (*stimulus set* properties; Broadbent, 1971) are not encoded into memory, but the properties that are expressed in the response subjects make (*response set* properties; Broadbent, 1971) are encoded.

Analyzer Selection

Logan (1990) presented subjects with words, pronounceable nonwords, and unpronounceable nonwords and varied the judgments they made about them. The *lexical decision* group decided whether or not the stimuli were words. The *pronunciation decision* group decided whether or not the stimuli were pronounceable. The *varied decision* group alternated between these decisions in successive blocks. The same stimuli were presented for 16 consecutive blocks. Subjects in the lexical decision group and subjects in the pronunciation decision group showed substantially more benefit from repetition over blocks than subjects in the varied decision group (also see Logan, 1988, Experiment 5). This suggests that subjects encode the interpretation given to a stimulus, which reflects the manner in which they attend to the stimulus (also see Franks, Bilbrey, Lien, & McNamara, 2000; Gorfein & Bubka, 1997).

Conditional Automaticity

The tests of the attention hypothesis suggest that attention determines what is encoded into memory during the acquisition of automaticity and what is retrieved from memory during the expression of automaticity. The results generally support the hypothesis and, consequently, support the obligatory-encoding and obligatory-retrieval assumptions of the instance theory. The assumptions and the results are important beyond the instance theory because they suggest that automaticity is conditional on attention (also see Bargh, 1992; DeJong, Liang, & Lauber, 1994). A lot of evidence suggests that Stroop and priming effects are strongly influenced by the spatial and conceptual direction of attention (e.g., Besner & Stolz, 1999; Kahneman & Henik, 1981; Neely, 1977; Smith, 1979). Researchers who assume that automaticity must be independent of attention interpret these results as evidence against the concept of automaticity (e.g., Besner, Stolz, & Boutilier, 1997). The instance theory in particular and memory-based theories of automaticity in general provide a coherent interpretation of these results, suggesting that attention determines what is retrieved from memory, and consequently, what automatisms are expressed in performance.

In normal vision, automaticity must be conditional on attention. Attention determines eye movements—we look at the things we attend to—and eye direction determines what we can see. A visual stimulus behind our heads cannot access memory no matter how familiar it is. A visual stimulus in a region of poor acuity will have poorer access than a visual stimulus in the fovea. The concept of conditional automaticity extends these ideas to the focus of spatial attention and the focus of conceptual attention, which may be covert and separate from eye direction.

Propositions and Attention

The experiments that tested the attention hypothesis addressed the nature of the representations that underlie automaticity. Following Kintsch's work

(Kintsch, 1974; Kintsch & van Dijk, 1978), I came to think of the representations as propositions. Propositions captured the associative nature of the memory traces underlying automaticity, connecting the stimulus with the goal the subject was trying to attain, the interpretation given to the stimulus in light of the goal, and the response given to the stimulus to communicate the interpretation to the experimenter. I came to think of the responses subjects make in experiments as speech acts that express their beliefs about the displays they experience (see Logan, 1990, 1995; Logan & Etherton, 1994; Logan & Zbrodoff, 1999). Pressing the *yes* key expresses the proposition *contains (display, target)*, which the subject believes to be true about a particular display and a particular target. Kintsch (1974) and others tell us that a proposition is a predicate with a truth value. A predicate is a relation between arguments, so the relation *contains* expresses a possible relation between the argument *display* and the argument *target*. Subjects begin a trial with that predicate in mind and assign a truth value to it by attending to the display. From this perspective, the function of attention is to assign truth values to predicates to create propositions, that is, to create beliefs about the world around us (Logan & Zbrodoff, 1999).

The idea that attention creates propositions provides a means for representations to control performance (Logan & Gordon, 2001; Logan & Zbrodoff, 1999). The predicate tells the subject what to look for: which arguments and which relation between them. It tells the subject when to stop processing: when enough information has been gathered to assign a truth value. The idea that attention creates propositions also provides a basis for linking research on perceptual attention to research on comprehension and memory for conceptual structures, such as those expressed in text.

Instance Theory of Attention and Memory

In the middle of the 1990s, my abiding interest in cognitive control led me to consider how instance theory might interface with theories of attention. To many people, automatic processing is the opposite of controlled processing (e.g., Schneider, 1985), so a theory of automaticity is not a theory of control. In my view, automatic processing is controlled—a person directs attention at task-relevant stimuli and goes with whatever comes out of memory—but it is only one kind of control. I wanted a theory with more options. I was attracted to Bundesen's (1990) *theory of visual attention* (TVA) because it was at the same level of abstraction as the instance theory and because it also involved a race. Whereas instance theory assumes that memory traces race to be retrieved, TVA assumes that perceptual objects race to be selected. I began applying TVA to problems of perceptual selection, interfacing it with a powerful theory of grouping by proximity to account for distance and grouping effects in a variety of attention tasks (Logan, 1996; Logan & Bundesen, 1996).

At the same time, Nosofsky and Palmeri (1997; Palmeri, 1997) began integrating Nosofsky's (1984, 1988) *generalized context model* (GCM) with my instance theory. They noted that GCM did not predict reaction times and the instance theory did not account for similarity effects or for response conflict.

They combined the two theories to form the *exemplar-based random walk model* (EBRW), which provides an excellent account of reaction times in categorization and automatization.

Palmeri (1997) documented the difficulty the instance theory had with response conflict. The race model inherent in the theory chooses the first instance to be retrieved, and in conflict situations, that is likely to lead to a fast response that is incorrect. To overcome the conflict, EBRW assumes that the runners that finish the race accumulate in response counters, and a response is not selected until one of the counters has K more runners in it than any other counter. In EBRW, performance is no longer dominated by the first trace to be retrieved, but rather depends on the strength of the evidence in favor of one response or the other. Conflict prolongs reaction time without unduly increasing error rate.

EBRW explains learning like instance theory did, in terms of the accumulation of instances with practice. It explains similarity in terms of distance in multidimensional space. That conception allows powerful tests of the theory. Distances estimated with one task (e.g., similarity judgments or confusions in perceptual identification tasks) can be used to predict performance in other tasks (e.g., categorization, recognition memory, or typicality judgments; Nosofsky, 1984, 1988).

In 2002, I proposed an *instance theory of attention and memory* (ITAM) that combined my extensions of TVA with Nosofsky and Palmeri's (1997) extensions of the instance theory and GCM (see Logan, 2002). My extensions of TVA solved the problem of selecting one object from a display of many objects but did not explain similarity. Nosofsky and Palmeri's (1997) EBRW explained similarity but did not account for selecting one of several objects. ITAM does both. It allows three kinds of attention: attention to objects, attention to categories, and attention to dimensions. Thus, it provides several mechanisms by which performance can be controlled. Moreover, ITAM relates EBRW and TVA formally to several theories of attention and categorization, tracing their ancestry back to seminal theories of similarity and choice by Shepard (1957) and Luce (1963). Each of the ancestors can be construed as a special case of the new theory, so ITAM inherits the successes of its ancestors, which are numerous and impressive.

Executive Control of Thought and Action

A theory of attention provides mechanisms by which control can be exercised but it is not yet a theory of control. In describing TVA, Bundesen (1990) said "no attempt is made to discard the notion that attentional selection is controlled by an intelligent agent, but a serious attempt is made to relieve the burden on the agent by placing a powerful mechanism at its disposal" (p. 523). In 2001, Rob Gordon and I proposed a theory by which TVA can be controlled, called *executive control of TVA* (ECTVA; Logan & Gordon, 2001). The same theory can explain how ITAM is controlled.

A key idea in many approaches to executive control is the notion that an executive process programs a subordinate (Logan, 1985; Norman & Shallice,

1986). This idea is empty without a theory of the subordinate process that explains how it can be programmed. ECTVA uses TVA and EBRW as subordinate processes and says how they are programmed (also see Gilbert & Shallice, 2002; Kieras, Meyer, Ballas, & Lauber, 2000; Sohn & Anderson, 2001). Following Kintsch (1974; Kintsch & van Dijk, 1978), ECTVA programs TVA and EBRW by deriving values of their homunculus-controlled parameters from a propositional representation of the task instructions (also see Logan & Zbrodoff, 1999).

There are six different kinds of parameters in the combination of TVA and EBRW. Two kinds of parameters are determined by the stimulus situation, the subject's history with the categories relevant to the task, and constraints on the processing system. One is determined partly by the stimulus situation and partly by the subject's homunculus, and three are determined entirely by the homunculus. ECTVA is a theory of how the latter four parameter types are set by the homunculus and transmitted to TVA and EBRW. In ECTVA, a task set is precisely a set of TVA and EBRW parameters that are sufficient to program TVA and EBRW to perform the task at hand. Task switching involves deriving a set of parameters from a propositional representation of the instructions or retrieving them from long-term memory and then transmitting them from working memory to TVA and EBRW. Simply placing the parameters in working memory is not sufficient to enable performance, just as having a program on a hard drive is not sufficient to execute it. The parameters must also be put into place in TVA and EBRW to enable performance, just as a program must be loaded into core memory to execute it.

Logan and Gordon (2001) applied ECTVA to a dual-task situation known as the *psychological refractory period* (PRP) procedure. We accounted for dual-task interference and crosstalk between the tasks, from the first task to the second and from the second task to the first. We noted that typical PRP procedures involve task switching, in that the second task is usually different from the first. We varied the similarity between the two tasks and found that reaction times for both tasks were substantially longer when the tasks were dissimilar than when they were similar. ECTVA accounted for this difference in terms of the time taken to transmit parameters from working memory to TVA and EBRW. More parameters had to be transmitted when the tasks were dissimilar, so reaction times were longer.

ECTVA provides a framework for understanding other acts of executive control in other task switching procedures. Logan and Bundesen (2003) applied it to the explicit task cuing procedure, in which subjects are given a cue that tells them which task to perform and then a target stimulus on which to perform the instructed task. We developed formal models of the time-course function that is generated in this procedure when the interval between the cue and the target is varied. Logan and Bundesen's modeling analyses suggested that subjects may not switch tasks in the explicit task cuing procedure. The cue and the target jointly provide enough information to uniquely specify the correct response, so subjects can adopt a compound-stimulus strategy and respond to all cues and targets with a single task set. The strategy involves encoding the cue, encoding the target, and retrieving the response associated with the combination of the two. Cue encoding is faster when the cue repeats than when it alternates, so repetitions are faster than alternations even though the same processes are engaged. Thus, the difference between repetitions and alternations may not reflect an endogenous act of control, as researchers often assume (e.g., Meiran, 1996; Sohn & Anderson, 2001).

ECTVA begins to cash in the idea that an executive process programs a subordinate but the theory has not yet cashed it in completely. The applications to the PRP procedure and the explicit task cuing procedure begin after TVA and EBRW parameters have been derived or retrieved into working memory. The predictions focus primarily on the time required to transmit those parameters from working memory to TVA and EBRW. An important question for future research is how those parameters can be derived from propositional representations of task instructions. When that question is answered, we will have a clearer idea of how propositions control thought and action. Work by Kintsch, Landauer, and Bourne will be essential in framing the answer.

Applications

My research has focused on basic issues rather than applications, but problems of attention and control are pervasive in applied settings. Many people think, "Nothing is as practical as a good theory." In that vein, I hope my work proves useful in applied settings beyond the ivory tower I call home.

References

Allport, D. A. (1980). Attention and performance. In G. Claxton (Ed.), *Cognitive psychology* (pp. 112–153). London: Routledge & Kegan Paul.

Anderson, J. R. (1982). Acquisition of cognitive skill. *Psychological Review, 89*, 369–406.

Bargh, J. A. (1992). The ecology of automaticity: Toward establishing the conditions needed to produce automatic processing effects. *American Journal of Psychology, 105*, 181–193.

Besner, D., & Stolz, J. A. (1999). What kind of attention modulates the Stroop effect? *Psychonomic Bulletin & Review, 6*, 99–104.

Besner, D., Stolz, J. A., & Boutilier, C. (1997). The Stroop effect and the myth of automaticity. *Psychonomic Bulletin & Review, 4*, 221–225.

Boronat, C. B., & Logan, G. D. (1997). The role of attention in automatization: Does attention operate at encoding, or retrieval, or both? *Memory & Cognition, 25*, 36–46.

Bourne, L. E., Jr. (1966). *Human conceptual behavior.* Boston: Allyn & Bacon.

Broadbent, D. E. (1971). *Decision and stress.* London: Academic Press.

Bundesen, C. (1990). A theory of visual attention. *Psychological Review, 97*, 523–547.

Cousineau, D., Goodman, V., & Shiffrin, R. M. (2002). Extending statistics of extreme values to distributions varying in position and scale and the implications for race models. *Journal of Mathematical Psychology, 46*, 431–454.

DeJong, R., Liang, C.-C., & Lauber, E. J. (1994). Conditional and unconditional automaticity: A dual-process model of stimulus–response correspondence. *Journal of Experimental Psychology: Human Perception and Performance, 20*, 731–750.

Franks, J. J., Bilbrey, C. W., Lien, K. G., & McNamara, T. P. (2000). Transfer-appropriate processing (TAP) and repetition priming. *Memory & Cognition, 28*, 1140–1151.

Gilbert, S., & Shallice, T. (2002). Task switching: A PDP model. *Cognitive Psychology, 44*, 193–251.

Gorfein, D. S., & Bubka, A. (1997). A transfer analysis of the repetition effect in the lexical decision and ambiguity detection tasks. *Psychonomic Bulletin & Review, 4*, 232–236.

Haygood, R. C., & Bourne, L. E., Jr. (1965). Attribute- and rule-learning aspects of conceptual behavior. *Psychological Review, 72,* 175–195.

Heathcote, A., Brown, S., & Mewhort, D. J. K. (2000). The power law repealed: The case for an exponential law of practice. *Psychonomic Bulletin & Review, 7,* 185–207.

Jacoby, L. L. (1983). Remembering the data: Analyzing interactive processes in reading. *Journal of Verbal Learning and Verbal Behavior, 22,* 485–508.

Jacoby, L. L., & Dallas, M. (1981). On the relationship between autobiographical memory and perceptual learning. *Journal of Experimental Psychology: General, 110,* 306–340.

Johansen, M. K., & Palmeri, T. J. (2002). Are there representational shifts during category learning? *Cognitive Psychology, 45,* 482–553.

Kahneman, D. (1973). *Attention and effort.* Englewood Cliffs, NJ: Prentice Hall.

Kahneman, D., & Henik, A. (1981). Perceptual organization and attention. In M. Kubovy & J. R. Pomerantz (Eds.), *Perceptual organization* (pp. 307–332). Hillsdale, NJ: Erlbaum.

Kieras, D. E., Meyer, D. E., Ballas, J. A., & Lauber, E. J. (2000). Modern computational perspectives on executive mental processes and cognitive control: Where to from here? In S. Monsell & J. Driver (Eds.), *Attention and performance XVIII* (pp. 681–712). Cambridge, MA: MIT Press.

Kintsch, W. (1974). *The representation of meaning in memory.* Hillsdale, NJ: Erlbaum.

Kintsch, W. (1988). The role of knowledge in discourse comprehension: A construction-integration model. *Psychological Review, 95,* 163–182.

Kintsch, W., & van Dijk, T. A. (1978). Toward a model of text comprehension and production. *Psychological Review, 85,* 363–394.

Landauer, T. K. (1975). Memory without organization: Properties of a model with random storage and undirected recall. *Cognitive Psychology, 7,* 495–531.

Landauer, T. K., & Dumais. S. T. (1995). A solution to Plato's problem: The latent semantic analysis theory of acquisition, induction, and representation of knowledge. *Psychological Review, 104,* 211–240.

Logan, G. D. (1978). Attention in character-classification tasks: Evidence for the automaticity of component stages. *Journal of Experimental Psychology: General, 107,* 32–63.

Logan, G. D. (1979). On the use of a concurrent memory load to measure attention and automaticity. *Journal of Experimental Psychology: Human Perception and Performance, 5,* 189–207.

Logan, G. D. (1985). Executive control of thought and action. *Acta Psychologica, 60,* 193–210.

Logan, G. D. (1988). Toward an instance theory of automatization. *Psychological Review, 95,* 492–527.

Logan, G. D. (1990). Repetition priming and automaticity: Common underlying mechanisms? *Cognitive Psychology, 22,* 1–35.

Logan, G. D. (1992). Shapes of reaction time distributions and shapes of learning curves: A test of the instance theory of automaticity. *Journal of Experimental Psychology: Learning, Memory, and Cognition, 18,* 883–914.

Logan, G. D. (1995). Linguistic and conceptual control of visual spatial attention. *Cognitive Psychology, 28,* 103–174.

Logan, G. D. (1996). The CODE theory of visual attention: An integration of space-based and object-based attention. *Psychological Review, 103,* 603–649.

Logan, G. D. (2002). An instance theory of attention and memory. *Psychological Review, 109,* 376–400.

Logan, G. D., & Bundesen, C. (1996). Spatial effects in the partial report paradigm: A challenge for theories of visual-spatial attention. In D. L. Medin (Ed.), *The psychology of learning and motivation* (Vol. 35, pp. 243–282). San Diego, CA: Academic Press.

Logan, G. D., & Bundesen, C. (2003). Clever homunculus: Is there an endogenous act of control in the explicit task-cuing procedure? *Journal of Experimental Psychology: Human Perception and Performance, 29,* 575–599.

Logan, G. D., & Etherton, J. L. (1994). What is learned in automatization? The role of attention in constructing an instance. *Journal of Experimental Psychology: Learning, Memory, and Cognition, 20,* 1022–1050.

Logan, G. D., & Gordon, R. D. (2001). Executive control of visual attention in dual-task situations. *Psychological Review, 108,* 393–434.

Logan, G. D., Taylor, S. E., & Etherton, J. L. (1996). Attention in the acquisition and expression of automaticity. *Journal of Experimental Psychology: Learning, Memory, and Cognition, 22,* 620–638.

Logan, G. D., Taylor, S. E., & Etherton, J. L. (1999). Attention and automaticity: Toward a theoretical integration. *Psychological Research, 62,* 165–181.

Logan, G. D., & Zbrodoff, N. J. (1999). Selection for cognition: Cognitive constraints on visual spatial attention. *Visual Cognition, 6,* 55–81.

Luce, R. D. (1963). Detection and recognition. In R. D. Luce, R. R. Bush, & E. Galanter (Eds.), *Handbook of mathematical psychology* (pp. 103–189). New York: Wiley.

Meiran, N. (1996). Reconfiguration of processing mode prior to task performance. *Journal of Experimental Psychology: Learning, Memory, and Cognition, 22,* 1423–1442.

Navon, D. (1984). Resources: A theoretical soup stone? *Psychological Review, 91,* 216–234.

Navon, D., & Gopher, D. (1979). On the economy of the human processing system. *Psychological Review, 86,* 214–255.

Neely, J. H. (1977). Semantic priming and retrieval from lexical memory: Roles of inhibitionless spreading activation and limited-capacity attention. *Journal of Experimental Psychology: General, 106,* 226–254.

Neisser, U. (1976). *Cognition and reality.* San Francisco: Freeman.

Newell, A., & Rosenbloom, P. S. (1981). Mechanisms of skill acquisition and the law of practice. In J. R. Anderson (Ed.), *Cognitive skills and their acquisition* (pp. 1–55). Hillsdale, NJ: Erlbaum.

Norman, D. A., & Shallice, T. (1986). Attention to action: Willed and automatic control of behaviour. In R. J. Davidson, G. E. Schwartz, & D. Shapiro (Eds.), *Consciousness and self-regulation* (Vol. 4, pp. 1–18). New York: Plenum Press.

Nosofsky, R. M. (1984). Choice, similarity, and the context theory of classification. *Journal of Experimental Psychology: Learning, Memory, and Cognition, 10,* 104–114.

Nosofsky, R. M. (1988). Exemplar-based accounts of relations between classification, recognition, and typicality. *Journal of Experimental Psychology: Learning, Memory, and Cognition, 14,* 700–708.

Nosofsky, R. M., & Palmeri, T. J. (1997). An exemplar-based random walk model of speeded classification. *Psychological Review, 104,* 266–300.

Palmeri, T. J. (1997). Exemplar similarity and the development of automaticity. *Journal of Experimental Psychology: Learning, Memory, and Cognition, 23,* 324–354.

Posner, M. I., & Boies, S. J. (1971). Components of attention. *Psychological Review, 78,* 391–408.

Schneider, W. (1985). Toward a model of attention and the development of automatic processing. In M. I. Posner & O. S. Marin (Eds.), *Attention and performance XI* (pp. 475–492). Hillsdale, NJ: Erlbaum.

Shepard, R. N. (1957). Stimulus and response generalization: A stochastic model relating generalization to distance in psychological space. *Psychometrika, 22,* 325–345.

Smith, M. C. (1979). Contextual facilitation in a letter search task depends on how the prime is processed. *Journal of Experimental Psychology: Human Perception and Performance, 5,* 239–251.

Sohn, M.-H., & Anderson, J. R. (2001). Task preparation and task repetition: Two-component model of task switching. *Journal of Experimental Psychology: General, 130,* 764–778.

Treisman, A. (1969). Strategies and models of selective attention. *Psychological Review, 76,* 282–299.

Tulving, E., Schacter, D. L., & Stark, H. A. (1982). Priming effects in word-fragment completion are independent of recognition memory. *Journal of Experimental Psychology: Learning, Memory, and Cognition, 8,* 336–342.

Wickens, C. D. (1980). The structure of attentional resources. In R. S. Nickerson (Ed.), *Attention and performance VIII* (pp. 239–257). Hillsdale, NJ: Erlbaum.

11

Roles of Task-Defined Associations and Reference Frames in Spatial Stimulus–Response Compatibility

Robert W. Proctor and Kim-Phuong L. Vu

More than 50 years have passed since the beginnings of contemporary cognitive psychology and engineering psychology, or human factors. One phenomenon at the forefront of these developments was stimulus–response compatibility (SRC), demonstrated and named in compelling studies conducted by Paul Fitts and colleagues in the early 1950s (Fitts & Deininger, 1954; Fitts & Seeger, 1953). These studies showed that performance was best when (a) the stimulus and response sets were configured similarly, (b) each member of the stimulus set was mapped to its corresponding response, and, if correspondence was not maintained, (c) the mapping between stimuli and responses could be described by a simple rule (e.g., respond at the mirror opposite location). The studies by Fitts and colleagues are regarded as classics in the areas of basic human performance and applied human factors. They have led to many investigations of SRC effects in a variety of tasks and to an improved understanding of the processes responsible for them.

Although research on SRC never disappeared entirely, there has been a resurgence of interest in SRC effects and related phenomena since about 1990. In that year, two important publications appeared: a theoretical article by Kornblum, Hasbroucq, and Osman (1990) that provided the first detailed taxonomy of SRC effects and a model to explain them, and an edited book by Proctor and Reeve (1990) with chapters summarizing research on SRC being conducted in a variety of basic and applied areas. Over the past 13 years, SRC effects have been the subject of an intense research effort devoted to understanding the relation between perception and action.

Research on SRC has stressed differences in performance with various stimulus–response (S-R) mappings for stimulus and response sets that are similar. Kornblum et al. (1990) used the term *dimensional overlap* to refer to similarity and identified two types: conceptual (e.g., stimuli and responses refer to left–right locations) and perceptual (or mode match, e.g., the left–right stimuli and responses are visuospatial–manual or verbal–vocal). Their dimensional overlap model specified two response-selection routes, the durations of which are affected by the S-R mapping for sets with dimensional overlap: In the automatic route, a stimulus automatically activates its corresponding response, regardless of the mapping; in the intentional identification (or translation) route, a response is identified faster when a rule can be applied (e.g., respond at the corresponding location) than when one cannot. SRC effects arise from conflict between the automatically activated response and the assigned response when they are not the same, and from differences in the time to generate the assigned response through the intentional route. Later models differ from Kornblum et al.'s model in some details, but most distinguish two response-selection routes and emphasize similarity as important (Hommel & Prinz, 1997). The automatic, or direct, route is often described as producing response activation through long-term associations that are innate or acquired through years of experience, and thus are not affected by the current task requirements, whereas the intentional route is presumed to produce response activation through the temporary associations or rules defined by the task instructions (Hommel & Prinz, 1997).

However, recent research from our laboratory and others has indicated that the distinction between intentional and automatic routes is not as sharp as suggested by the standard depiction. Task-defined associations can override the effects of long-term associations, both when they are currently in effect and when they were in effect in the immediate past. Also, because responses can be coded with respect to different frames of reference, the effects of automatic activation and intentional translation depend on task instructions and goals. We elaborate on these points in the next two sections and then discuss their implications for cognitive theory and design applications.

Influence of Task-Defined Associations

Most studies of SRC proper examine situations in which a single S-R mapping is in effect for a block of trials. Mapping is varied within or between subjects, and performance with the different mappings is compared. For two-choice spatial tasks, left–right stimulus locations are mapped compatibly or incompatibly to left–right responses, with reaction time (RT) being 50–100 ms faster with the compatible mapping than with the incompatible mapping. In a variant called the *Simon effect*, a nonspatial stimulus dimension (e.g., the color red or green) is mapped to left and right responses, and the stimuli can occur in a left or right location. Although stimulus location is irrelevant, RT is still shorter when the stimulus location corresponds with that of the response than when it does not. For both SRC proper and the Simon effect, activation of the corresponding response through the long-term associations is presumed to be a major factor.

Mixed Mappings and Tasks

In a study that has received little notice, Shaffer (1965) found that the two-choice SRC effect was eliminated, and responses slowed overall, when the S-R mapping varied randomly from trial to trial, being indicated by a simultaneously presented mapping signal (a horizontal or vertical line). We replicated this finding for left–right locations using stimulus color (white or red) as the mapping signal (Vu & Proctor, 2004) and found similar results when the stimuli were left–right pointing arrows. With the words *left* and *right* mapped to vocal "left"–"right" responses, mixing the mappings also reduced the SRC effect, although the effect was not eliminated entirely because the baseline SRC effect was larger. Moreover, we found that the SRC effect is eliminated when only one location mapping is in effect for the trial block, but stimulus location (signaled by a white color) is relevant on half of the trials and stimulus color (red or green) on the other half (Proctor & Vu, 2002; Proctor, Vu, & Marble, 2003). Thus, contrary to the implication of many models of SRC, the spatially corresponding response often receives little benefit when mappings or trial types are mixed. These findings are consistent with the possibility that the "automatic" route is inhibited under mixed conditions.

Elimination or reduction of the SRC effect with mixed mappings or tasks is not found in some cases. For mixed mappings, the SRC effect is not reduced for S-R sets that have only conceptual similarity: With physical locations and arrows mapped to "left"–"right" utterances, the SRC effect is not reduced significantly, and with location words mapped to keypresses, it increases substantially (Proctor & Vu, 2002). For mixed tasks, the SRC effect is eliminated only when the S-R sets are visuospatial–manual, and the effect increases substantially for all three stimulus modes (physical locations, arrows, and location words) when the responses are vocal and for location words when the responses are keypresses. If it is assumed that the reduction with mixing reflects suppression of the automatic route, then conceptual similarity alone must not be sufficient to produce automatic activation.

Another interesting finding obtained with the mixed-tasks procedure is that the S-R mapping in effect for the location-relevant trials influences the Simon effect for trials on which stimulus color is relevant (Marble & Proctor, 2000; Proctor, Marble, & Vu, 2000). For all stimulus and response modes, the Simon effect is larger when the location mapping is compatible than when it is incompatible. For physical location and arrow stimuli, the Simon effect reverses to favor noncorresponding responses when the mapping is incompatible. For physical locations mapped to keypresses, the reversed effect is as large as the positive effect obtained when the mapping is compatible, implying that only the task-defined location associations are determining the Simon effect. The tendency for the Simon effect to reverse when the location-relevant mapping is incompatible is not as large for other combinations of stimulus and response modes, leaving open the possibility that the long-term associations still affect performance in those cases.

Influence of Prior Location Mappings

It is perhaps not too surprising that a location mapping in effect during a block of trials affects performance on trials for which stimulus location is irrelevant. However, the mapping has been shown to continue to influence performance when it is no longer in effect. Proctor and Lu (1999) found that, after practice for over 900 trials with an incompatible location mapping over 3 days, the Simon effect reversed in a transfer session. This reversal was still evident in the final 250 trials of the 600-trial transfer session. Tagliabue, Zorzi, Umiltà, and Bassignani (2000) showed that the Simon effect is eliminated after only 72 trials of practice with an incompatible mapping 5 minutes or a day prior to the Simon transfer session. Furthermore, the Simon effect reversed after a 1-week delay, which they attributed to consolidation of the task-defined associations. The impact of the prior incompatible mapping indicates that the associations between S-R locations defined for the SRC task are not disabled when they are no longer relevant and continue to exert an influence even a week later.

Tagliabue, Zorzi, and Umiltà (2002) showed that practice with an incompatible mapping of auditory stimuli to keypresses also eliminated the visual Simon effect in a transfer session, and they concluded that the remapping of the S-R associations that occurs during practice is not modality specific. However, Vu, Proctor, and Urcuioli (2003) showed that there is a modality-specific component to the transfer effect in addition to a general component. At 5-minute and 1-week delays, the transfer effect was largest when both the practice and the transfer modalities were visual. However, unlike Tagliabue et al. (2000), the effect did not get stronger after the 1-week delay, showing no sign of consolidation. Furthermore, when transfer was to an auditory Simon task, for which a tone occurred in the left or right ear and tone-pitch was relevant, the prior practice with either auditory or visual stimuli reduced the Simon effect after 5 minutes but not after a week.

Vu (2003) examined factors underlying the transfer of the prior incompatible mapping to the Simon task when the practice and transfer modalities were visual. Although practicing 72 trials with an incompatible mapping eliminated the Simon effect in the transfer session when the stimulus and response sets varied on the horizontal dimension, it did not have an effect when the stimulus and response sets varied on the vertical dimension. Because the vertical Simon effect tended to be larger than the horizontal effect at baseline, the long-term associations may be stronger for the vertical dimension and thus more difficult to override. Consistent with this hypothesis, the vertical Simon effect was eliminated when the practice was increased from 72 to 600 trials. Furthermore, when the stimulus and response sets varied along the vertical dimension in the practice session and along the horizontal dimension in the transfer session, or vice versa, the Simon effect was unaffected after 72 practice trials but was eliminated after 600 trials. This finding suggests that a small amount of practice primarily strengthens specific S-R associations, but larger amounts promote learning of a general response-selection rule (e.g., "respond opposite") or remapping of S-R locations.

Vu (2003) showed that awareness of the incompatible S-R relation is necessary to produce the transfer effect with 72 trials of practice. Subjects practiced a Simon task for which all trials were noncorresponding (which is equivalent to a spatially incompatible mapping) and transferred to a Simon task in which half of the trials were corresponding and half noncorresponding. Only half of the subjects reported realizing that the correct response in the practice session was always opposite the stimulus location. The subjects who reported awareness of this relation showed shorter RTs in the practice session than those who did not, confirming that their responses were based on location and not color. More important, the Simon effect was only eliminated for those who reported awareness of the incompatible S-R relation. Those who did not notice this relation showed a standard Simon effect. Thus, the influence of the prior spatial relation is not a direct consequence of performing the incompatible responses in the practice session but of subjects explicitly representing the practice task in terms of the incompatible spatial mapping.

Frames of Reference

SRC effects are influenced not only by the S-R mappings that are currently in effect, or were previously, but also by other aspects of the task environment. Specifically, location can be coded with respect to different frames of reference, and the reference frames on which coding is based determine the direction and magnitudes of effects (Hommel & Prinz, 1997). We illustrate this point for two-dimensional S-R sets, orthogonal S-R dimensions, and wheel-rotation responses.

Two-Dimensional Stimulus–Response Sets

When the two stimulus locations are the endpoints of one diagonal of an imaginary square, and the response locations the endpoints of one diagonal or the other of another imaginary square, the stimulus and response locations can be coded in terms of both the horizontal and the vertical dimensions. SRC effects are obtained for both dimensions, indicating that multiple spatial codes are formed at stimulus presentation. However, the SRC effect is typically larger for the horizontal dimension than for the vertical dimension (even though the effects are of similar magnitude for unidimensional S-R sets), a phenomenon known as *right–left prevalence* (Nicoletti & Umiltà, 1984; Vu, Proctor, & Pick, 2000). The relative advantage for the horizontal or vertical dimension is affected by instructions: When instructed in terms of the vertical dimension, the advantage for horizontal compatibility is reduced or eliminated compared with when instructed in terms of the horizontal dimension, but right–left prevalence is evident when collapsed across instructions (Vu & Proctor, 2001).

Hommel (1996) demonstrated that responding with right–left effectors is crucial for producing right–left prevalence: When subjects responded with unimanual joystick movements along a diagonal, no right–left prevalence was evident. Vu and Proctor (2001) replicated this finding but also found no prevalence effect when the responses were made with two fingers on one hand, although the two fingers can be coded as left–right effectors and yield unidimensional SRC effects. This finding suggests that right–left prevalence is not due to use of right–left effectors, per se, but to the hands providing a salient frame of reference for horizontal coding.

Consistent with this hypothesis, Vu and Proctor (2001) showed that the prevalence effect is a consequence of the horizontal dimension being more salient than the vertical dimension in most task environments. When responding with a hand and foot, right–left prevalence was obtained when the effectors were contralateral and top–bottom prevalence when they were ipsilateral. Even though the hand and foot are top–bottom effectors, the left–right distinction for the contralateral condition provided a reference frame for horizontal coding of sufficient salience to produce right–left prevalence. Top–bottom prevalence only occurred when the horizontal reference frame was removed. Vu and Proctor also showed that top–bottom prevalence can be obtained when responses are made with the left and right hands, if the vertical dimension is made more salient than the horizontal one by having subjects place one hand on top of the other. Manipulations of display salience produced similar effects, with the horizontal and vertical SRC effects being largest when the same dimension was salient for both the display and the response arrangements (Vu & Proctor, 2002). When the S-R environment did not provide a salient frame of reference for horizontal or vertical coding, an advantage was obtained for the instructed dimension. However, when the display and response salience of both favored the same dimension, a prevalence effect occurred for that dimension regardless of the task instructions.

Proctor, Vu, and Nicoletti (2003) examined whether the prevalence effect is based on automatic or intentional coding of the salient dimension by using a two-dimensional Simon task. Because the relevant stimulus dimension was color and not location, stimulus location should undergo automatic but not intentional processing. There was no overall prevalence effect for the Simon task, indicating that the prevalence effect is due to intentional coding of the salient dimension. However, an advantage for one dimension over the other was created when the salient features of the stimulus and response sets corresponded to that dimension, although the effects were smaller than those obtained when location was relevant. This outcome implies that salience manipulations affect both the automatic and the intentional response-selection routes.

Orthogonal Stimulus–Response Dimensions

For many years it was thought that SRC effects would not occur when the stimulus and response dimensions are orthogonal. However, there have now been numerous demonstrations of SRC effects for orthogonal S-R arrangements in two-choice tasks (Cho & Proctor, 2003). When the stimulus dimension is vertical and the response dimension horizontal, the SRC effects have two major characteristics. First, an overall advantage for the mapping of up to right and down to left is obtained when the stimuli are up–down physical locations, up–down pointing arrows, or *up–down (above–below)* location words, and the responses are bimanual keypresses, unimanual aimed or switch movements, or vocal responses (Proctor, Wang, & Vu, 2002; Weeks & Proctor, 1990). Weeks and Proctor attributed this up–right/down–left advantage to asymmetric coding of the stimulus and response alternatives, with up and right coded as positive polarity, or salient, and down and left coded as negative polarity. Each stimulus is mapped to the response of corresponding polarity for the up–right/down–left mapping but not for the up–left/down–right mapping. No alternative account of the up–right/down–left advantage has been proposed, and debate has focused only on whether asymmetric coding is a general property of spatial representation or restricted to verbal codes, with the evidence favoring the former view (Cho & Proctor, 2003).

The second major characteristic is that, with unimanual responses, the orthogonal SRC effect varies with the position at which the responses are made. The up–right/down–left advantage is evident when responding at body midline, but it shifts to a much larger advantage when responding in the right hemispace and to an up–left/down–right advantage when responding in the left hemispace (Cho & Proctor, 2003). This phenomenon is called the *response eccentricity effect*. Moreover, the up–right/down–left advantage is larger when responding with the left hand than with the right hand, and this pattern reverses when the hand is placed in a supine posture. Because the variables affecting orthogonal SRC entail effectors and their placement, some researchers have proposed that the effects are due primarily to properties of the motor system (e.g., Lippa & Adam, 2001). However, considerable evidence indicates that the effects of these variables on orthogonal SRC can be explained in the same way as the overall up–right/down–left advantage, that is, by correspondence of asymmetric S-R codes (Cho & Proctor, 2003).

The central idea behind Cho and Proctor's (2003) explanation is that response position is represented in relation to various referent objects. The response alternative that is consistent with a particular representation of response position is coded as positive polarity. The multiple response codes contribute to performance in an approximately additive manner, such that their combined effects determine the direction and size of the orthogonal SRC effect. As an example, unimanual responses at body midline show an effect of location in relation to an inactive response device similar to the response eccentricity effect (Proctor & Cho, 2003; Weeks, Proctor, & Beyak, 1995): A sizable up–right/down–left advantage occurs when the inactive switch is left (and the response position is right in relation to it), and this changes to a tendency toward a small up–left/down–right advantage when the inactive switch is to the right.

The response eccentricity effect is explained in the following manner. When responding in the left hemispace, the response position is left in relation to the display and body midline, and the left response is thus coded as positive polarity and the right response as negative polarity; when responding in the right hemispace, the relations are opposite. Experiments dissociating the display and body midline as reference frames indicate that the display is the primary referent determining the response eccentricity effect (Cho & Proctor, in press): A large effect occurs when the participant's position covaries with the location of the response device in relation to the display, such that the response position is always at body midline. In contrast, no significant effect is found when the display position covaries with the response position, such that when the response position is in the left or right hemispace, the display is still aligned with it. These effects occur not only for unimanual switch movements but also for keypresses made with the left and right hands and vocal "left"–"right" responses, indicating that they are not effector based.

The effects of hand and hand posture, which are additive with those of response eccentricity, are due at least in part to coding the position of the response switch in relation to the main part of the hand. When the switch is grasped with the index finger and thumb in a normal, prone hand posture, it is located to the left side of the right hand and the right side of the left hand, which should produce negative and positive response codes, respectively, resulting in a smaller up–right/down–left advantage with the right hand, as is found. Cho and Proctor (2002) showed that when the hand is in a supine posture, which reverses the switch position in relation to the main part of the hand, the right hand now yields the larger up–right/down–left advantage, and when the switch is grasped between the little and ring fingers, which also alters the relation between the response position and hand, the effect magnitudes vary in a similar manner.

Wheel-Rotation Responses

Rotations of a steering wheel are clockwise and counterclockwise and do not overlap with the horizontal dimension along which left–right stimuli vary. However, several relations between wheel-rotation responses and the left–right distinction exist: Clockwise rotations are associated with turning a vehicle right and counterclockwise rotations with turning it left; the top of the wheel (which is near the line of sight) moves right for clockwise rotation and left for counterclockwise rotation; both hands move left or right when placed at the top or bottom of the wheel, with the direction of hand movement being opposite that of the wheel movement when the wheel is held at the bottom. Thus, both wheel- and hand-referenced frames could provide a basis for SRC effects.

Guiard (1983) reported several experiments examining the Simon effect for wheel-rotation responses: One response was to be made to a high pitch tone and the other to a low pitch tone, with the ear in which the tone was presented being irrelevant. Wang, Proctor, and Pick (2003) recently replicated and extended these findings, the major ones of which are as follows: First, the Simon effect (faster responses when tone location corresponds with the typical direction of rotation) occurs when the wheel is held at its sides, as well as when the hands are at the top. Second, no overall Simon effect is obtained when the hands are at the bottom of the wheel. This absence of an overall effect is due to approximately half of the subjects showing a Simon effect and half a reverse Simon effect (faster responses when the clockwise response is made to a tone in the left ear and the counterclockwise response to a tone in the right ear). These individual differences indicate that, when hand- and wheel-referenced frames are in opposition, some subjects code responses relative to one and other subjects relative to the other.

Wang et al. (2003) instructed subjects using the bottom hand placement in terms of the direction of hand movement or wheel movement. The hand-movement instructions were sufficient to induce a reverse Simon effect for all subjects, indicating that these instructions caused everyone to code the responses with respect to the direction of hand movement. In contrast, wheel-movement instructions did not produce a similar effect: As with neutral instructions, only about half of the subjects showed a positive Simon effect indicative of wheel-referenced coding, and half showed a reversed Simon effect indicative of hand-reference coding. This asymmetry for the instruction manipulation implies that subjects who tend to use wheel-referenced coding can be induced through instructions to use hand-referenced coding, but not vice versa.

The third major finding evident in both Guiard's (1983) and Wang et al.'s (2003) studies is that even with the hands at the bottom of the wheel, all subjects show a positive Simon effect when the wheel controls a cursor that moves in a direction compatible with wheel rotation. In contrast, Wang et al. found that movement of a visual cursor triggered at completion of the wheel rotation (an 8° rotation) did not influence the Simon effect, with approximately half of the subjects showing a positive effect and half a reversed effect, as when no cursor is visible. Thus, responses are coded in terms of left–right cursor movements when the cursor movement is visible during the response but not when it occurs as a subsequent outcome.

Similar effects for coding wheel-rotation responses occur when stimulus location is relevant (Proctor, Wang, & Pick, in press; Stins & Michaels, 1997). As for the Simon effect, an SRC effect is obtained with the hands at the top or sides of the wheel: RT is shorter when the right stimulus is mapped to the clockwise response and the left stimulus to the counterclockwise response. With the hands at the bottom of the wheel, no overall SRC effect occurs. Unlike the Simon effect, the absence of an overall SRC effect is not due to some subjects coding responses in relation to a wheel-referenced frame and others a hand-referenced frame. Responses are accurate and fast with both mappings, implying that subjects code the responses relative to the reference frame that yields a compatible S-R relation (wheel movement for the right–clockwise/left–counterclockwise mapping and hand movement for the right–counterclockwise/left–clockwise mapping).

For the bottom hand placement, instructions that emphasize direction of hand movement yield a large SRC effect with respect to the hands, and a visual cursor controlled by the wheel yields a large SRC effect with respect to cursor direction. Although these results are similar to those for the Simon effect, the interesting aspect is that the subjects code the responses in the manner consistent with the hand instructions or cursor even when the S-R mapping is incompatible relative to that reference frame. Thus, the coding of responses may be determined by instructions or a salient event in the environment when an alternative coding would be more beneficial.

Conclusions

Spatial SRC effects have been studied for the past 50 years because they provide essential insights into the relation between perception and action. Despite this fact, many cognitive and engineering psychologists' knowledge of SRC is limited to the rule that performance is best when spatial correspondence is maintained. Yet, research on SRC indicates that, even for a task as basic as two-choice reactions, response selection is a goal-directed act that is affected by the way that the stimuli and responses are coded and associated with each other. The research reviewed in this chapter alone shows the following: (a) Complex interactions occur when tasks with different S-R mappings are mixed; (b) location mappings for one task affect performance on a subsequent task for which stimulus location is irrelevant up to at least a week later; (c) task environments and instructions can affect the way in which stimuli and responses are coded; and (d) complex, but systematic, patterns of SRC occur for situations in which the stimulus and response sets vary along different dimensions.

The unintuitive nature of these effects is illustrated by a study we conducted in which naïve subjects predicted the RT and error rate for each of several different mapping conditions and S-R sets (Vu & Proctor, 2003). They correctly predicted that performance is better with a pure compatible mapping than a pure incompatible mapping. However, they did not predict virtually any other effect that is typically found, including several of those reviewed in this chapter. The subjects did not correctly predict that the two-choice SRC effect for pure mappings is larger for S-R sets that have both perceptual and conceptual similarity than for those that have only conceptual similarity. Moreover, they estimated SRC effects for all stimulus modes mapped to keypresses to be about the same size with mixed mappings as with pure mappings. Thus, the subjects did not realize that, with mixed mappings, the SRC effect would be eliminated for physical locations or arrows and enhanced for location words. The subjects also did not predict an SRC effect for up–down stimuli mapped to left–right responses, nor that performance in a four-choice task is better for an S-R mapping that conforms to a "respond opposite" rule than for a random one. An encouraging outcome of the study, though, was that the predictions of relative performance became significantly more accurate after performing the judged task for 100 trials.

Contemporary research on SRC effects has yet to have much impact on human factors guidelines and principles. Guidelines indicate that display–control compatibility should be maintained, a control should be placed close to the display with which it is associated, and displays and controls should be compatible with users' expectancies and learning characteristics (e.g., Andre & Wickens, 1990; ISO 9355-1, 1999; Proctor & Vu, in press). However, they do not mention that SRC effects are often eliminated or reduced when mappings and tasks are mixed, nor do they convey that the users' task representation is crucial and the factors that can affect that representation. Below we summarize the major implications of the research covered in this chapter for interface design. Although these points may be used as general guidelines, the specific task environment and goals must be taken into account to predict performance accurately.

1. Performance on mixed tasks differs from performance on pure tasks.

- When compatible and incompatible spatial mappings are mixed, responding is slowed overall, and the advantage for the compatible mapping is eliminated for S-R sets that have conceptual and perceptual similarity.
- When a task for which stimulus location is relevant is mixed with one for which it is irrelevant, the SRC effect for the location-relevant task is eliminated if the S-R set is visuospatial–manual and enhanced if the stimuli or responses are verbal. The location mapping influences the

direction and magnitude of the Simon effect for the location-irrelevant task: When the location mapping is incompatible, the spatially noncorresponding response tends to be made faster and more accurately than the corresponding response.

2. The location mapping defined for a spatial task can influence performance on a subsequent task for which stimulus location is irrelevant.

- An incompatible mapping for a location-relevant task can eliminate or reverse the typical tendency to make the corresponding response.
- The influence of the prior incompatible mapping can be eliminated or minimized by varying the sensory modality of the stimulus and response sets for the different conditions.

3. For stimulus and response sets that vary along two dimensions, prevalence effects occur or can be induced when the task environment makes one dimension more salient than the other.

- When the stimulus and response sets can be coded along both horizontal and vertical dimensions, right–left prevalence often occurs when stimulus location is relevant and left–right effectors in their natural adjacent positions are used for responding.
- The advantage or prevalence of one dimension over another is greatest when the same dimension is salient for both the display and the response configuration.

4. SRC effects occur when the stimulus and response sets vary along orthogonal dimensions.

- There is an overall tendency for the up–right/down–left mapping to yield better performance than the alternative mapping.
- The direction and magnitude of orthogonal SRC effects vary systematically as a function of response position in relation to various frames of reference.

5. SRC effects occur for wheel-rotation responses to stimuli in left and right locations.

- When the reference frame for response coding is ambiguous, some people code responses relative to the hands and others relative to the wheel.
- Coding of wheel-rotation responses is influenced by instructions and salient display features, such as a cursor controlled by the wheel.

The central message from the research on SRC is that responses are coded in a manner similar to stimuli, and the relations between the stimulus and response codes are crucial in determining performance. Both researchers and practitioners can benefit from heeding this message.

References

Andre, A. D., & Wickens, C. D. (1990). *Display-control compatibility in the cockpit: Guidelines for display layout analysis* (Aviation Research Laboratory Technical Report ARL-90-12/NASA-A³I-90-1). Champaign: University of Illinois.

Cho, Y. S., & Proctor, R. W. (2002). Influences of hand posture and hand position on compatibility effects for up-down stimuli mapped to left-right responses. *Perception & Psychophysics, 64,* 1301–1315.

Cho, Y. S., & Proctor, R. W. (2003). Stimulus and response representations underlying orthogonal stimulus–response compatibility effects. *Psychonomic Bulletin & Review, 10,* 45–73.

Cho, Y. S., & Proctor, R. W. (in press). Representing response position relative to display location: Influence on orthogonal stimulus–response compatibility. *Quarterly Journal of Experimental Psychology.*

Fitts, P. M., & Deininger, R. L. (1954). S-R compatibility: Correspondence among paired elements within stimulus and response codes. *Journal of Experimental Psychology, 48,* 483–492.

Fitts, P. M., & Seeger, C. M. (1953). S-R compatibility: Spatial characteristics of stimulus and response codes. *Journal of Experimental Psychology, 46,* 199–210.

Guiard, Y. (1983). The lateral coding of rotation: A study of the Simon effect with wheel-rotation responses. *Journal of Motor Behavior, 15,* 331–342.

Hommel, B. (1996). No prevalence of right-left over top-bottom spatial codes. *Perception & Psychophysics, 43,* 102–110.

Hommel, B., & Prinz, W. (Eds.). (1997). *Theoretical issues in stimulus–response compatibility.* Amsterdam: North-Holland.

ISO 9355-1. (1999). *Ergonomic requirements for the design of display and control actuators: Part 1. Human interactions with displays and control actuators.* Geneva, Switzerland: International Standards Organization.

Kornblum, S., Hasbroucq, T., & Osman, A. (1990). Dimensional overlap: Cognitive basis for stimulus–response compatibility—A model and taxonomy. *Psychological Review, 97,* 253–270.

Lippa, Y., & Adam, J. J. (2001). An explanation of orthogonal S-R compatibility effects that vary with hand or response position: The end-state comfort hypothesis. *Perception & Psychophysics, 63,* 156–174.

Marble J. G., & Proctor, R. W. (2000). Mixing location-relevant and location-irrelevant choice-reaction tasks: Influences of location mapping on the Simon effect. *Journal of Experimental Psychology: Human Perception and Performance, 26,* 1515–1533.

Nicoletti, R., & Umiltà, C. (1984). Right-left prevalence in spatial compatibility. *Perception & Psychophysics, 35,* 333–343.

Proctor, R. W., & Cho, Y. S. (2003). Effects of response eccentricity and relative position on orthogonal stimulus–response compatibility with joystick and keypress responses. *Quarterly Journal of Experimental Psychology, 56A,* 309–328.

Proctor, R. W., & Lu, C.-H. (1999). Processing irrelevant location information: Practice and transfer effects in choice-reaction tasks. *Memory & Cognition, 27,* 63–77.

Proctor, R. W., Marble, J. G., & Vu, K.-P. L. (2000). Mixing incompatibly mapped location-relevant trials with location-irrelevant trials: Effects of stimulus mode on the reverse Simon effect. *Psychological Research, 64,* 11–24.

Proctor, R. W., & Reeve, T. G. (Eds.). (1990). *Stimulus–response compatibility: An integrated perspective.* Amsterdam: North-Holland.

Proctor, R. W., & Vu, K.-P. L. (2002). Mixing location-irrelevant and location-relevant trials: Influence of stimulus mode on spatial compatibility effects. *Memory & Cognition, 30,* 281–293.

Proctor, R. W., & Vu, K.-P. L. (in press). Location and arrangement of displays and control actuators. In W. Karwowski (Ed.), *Handbook of human factors and ergonomics standards.* Mahwah, NJ: Erlbaum.

Proctor, R. W., Vu, K.-P. L., & Marble, J. G. (2003). Eliminating spatial compatibility effects for location-relevant trials by intermixing location-irrelevant trials. *Visual Cognition, 10,* 15–50.

Proctor, R. W., Vu, K.-P. L., & Nicoletti, R. (2003). Does right-left prevalence occur for the Simon effect? *Perception & Psychophysics, 65,* 1318–1329.

Proctor, R. W., Wang, D.-Y. D., & Pick, D. F. (in press). Stimulus–response compatibility with wheel-rotation responses: Will an incompatible response coding be used when a compatible coding is possible? *Psychonomic Bulletin & Review.*

Proctor, R. W., Wang, H., & Vu, K.-P. L. (2002). Influences of different combinations of conceptual, perceptual, and structural similarity on stimulus–response compatibility. *Quarterly Journal of Experimental Psychology, 55A,* 59–74.

Shaffer, L. H. (1965). Choice reaction with variable S-R mapping. *Journal of Experimental Psychology, 70,* 284–288.

Stins, J. F., & Michaels, C. F. (1997). Stimulus–response compatibility is information-action compatibility. *Ecological Psychology, 9,* 25–45.

Tagliabue, M., Zorzi, M., & Umiltà, C. (2002). Cross-modal re-mapping influences the Simon effect. *Memory & Cognition, 30,* 18–23.

Tagliabue, M., Zorzi, M., Umiltà, C., & Bassignani, F. (2000). The role of LTM links and STM links in the Simon effect. *Journal of Experimental Psychology: Human Perception and Performance, 26,* 648–670.

Vu, K.-P. L. (2003). *Determinants of the transfer effect of an incompatible location mapping to the Simon task.* Unpublished doctoral dissertation, Purdue University, West Lafayette, Indiana.

Vu, K.-P. L., & Proctor, R. W. (2001). Determinants of right–left and top–bottom prevalence for two-dimensional spatial compatibility. *Journal of Experimental Psychology: Human Perception and Performance, 27,* 813–828.

Vu, K.-P. L., & Proctor, R. W. (2002). The prevalence effect in two-dimensional stimulus–response compatibility is a function of the relative salience of the dimensions. *Perception & Psychophysics, 64,* 815–828.

Vu, K.-P. L., & Proctor, R. W. (2003). Naïve and experienced judgments of stimulus–response compatibility: Implications for interface design. *Ergonomics, 46,* 169–187.

Vu, K.-P. L., & Proctor, R. W. (2004). Mixing compatible and incompatible mappings: Elimination, reduction, and enhancement of spatial compatibility effects. *Quarterly Journal of Experimental Psychology, 57A,* 539–556.

Vu, K.-P. L., Proctor, R. W., & Pick, D. F. (2000). Vertical versus horizontal spatial compatibility: Right-left prevalence with bimanual responses. *Psychological Research, 64,* 25–40.

Vu, K.-P. L., Proctor, R. W., & Urcuioli, P. (2003). Transfer effects of incompatible location-relevant mappings on subsequent visual or auditory Simon tasks. *Memory & Cognition, 31,* 1146–1152.

Wang, D.-Y. D., Proctor, R. W., & Pick, D. F. (2003). The Simon effect with wheel-rotation responses. *Journal of Motor Behavior, 35,* 261–273.

Weeks, D. J., & Proctor, R. W. (1990). Salient-features coding in the translation between orthogonal stimulus and response dimensions. *Journal of Experimental Psychology: General, 119,* 355–366.

Weeks, D. J., Proctor, R. W., & Beyak, B. (1995). Stimulus–response compatibility for vertically oriented stimuli and horizontally oriented responses: Evidence for spatial coding. *Quarterly Journal of Experimental Psychology, 48A,* 367–383.

Part V

Discourse

12

Watching the Brain Comprehend Discourse

Morton Ann Gernsbacher and David A. Robertson

When the first author (Morton Ann Gernsbacher) was in graduate school, she once sat in on an undergraduate entry-level cognition course to see how one of the department's best teachers conveyed the excitement and exquisiteness of cognitive psychology to an audience of 19-year-olds. This professor began the first day by posing the following challenge: Imagine that you were sent to some faraway planet, and your mission on this planet was to discern the workings of a mysterious—at least to you—structure, what here on earth we might call a building. However, you were prohibited or otherwise unable to enter the structure. How would you discern what work went on inside the structure?

With guidance, the students arrived at recommendations such as to first carefully observe what entered the structure, and then carefully observe what exited the structure, and from those observations infer what work must go on inside the structure. Thus, if one saw sheet metal, rubber, and glass entering the structure and one observed Subaru vehicles leaving the structure, one might infer something different than if one saw denim cloth, thread, and zippers entering the structure and men's blue jeans coming out.

At this point the professor skillfully introduced some of the rudimentary concepts of experimental design: How, if clever enough, one might manipulate certain aspects of the input to the structure while controlling as many extraneous variables as possible, then measure qualitatively or quantitatively the output and thereby allow sharper inferences of what type of work went on inside the structure. At this point students suggested other covert techniques, for example, sneaking in at night or some time when their presence would not be detected—in other words, observing the structure "at rest." Trying to obtain a blueprint or floor plan of the structure was also suggested. Even bombing a section of the structure to see how that affects the output (an idea not so far

The research described in this chapter was supported primarily by a grant to Morton Ann Gernsbacher from the National Institute of Health (RO1 NS29926), a University of Wisconsin–Madison Faculty Development Award to Morton Ann Gernsbacher, and a National Institute of Mental Health predoctoral traineeship (T32 MH18931) to David A. Robertson.

removed from our U.S. military reconnaissance) was proposed. These approaches resemble techniques of neuroanatomical inquiry: postmortem analyses, nonfunctional imaging, lesion studies. However, as the professor pointed out, none of those approaches would portray the structure at work. And indeed, over 20 years ago, when the first author sat in on this classroom activity, the opportunity to see the brain at work eluded cognitive psychologists.

Times have changed. Now, the ability to answer questions such as how humans plan, learn, remember, represent experience, and comprehend language is aided by the ability to watch the brain at work (Posner & Raichle, 1994). We can generate visual images of that mysterious structure while these higher level processes are occurring. In this chapter, we provide (a) a claim—that a picture can be worth a thousand milliseconds; (b) a testimonial—that one can find hay in a haystack; and (c) a caveat—from a lesson learned from drinking scotch.

A Claim

The claim we want to make is that "A picture can be worth a thousand milliseconds," which could be subtitled "Why doing brain-imaging experiments can be more than redoing old reaction time experiments with more expensive apparatus." We substantiate this claim with some of our own research. The brain imaging technique we have used most frequently is functional magnetic resonance imaging (fMRI), and the goal of many of our fMRI experiments has been to observe the brain at work while it processed coherent discourse. In one experiment (Robertson et al., 2000), we manipulated a subtle marker of discourse coherence: the English definite article *the*. In languages that use an article system, the definite article signals repeated reference, which typically leads to coherence. For example, the use of the definite article *the* in these two sentences,

> *The conference speaker was talking very fast.*
> *The conference speaker was showing a bunch of overheads.*

suggests that the woman who was showing a lot of overheads was the same as the woman who was talking very fast. In contrast, the use of the indefinite article *a* in these two sentences,

> *A member of the audience was listening.*
> *A member of the audience was yawning.*

makes it unclear whether the member of the audience who was listening was also the member of the audience who was yawning. However, if we substitute the definite article *the* for the indefinite article *a,* this unfortunate situation becomes clear.

> *A member of the audience was listening.*
> *The member of the audience was yawning.*

In fact, the definite article *the* can signal coreference even when the noun it modifies is only a synonym of the previously mentioned noun, as in

> *A member of the audience was getting bored.*
> *The clod began thumbing through his program looking for another talk to attend.*

As these examples illustrate, the definite article *the* promotes coherence.

Gernsbacher and Robertson (2002) collected empirical data to evaluate these intuitions. We created 10 series of sentences. One version of each series contained only the definite article, and the other version contained only indefinite articles. In one experiment we measured subjects' reading time and their recall, and in another experiment we measured subjects' reading time and their speeded recognition, using a priming-in-item recognition task (McKoon & Ratcliff, 1980). We observed that when the sentences were presented with the definite article, they were read considerably more rapidly, about 25% faster (as Haviland & Clark, 1974, had observed over 25 years earlier); they were perceived as being more narrativelike (as de Villiers, 1974, had observed over 25 years earlier), they were recalled in a more integrative fashion, and they showed a priming-in-item recognition advantage, meaning that recognition of one sentence from a series was speeded if preceded by another sentence from that series. Sentences presented with indefinite articles did not show this priming advantage.

All these data led us to believe that the definite article *the* signals the recurrence of concepts and therefore their interrelations, and that discourse comprehension must involve capturing those interrelations. However, those were just our educated speculations from carefully controlling what we sent into the unknown structure and carefully observing what came out. Therefore, we conducted an fMRI experiment in which we presented several series of sentences that contained only indefinite articles, such as

> *A grandmother sat at a table.*
> *A young child played in a backyard.*
> *A mother talked on a telephone.*
> *A husband drove a tractor.*
> *A grandchild walked up to a door.*
> *A little boy pouted and acted bored.*
> *A grandmother promised to bake cookies.*
> *A wife looked out at a field.*
> *A family was worried about some crops.*

Or we presented the same sentences, with the indefinite articles replaced by the definite article, as in the following examples:

> *The grandmother sat at the table.*
> *The young child played in the backyard.*
> *The mother talked on the telephone.*
> *The husband drove the tractor.*
> *The grandchild walked up to the door.*

The little boy pouted and acted bored.
The grandmother promised to bake cookies.
The wife looked out at the field.
The family was worried about the crops.

Although as psycholinguists we wanted to directly compare these two conditions, the Wisconsin medical physicists with whom we consulted could not believe that such a "subtle" comparison would lead to any observable differences in brain activity. Given their skepticism and to conform to the fMRI literature of that time, we also included a "loose" control condition, in which we replaced the letters of the sentences with nonletter characters while retaining interword spacing and string length (e.g., <` <^#%} |<-|*))#~/ <>*{+-*^~?)*(-.). This combination of tight and loose comparisons turned out to be very fruitful. We collected whole brain functional images in 23 coronal slices from 8 right-handed subjects and observed two main findings.

First, we observed that reading sentences compared with viewing nonletter strings led to a robust region of activation in the left hemisphere extending from the angular gyrus rostrally to the left anterior temporal pole along the middle temporal gyrus; a smaller region of activation was also observed in the right-hemisphere homologue of Wernicke's area, as shown in Figure 12.1. These data replicate several other sets in the literature, including those of Bavelier et al. (1997), who examined the contrast of reading sentences versus consonant strings. We were encouraged by the very similar results across laboratories despite different tasks and different analysis techniques.

However, in contrast to our comparison between reading sentences and viewing nonletter strings, our comparison between reading sentences that contained definite articles and reading sentences that contained indefinite articles revealed virtually no differences in left-hemisphere activation. Instead,

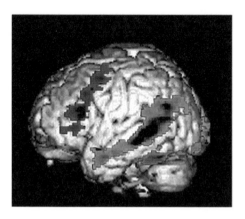 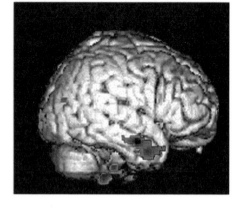

Left   Right

Figure 12.1.   Brain activation patterns from Robertson et al. (2000). Illustrated is the contrast between subjects reading sentences (left) and viewing nonletter character strings (right); data are averaged across all subjects.

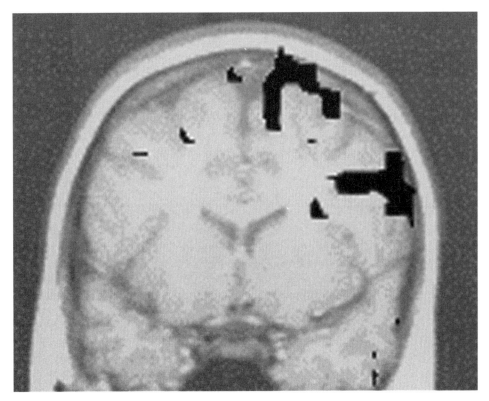

Left   Right

Figure 12.2. Brain activation pattern for one example subject in Robertson et al. (2000). Illustrated is the contrast between reading sentences that contained the definite article (*the* [left]) and sentences that contained indefinite articles (*a, an, some* [right]).

differential activation was observed in frontal regions, particularly in the right superior and medial frontal gyri. Figure 12.2 illustrates the pronouncedly right-lateralized activation in one of our subjects, from a coronal view through the frontal lobes and anterior temporal lobes. This finding corroborates a wealth of lesion studies, which demonstrate that people with right-hemisphere damage are often described as "not getting the point," less able to integrate information, and unaware of inconsistencies; in short, they are described as often oblivious to and challenged by discourse coherence (Brownell, Carroll, Rehak, & Wingfield, 1992; van Lancker & Kempler, 1987; Winner & Gardner, 1977; Zaidel, Zaidel, Oxbury, & Oxbury, 1995).

Thus, our finding that the processing of coherent discourse is manifested by more right- rather than left-hemisphere activation corroborates the behavioral challenges that people with right-hemisphere brain damage exhibit during discourse comprehension. We can then turn to other functional imaging studies to ask: Why right frontal? Other functional imaging work suggests that right frontal regions support the allocation of attention (e.g., Knight & Grabowesky, 1995); we have suggested that the definite article acts as a cue for coherence. Therefore, the behavioral advantages that we previously observed might be advantages of attention to that cue. Could we have arrived at the same conclusions through reaction time experiments? Granted, this experiment was not as unique as Blakemore, Wolpert, and Frith's (2000) study in which they collected fMRI data to explain why tickling yourself is never as ticklish as someone else tickling you. Nonetheless, we claim that watching the brain at work provides insights that reaction time studies cannot.

A Testimonial

Our testimonial is that one can look for hay in a haystack, or perhaps more accurately, one can find hay in a haystack. We often think of functional imaging as a wonderful vehicle for isolating unique neural circuits, distinguishing independent systems, and otherwise identifying differences, but one can also use the technique to identify commonalities. We illustrate this point by sharing another research study from our lab.

In much of our behavioral work, we have been interested in identifying the common processes involved in comprehending different media (Gernsbacher, 1990, 1997). This is not to deny that there are language-specific processes; rather our goal has been to identify the processes and mechanisms that might be common across the comprehension of various media. We have known for almost 30 years that for adults without any known impairments, written comprehension, measured by performance on a comprehension test after reading, is highly correlated with spoken language comprehension, measured by performance on a comprehension test after listening (Daneman & Carpenter, 1983; Jackson & McClelland, 1979; Palmer, MacLeod, Hunt, & Davidson, 1985; Perfetti & Lesgold, 1977; Sticht, 1972).

For example, Palmer et al. (1985) reported that the correlation between written language comprehension, measured by visually presenting the comprehension sections of the Davis reading test, and spoken language comprehension, measured by auditorily presenting the comprehension sections of the Davis reading test, was .80. The correlations were only slightly lower for written comprehension measured by the Nelson–Denny or the Washington Pre-College Scholastic Aptitude test and spoken comprehension, measured by auditorily presenting the Davis reading test. Over a decade ago, my lab extended these findings by demonstrating that comprehension of written narratives was highly correlated with comprehension of spoken narratives, and more strikingly, that both were highly correlated with comprehension of narratives told without any words, that is, picture-only narratives. We (Gernsbacher, Varner, & Faust, 1990) reported correlations corrected for reliability of .92, .82, and .72 for the relation between written and spoken, written and picture, and picture and spoken comprehension, based on our Multi-Media Comprehension Battery.

These correlations support the hypothesis that many of the cognitive processes and mechanisms underlying discourse comprehension are general enough to be involved in the comprehension of nonverbal media. More discrete laboratory behaviors also support this hypothesis. For example, after viewing a narrative as a movie without dialogue or listening to the narrative as text, comprehenders mark off the same episode structure (Baggett, 1979; Gernsbacher, 1985); comprehenders draw the same inferences after they view nonverbal cartoon sequences as when they read verbal descriptions of those sequences (Baggett, 1975); and when recalling a narrative viewed as a movie without dialog or listened to as a text, comprehenders emphasize, elaborate, and omit the same information (Poulsen, Kintsch, Kintsch, & Premack, 1979).

Therefore, in a recent fMRI experiment (Robertson, Guidotti, & Gernsbacher, 2003) we measured subjects' brain activity while we presented six narratives. Two were presented by means of written sentences, two were presented by means of spoken sentences, and two were presented by means of line-drawn pictures. The subjects' comprehension task was oddball detection. During each narrative segment, which comprised six or seven narrative stimuli—that is, six or seven written sentences, six or seven spoken sentences, or six or seven pictures—one or two oddball stimuli occurred. The subjects' task was to detect these oddballs. For the narratives presented by means of written sentences, these oddball stimuli were sentences that were semantically and syntactically coherent but they did not fit the content of the ongoing narrative. For the narratives presented by means of pictures, oddball stimuli were pictures that were taken from other picture books and therefore did not fit the ongoing narrative. We used as a comparison task the comprehension of unconnected stimuli: By this, we mean written sentences, spoken sentences, or pictures that were unrelated to each other. Oddballs for the comparison task were sentences or pictures that contained a local anomaly, such as the Kutas and Hillyard (1980) sentences (e.g., *He drank his coffee with milk and socks*) or the Biederman, Glass, and Stacy (1973) pictures, in which a common object is misplaced in a familiar scene (e.g., a fire hydrant in a living room scene). We collected whole brain functional images in 23 coronal slices from nine right-handed subjects and observed the activation patterns illustrated in Figure 12.3. The striking similarity among the images representing the brain activity while comprehending picture narratives, written narratives, and spoken narratives suggests that there is a lot of hay in that haystack, but it is not all hay.

A Caution

The penultimate point we want to make briefly draws back to the old joke about the man who one night drank a lot of scotch and water, and the next morning he had a terrible hangover; the next night he drank a lot of whiskey and water, and the next morning he had a terrible hangover; the third night he drank a lot of bourbon and water, and the next morning he had a terrible hangover. He therefore decided that he just had to stop drinking so much water. Those of us who are corny enough to tell this riddle in experimental methods courses do so in the service of illustrating the importance of one's control condition. When interpreting functional imaging experiments, it is just as crucial to ask what the control or comparison task is as it is when interpreting more traditional cognitive psychology experiments.

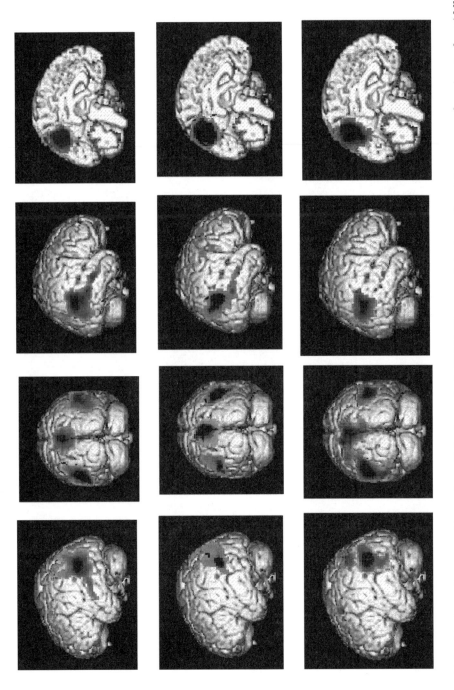

Figure 12.3. Brain activation patterns from Robertson et al. (2003). Top row: data from the picture comprehension task; middle row: data from the written comprehension task; bottom row: data from the spoken comprehension task. The first picture of each row shows a left view, the second picture a posterior view, the third picture a right view, and the fourth picture a medial view. All views are contrasts between comprehending connected stimuli (picture stories, written stories, spoken stories) and comprehending unconnected stimuli. Data are averaged across all subjects.

As we look forward to the future of cognitive psychology, we are inspired to wonder how the field will be affected by the advent of functional imaging. One effect is that we are going to see a lot more color: lots of reds, yellows, and oranges, if those remain our colors for symbolizing the brain at work. To interpret those vivid images of the brain at work, we need to ask the same questions that we have asked since the dawn of experimental psychology, including what was the comparison task? Indeed, this one caution exemplifies our strong belief that good functional brain imaging cannot be done without good cognitive psychology, both methodologically and theoretically, and we predict that soon we shall see that the opposite will be the case as well. Good cognitive psychology will need good functional brain imaging for generating and testing hypotheses.

The Applications

Last, we bring ourselves to discuss briefly the real-world applications of the findings we have reviewed here. Both our empirical data and our methodology suggest direct applications. First, we have argued here and elsewhere for the construct of general comprehension; our neuroimaging data strongly support the hypothesis that there are common brain regions underlying the comprehension of connected discourse—regardless of the medium in which the discourse occurred. Thus, instructional materials and assessments of instructional accomplishment should take advantage of the common mechanisms underlying comprehension of different media. For instance, instruction materials can indeed be multimedia without too great of a concern (particularly in a normative population) that one medium will be comprehended more poorly or differentially than another. Instructional assessment can even be cross-modality as a way to assess a general or "higher level" understanding that is independent of input modality.

Second, our methodology suggests another application, that of using brain imaging for assessing comprehension, development of comprehension, or even impairment of comprehension (Eden & Moats, 2002). Within the more prescribed realm of reading comprehension, we are already seeing brain imaging used this way. For instance, brain imaging has been used to differentiate readers who were described behaviorally as "poor readers as children who retained persistent reading problems in adulthood" as opposed to "poor readers as children who compensated as adults" (Shaywitz et al., 2003). Furthermore, brain imaging has documented changes in neural activity among poor readers who underwent successful behavioral intervention and those who did not (Temple et al., 2003). Thus, cognitive psychologists' current ability to watch the brain at work means that they can also watch the brain work better. These are quite exciting times.

References

Baggett, P. (1975). Memory for explicit and implicit information in picture stories. *Journal of Verbal Learning and Verbal Behavior, 14,* 538–548.

Baggett, P. (1979). Structurally equivalent stories in movie and text and the effect of the medium on recall. *Journal of Verbal Learning and Verbal Behavior, 18,* 333–356.

Bavelier, D., Corina, D., Jezzard, P., Padmanabhan, S., Clark, V. P., Karni, A., et al. (1997). Sentence reading: A functional MRI study at 4 Tesla. *Journal of Cognitive Neuroscience, 9,* 664–686.

Biederman, I., Glass, A. L., & Stacy, E. W., Jr. (1973). Searching for objects in real world scenes. *Journal of Experimental Psychology, 97,* 22–27.

Blakemore, S. J., Wolpert, D., & Frith, C. (2000). Why can't you tickle yourself? *Neuroreport, 3,* R11–R16.

Brownell, H. H., Carroll, J. J., Rehak, A., & Wingfield, A. (1992). The use of pronoun anaphora and speaker mood in the interpretation of conversational utterances by right hemisphere-damaged patients. *Brain and Language, 43,* 121–147.

Daneman, M., & Carpenter, P. A. (1983). Individual differences in integrating information between and within sentences. *Journal of Experimental Psychology: Learning, Memory, and Cognition, 9,* 561–585.

de Villiers, P. A. (1974). Imagery and theme in recall of connected discourse. *Journal of Experimental Psychology, 103,* 263–268.

Eden, G. F., & Moats, L. (2002). The role of neuroscience in the remediation of students with dyslexia. *Nature Neuroscience, 5S,* 1080–1084.

Gernsbacher, M. A. (1985). Surface information loss in comprehension. *Cognitive Psychology, 17,* 324–363.

Gernsbacher, M. A. (1990). *Language comprehension as structure building.* Hillsdale, NJ: Erlbaum.

Gernsbacher, M. A. (1997). Two decades of structure building. *Discourse Processes, 23,* 265–304.

Gernsbacher, M. A., & Robertson, R. R. W. (2002). The definite article "the" as a cue to map thematic information. In M. M. Louwerse & W. Van Peer (Eds.), *Thematics: Interdisciplinary studies* (pp. 119–136). Philadelphia: John Benjamins.

Gernsbacher, M. A., Varner, K. R., & Faust, M. (1990). Investigating differences in general comprehension skill. *Journal of Experimental Psychology: Learning, Memory, and Cognition, 16,* 430–445.

Haviland, S. E., & Clark, H. H. (1974). What's new? Acquiring new information as a process in comprehension. *Journal of Verbal Learning and Verbal Behavior, 13,* 512–521.

Jackson, M. D., & McClelland, J. L. (1979). Processing determinants of reading speech. *Journal of Experimental Psychology: General, 108,* 151–181.

Knight, R. T., & Grabowesky, M. (1995). Escape from linear time: Prefrontal cortex and conscious experience. In M. S. Gazzaniga (Ed.), *The cognitive neurosciences* (pp. 1357–1371). Cambridge, MA: MIT Press.

Kutas, M., & Hillyard, S. A. (1980, January 11). Reading senseless sentences: Brain potentials reflect semantic incongruity. *Science, 207,* 203–205.

McKoon, G., & Ratcliff, R. (1980). Priming in item recognition: The organization of propositions in memory for text. *Journal of Verbal Learning and Verbal Behavior, 19,* 369–386.

Palmer, J., MacLeod, C. M., Hunt, E., & Davidson, J. E. (1985). Information processing correlates of reading. *Journal of Memory and Language, 24,* 59–88.

Perfetti, C. A., & Lesgold, A. L. (1977). Discourse comprehension and sources of individual differences. In M. A. Just & P. A. Carpenter (Eds.), *Cognitive processes in comprehension* (pp. 141–183). Hillsdale, NJ: Erlbaum.

Posner, M. I., & Raichle, M. E. (1994). *Images of mind.* New York: Freeman.

Poulsen, D., Kintsch, E., Kintsch, W., & Premack, D. (1979). Children's comprehension and memory for stories. *Journal of Experimental Child Psychology, 28,* 379–403.

Robertson, D. A., Gernsbacher, M. A., Guidotti, S. J., Robertson, R. R. W., Irwin, W., Mock, B. J., & Campana, M. E. (2000). Functional neuroanatomy of the cognitive process of mapping during discourse comprehension. *Psychological Science, 11,* 255–260.

Robertson, D. A, Guidotti, S. J., & Gernsbacher, M. A. (2003). *A modality-independent network of brain regions supporting narrative comprehension.* Manuscript submitted for publication.

Shaywitz, S. E., Shaywitz, B. A., Fulbright, R. K., Skudlarski, P., Mencle, W. E., Constable, R. T., et al. (2003). Neural systems for compensation and persistence: Young adult outcome of childhood reading disability. *Biological Psychiatry, 54,* 25–33.

Sticht, T. G. (1972). Learning by listening. In R. O. Freedle & J. B. Carroll (Eds.), *Language comprehension and the acquisition of knowledge* (pp. 285–314). Washington, DC: Winston.

Temple, E., Deutsch, G. K., Poldrack, R. A., Miller, S. L., Tallal, P., Merzenich, M. M., & Gabrieli, J. D. E. (2003). Neural deficits in children with dyslexia ameliorated by behavioral remediation: Evidence from functional MRI. *Proceedings of the National Academy of Sciences, 100,* 2860–2865.

van Lancker, D. R., & Kempler, D. (1987). Comprehension of familiar phrases by left- but not right-hemisphere damaged patients. *Brain and Language, 32,* 256–277.

Winner, E., & Gardner, H. (1977). The comprehension of metaphor in brain-damaged patients. *Brain, 100,* 717–729.

Zaidel, D. W., Zaidel, E., Oxbury, S. M., & Oxbury, J. M. (1995). The interpretation of sentence ambiguity in patients with unilateral focal brain surgery. *Brain and Language, 51,* 458–468.

13

Learning to Construct and Integrate

Susan R. Goldman and David M. Bloome

No one can deny the profound impact of the theoretical and empirical work generated by Walter Kintsch and colleagues. The influence of the work is seen in numerous studies of the processing, comprehension, memory, representation, retrieval, and use of information acquired from text in learning and problem-solving situations. The work has also inspired investigations that identify and document differences in the text processing and comprehension by more as compared with less proficient readers, high as compared with low knowledge readers, and younger as compared with older readers. However, there is relatively little work that examines why those differences exist and how they came to be. At the same time, but largely in parallel, a significant amount of attention has been devoted to developing and implementing strategies for teaching comprehension. Nevertheless, two recent reports have concluded that research provides scant scientific evidence regarding how to teach comprehension effectively (National Institute of Child Health and Human Development, 2000; Snow, 2002). We do not debate the merits of these conclusions here because debates about them are readily available elsewhere (Coles, 2003; Yatvin, 2002). Rather, in this chapter we use Kintsch-inspired theoretical and empirical work on comprehension to provide new insights into the "art" of effective comprehension instruction through the analysis of the instructional practices of two language arts teachers.

We first provide a brief summary of the development of Kintsch's theory. The bulk of the chapter reports our interpretive analysis of comprehension instruction in two language arts classrooms. We focus on the discursive practices of the teachers and how they afford opportunities for students to learn how to construct meaning from text and appropriately integrate it with their prior knowledge and experiences.

The research discussed in this chapter was supported, in part, by a grant from the Spencer Foundation. However, the opinions expressed are those of the authors and should not be attributed to the funding agency. We express our appreciation to the teachers with whom we have collaborated in this work as well as to the other members of the research team, Cynthia Mayfield, Peter Meyerson, and Michael Wolfe.

Summary of the Evolution of the
Construction–Integration Model

Two Kintsch publications (Kintsch, 1974; Kintsch & van Dijk, 1978) constitute seminal works in the development of what later became the construction–integration model. Especially the 1978 article was foundational for interactive models of comprehension and learning from text because it laid out a clear representational format for the text input, a processing model, and mechanisms for incorporating prior knowledge, comprehension goals, and strategies. It "located" comprehension in the interaction of the text, the reader, and the task, although at that time attention was primarily focused on the text. Later work by Kintsch and others investigated the impact on processing and representation of (a) individual differences in knowledge and reading skill, (b) tasks (e.g., recall vs. summarization), (c) text difficulty and coherence, and (d) interactions among the three. (For a summary of this work, see Goldman, 1997.)

With further development of the text comprehension theory, Kintsch and colleagues (Kintsch et al., 1993; van Dijk & Kintsch, 1983) drew a distinction between processing that resulted in information that could be reproduced in a more or less rote and veridical form as compared with information that could be used in new situations and learning tasks. The theory connected these differences in behavioral outcomes to differences in aspects of mental representations that had been constructed during processing of the information. Van Dijk and Kintsch proposed that mental representations had multiple layers that captured different aspects of text, including the surface form (the specific words, sentences, layout of the text), the meaning of the text itself (textbase), and the interpretation or model of the world referred to by the text (mental or situation model). The textbase captured the referential and intra- and inter-sentential relations among the words in the text. Research indicated that textbase representations were relatively encapsulated in episodic memory and therefore difficult to access and use in new situations, that is, in learning tasks (Coté & Goldman, 1999; Kintsch et al., 1993). The situation model reflected the integration of prior knowledge with the information explicitly "in" the text. Situation model construction increased the likelihood that the information could be used in new situations.

Kintsch (1988) embodied interactive comprehension in a computational formalism called construction–integration (CI). CI is a two-phase, constraint satisfaction process model. The *construction* phase is a text-based, bottom-up process that results in an initial and frequently incoherent representation of the concepts and ideas in the text plus those elements of prior knowledge that are activated by the concepts and ideas from the text. This initial set of nodes and links forms a network. During the *integration* phase, activation is distributed among the nodes and links according to a connectionist algorithm that has the effect of strengthening the concepts that have a lot of connections and are therefore central to the meaning and situation and neglecting those with few connections. Nodes with few connections are often associates to an individual concept but irrelevant to the meaning in the context of the developing network, or are inconsistent with the core meaning. In effect, concepts that are compatible mutually enhance one another and ones that are incompatible or irrelevant are "ignored." Thus, during integration, relevant knowledge becomes more strongly connected to ideas from the text and gaps among ideas are filled in. Resulting representations have good predictive ability for human performance in a range of comprehension and learning tasks (Halldorson & Singer, 2002; Kintsch, 1998; Kintsch & Greeno, 1985; Wolfe & Goldman, 2003).

One question about the CI model is the degree of intentionality and explicitness involved in comprehension and learning. Although it can be argued that in proficient readers and learners, the sense-making process appears to operate without a great deal of strategic or intentional activity, when such learners encounter difficulty making sense they have available a repertoire of strategies that they intentionally deploy and that can be revealed through think-aloud protocols taken during the comprehension process (Chi, 2000; Coté, Goldman, & Saul, 1998; McNamara, 2001). Data from think-aloud studies indicate that "better" comprehension and learning are associated with learners who self-explain, connect information within and across texts, and monitor what they do and do not understand (Chi, 2000; Coté et al., 1998; McNamara, 2001; Wolfe & Goldman, 2003). Thus, the CI model does not obviate the need to understand what it is that proficient comprehenders do when they make sense of text and how those who are less proficient can learn what it takes.

Classroom Discourse That Supports Learning to Construct and Integrate

Elsewhere we have argued that reading and learning from text are fundamentally intertextual processes (Bloome & Goldman, 1999; Goldman, in press), an insight consistent with latent semantic analysis, an approach to text analysis that Kintsch and colleagues have used to simulate knowledge activation in CI (e.g., Kintsch, 1998; Landauer & Dumais, 1997). One aspect of our research on intertextual processes in comprehension and learning from multiple texts has been a collaboration with two language arts teachers, one a seventh-grade and the other a ninth-grade teacher. Each teacher developed and enacted an instructional unit that had the goal of making the intertextual character of learning from text explicit to students. In part, on the basis of the theoretical work of Kintsch and others, we argued that by making explicit the intertextual nature of learning from text, opportunities are provided to deepen comprehension and learning in ways that are not typically achieved through single-text models (Bloome & Goldman, 1999; Goldman, in press; Bloome & Goldman, 2004). The units the teachers developed approached intertextuality differently. The differences reflected a number of contextual variables, including differences in cognitive and social development issues facing students in seventh as compared with ninth grade, school-level emphases, learning objectives for which they were held accountable at school and district levels, and their personal goals for the students. Nevertheless, there were also a number of consistent patterns in the enactment of the intertextual units that relate to what we refer to as the academic discourse of literary analysis.

By academic discourse, we refer to those discourse practices associated with the teaching and learning of an academic area in a classroom, which in the present case is the analysis of literature. Literary analysis as a discipline has associated with it an established set of discourse practices—the set of linguistic, cultural, social, and cognitive practices that members of a disciplinary community use to constitute their community and to pursue the goals of that community. Academic discourse is oriented to the purposes of the classroom community, as opposed to the purposes of a disciplinary community. Thus, although teachers may "pull" on the discourse practices of a discipline in their classrooms, teachers and students are engaged in academic discourse, not disciplinary discourse.

What we see in the academic discourse of literary analysis that was enacted in these classrooms makes public the forms of thinking and reasoning with and about text that serve to establish textbase and situation model representations. Furthermore, because of the explicit emphasis on intertextuality, the classroom discourse makes visible ways in which representations of individual texts might become integrated across a set of texts. Perfetti and colleagues referred to such intertext representations in history and in science as the *documents model* (Perfetti, Rouet, & Britt, 1999). Each discipline has rules that govern how multiple texts are related to one another and what the integrated representation represents. For example, in history, rules of integration depend on corroborating evidence across documents, the source of the text (including biases and purposes for writing), and the temporal–spatial context in which the text was written (Wineburg, 1991). The integrated interpretation is an account of some actual historical event. Unlike history texts, across multiple literary works there is rarely a single event or phenomenon to be interpreted or understood. Rather literary works tend to reflect similarities and differences in ways that people experience various life events and how different authors and genres embody them. Meaning making and interpretation across multiple texts include identifying and understanding points of similarity and points of difference across texts and contribute to emergent understandings of themes of the human condition (e.g., survival, courage, persistence, overcoming adversity). This process creates a layer of representation that captures dimensions of comparison, emergent themes, and relevance and potential connections to readers' understanding of themselves (their identities) and their pasts, presents, and futures. We refer to this as the *intertextual level* (Goldman & Bloome, 2001).

Despite room for personal experiences and interpretations in relating multiple literary works, it is not a "no holds barred" process. What we see in the academic discourse of literary analysis in the seventh- and ninth-grade classrooms discussed here makes clear what the rules are for constructing meaning and interpretation within and across literary texts. The process is constrained: A reader needs to understand the claims in the text and that inferences and reasoning "from" the text must be constrained by what the text actually said. In other words, through engagement with multiple literary texts, the academic discourse of these classrooms provides opportunities for students to learn to construct and integrate within and across texts. Further, it scaffolds the learning process for individuals by relying on the social context of the classroom community, drawing on the pooled set of resources for making meaning and creating interpretations.

The Corpus

We present segments of classroom lessons here that are excerpted from a larger corpus that was collected to document the enactment of the units the two teachers had developed in collaboration with us for use as the first unit of the school year. Both classrooms are in an urban school district. The seventh-grade class of 30 students (16 boys and 14 girls) was located in a middle school (Grades 7 and 8) that served a predominately low-income, African American urban community. The ninth-grade classroom was located in a Grades 5–12 magnet school focused on literature (although it was not an academic magnet school). In the ninth-grade class there were 20 students (11 boys and 9 girls). Each teacher designed a 6- to 8-week unit that explicitly foregrounded intertextuality. Each classroom was videotaped daily for the unit's duration. A subset of the students were interviewed, and students' written work was collected. The teachers were frequently interviewed and assisted in data analysis. Elsewhere we have described our data analysis procedures (Bloome, 1989; Bloome & Goldman, 2002; Bloome et al., 1999; Goldman, in press; Goldman & Bloome, 2001). We focus only on the videotaped data in this chapter. As indicated previously, the seventh- and the ninth-grade units instantiated intertextuality differently.

The Seventh-Grade Classroom: Simultaneous Intertextuality

AW, the seventh-grade teacher, planned to have the students read two novels at the same time, one during class time and one at home. The two novels, *The Outsiders* (Hinton, 1967) and *Lottery Rose* (Hunt, 1976), deal with young people of different ages who are not living in typical family situations. The superficial characteristics of the books differ on a number of dimensions, but there are similarities in several underlying themes. The protagonists in each of the books can be considered "victims of circumstances" yet each finds a way to overcome these circumstances, with the help and support of others. The circumstances include socioeconomic conditions like those that confronted some of AW's students (e.g., school performance, violence, and struggles with personal identity in *The Outsiders*; school performance, alcoholism, physical abuse, acting out, and placement in foster care in *Lottery Rose*). Important to AW was that her students come to see themselves as instrumental in their worlds rather than as victims, as needing to take responsibility for themselves, and as having agency and the ability to make changes in their lives. She wanted her students to see that they too could and should be proactive—that they had choices to make in terms of what they did in her class, school in general, and in the larger community. In addition to the literature aspect of the class, there were also a variety of learning objectives around English grammar, writing the five-paragraph essay, and the like that were part of the seventh-grade curriculum. To accomplish these goals, AW created an instructional context that moved back and forth between instructional conversations and activities that focused on the texts of the novels and those that drew on prior experiences.

Table 13.1. Percentage of Class Time Devoted to Various Activities: Seventh-Grade Classroom

Instructional time[a]	Read aloud, book discussion, or both interleaved	Writing about novels	Mechanics, grammar, vocabulary	Procedural/ administrative
Week 1 (290)	41	3	34	20
Week 2 (300)	40	7	50	3
Week 3 (230)	17	13	61	8
Week 4 (240)	25	0	38	37
Week 5 (280)	7	75	14	4
Week 6 (190)	48	32	0	21

[a] In minutes per week: Fluctuations in minutes of instructional time reflect out of class time due to other school activities and administrative and in-service days when students were not in class.

The seventh-grade intertextuality unit extended over a 5-week period. We videotaped a total of 27 sessions of 50–55 minutes each and coded each video-taped lesson in terms of focal activities and their duration using a 10-minute time-sampling method. The typical structure of AW's classes was to begin with a phase that ranged from 10 to 30 minutes and that focused on grammar, vocabulary, sentence, or paragraph structure. The focus for the remaining part of the class sessions varied somewhat but typically included some time devoted to a read-aloud of *The Outsiders,* discussion of one or both books, occasional writing assignments (logs, paragraphs, essays), a small amount of group work, and occasional sharing of material they had written. Table 13.1 shows the proportion of time per week devoted to the various aspects of the curriculum. The culminating assignment for the unit was a five-paragraph essay that integrated the two books plus information on a social issues topic.

The reading and discussion time provided a forum for AW to model and scaffold students into the academic discourse of literary analysis within and across texts and the ways of thinking about text that accomplish this analysis. She emphasized attention to what the texts said, what they did not say, and what students could do to fill in content when the text did not provide it. She emphasized that students had a responsibility to communicate with the whole class during discussion: Students needed to speak so they could be heard by everyone. Our claim is these emphases created a learning environment that provided opportunities for students to learn to construct and integrate within and across texts. In this chapter we can only illustrate the evidence for our claim.

We focus on a segment of a class session from the 5th day of school. The segment begins about halfway through the class session and after AW had introduced the idea of reading two books at the same time and the ways in which students should be thinking and talking about them. The students had taken out their copies of each of the books to read the summaries on the back cover. From the outset, AW emphasized that they were to take an active stance toward the reading. She told them to think about any way the books are similar and any way they are different and that they were to sincerely attempt to do this. After they had read the summaries, AW asked them to use what was in the text or what they already knew about the books to come up with a similarity. In response to the first student comment, AW provided a discourse template that she wanted the students to use when responding: "In the book *The Outsiders* so and so Joe Smith is blah blah blah. In the book *Lottery Rose* so and so blah blah blah is blah blah blah," and concluded by emphasizing that they should "Refer to the text when you speak of the text." Thus, the discourse template marked the importance of indicating the source text on which comments are based. AW broke down this template further when the same student again responded with a single-word answer. Later in the segment, the desired form of responding was again mirrored back to the students. The presentation of a discourse template for responding was representative of AW's instruction. She used the same strategy of providing a template each time she introduced a new discourse form that she wanted students to use. For example, she introduced a template for their culminating five-paragraph essay task.

At the same time that AW put in place a template for academic discourse, she reiterated norms for discussion in the class: The public nature of the discussion made it necessary for students to speak loud enough to be heard by everyone. This request could be interpreted by students as negative evaluation of content but AW took steps to avoid this interpretation by establishing the validity of what each individual had to say, even if they were not saying it loud enough. Thus, AW encouraged the active construction of meaning, scaffolded the expression of it, and located the conversation in a public, shared space—the community in the classroom.

Expectations for how meaning was constructed were also made explicit for students. A primary expectation was that responses needed to be backed up with reasons or explanations. When students indicated that a similarity between Georgie and Ponyboy was that they were both sensitive, AW asked them how they knew and why they felt that way. This was the first of many times over the course of the unit that AW invoked the norm of literary analysis that assertions need to be grounded in evidence and be capable of being explained. The how and why comments permitted students to respond either from text or from personal experience, consistent with AW's request at the start of the segment to respond "based on what you've read or what you already know." As the students tried to relate sensitivity to hiding feelings, AW helped them focus their thinking directly on the issue of how these two ideas related, and she indicated that she needed them to help her see what they meant. In so doing, AW challenged the students to think more deeply about sensitivity as a similarity at the same time that she accepted the answer. This respect for student thinking is important if we expect students to risk putting their own ideas forward and move beyond answering with the response they think the teacher wants to hear. One of the students provided additional information, with AW continuing to scaffold the form of the response. This segment concluded with AW drawing it to a close by making public the unstated inference of the argument. She commented on this thinking with the word *Possible*.

In subsequent parts of this same lesson, AW reiterated the request to relate the two books and make reasoning public. Students discussed a concrete similarity for which the evidence was obvious—they are both male. Then AW asked about age. This information was given explicitly in the summary for one of the protagonists but not in the summary of the other book. When one of the students offered the answer "seven and one-half," AW reiterated the norm of providing evidence for the response and then modeled how to reason from what *was* provided in the text to fill in the gaps in what was not given. Because of space constraints, we only provide a snippet of that discussion here.

> AW: Why do you think he's seven and a half? What told you that he's seven and a half? How did you get that part? Help me out, [Student Sb.]. You don't know? (inaudible) She's guessed that he's about seven, seven and a half. What gave you the idea that he's seven? Anybody? Yes ma'am.
> S: He's in first grade . . .
> AW: I am sorry keep going . . .
> S: . . . and he spent over two years . . .
> AW: OK he's in the first grade. OK. Let's think kindergarten. He started kindergarten at what age?
> (ALL RESPOND FIVE.)
> AW: . . . first grade you're about . . .
> (ALL REPLY SIX.)
> AW: . . . six you might turn seven but he's repeating the first grade. So he's about seven going on possibly eight.

The discussion of the two books continued in a similar fashion exploring other similarities and then moving on to differences. In the context of discussing differences, AW had an opportunity to model some of the constraints on associations and interpretations. This is an important aspect of learning how to construct and integrate because irrelevant associations are not helpful to meaning making. One of the students pointed out that there was a knife on the cover of *The Outsiders*. AW asked the class what the knife could symbolize, and "death" was the response. AW used this opportunity to discuss how the context of the story limited the range of things the knife might symbolize.

> AW: Humm . . . what could a knife symbolize? Could it symbolize death? What else could a knife symbolize?
> S: A gang.
> AW: It could symbolize possibly a gang. Could it symbolize cutting meat at the grocery store? Could the symbol be used in Kroger for the deli? I mean don't people slice up salami and take it home. OK so you're saying what SJ's saying is that in the context of this cover this knife is not symbolizing that he wants to be a surgeon, and he's carrying this around because he's ready to do his first dissection, that's not what this is about.

In this excerpt, AW modeled thinking that is appropriately constrained by the text. Not all associations to knife are appropriate; interpretations of symbols must be plausible within the context.

In summary, AW provided opportunities for students to learn to construct and integrate, through the simultaneous reading and discussion of two novels.

The read-alouds and discussions established a public textbase and provided access to content that struggling readers may not have been able to get any other way. Interleaved with reading sections of the novel were teacher-posed questions. The questions "tested" comprehension but more importantly modeled for the students ways to think and talk about the events in text. Some of the questions were literal in the sense that the answers were directly in the books. But many involved having to make inferences from what was in the book, often bringing prior knowledge to bear. By externalizing ways of thinking and talking, the teacher provided opportunities for children to understand how to use text and prior knowledge in the service of making sense of the texts.

The Ninth-Grade Classroom: Successive Intertextuality

VS, the ninth-grade teacher, designed a unit in which intertextuality was explicitly established by having students work with a main reading juxtaposed with other short texts. The main reading was the book *House on Mango Street* by Sandra Cisneros (1984), which consists of a series of 44 short vignettes narrated in first person by the main character Esperanza. The vignettes are about topics that adolescents think about. Some are mundane, some are profound, but all deal with the fabric of being and becoming an individual, identity, and making one's mark on the world. The juxtaposed texts were excerpts from books, short stories, or poems that VS typically paired with a vignette on a similar theme from *House on Mango Street*. Thus, in contrast to the seventh-grade class, the ninth-grade class did not read a novel but worked across a series of relatively short texts of different genres. These were sequentially juxtaposed; that is, the students read them one at a time in sequence. For the culminating assignment of the unit, students were to write stories inspired by the vignettes in *House on Mango Street*. Preparation for this assignment was scaffolded throughout the unit in that the students did a lot of writing "for homework" that was in the style of a text they had read and discussed in class. The writing assignments also juxtaposed texts—those generated by the students with the published ones they were reading. These assignments used genre to constrain students' writing and were potential opportunities for students to become aware of document-level differences and disciplinary genre norms. Students' writing provided some evidence of partial uptake of these forms.

The ninth-grade intertextuality unit extended over a 9-week period, during which we taped 39 lessons of 55–60 minutes in duration. The results of the activity coding are shown in Table 13.2. Class activities were dominated by discussion of the themes in the readings and writings students were doing, with class time sometimes devoted to reading short texts that were given out in class. Sometimes the focus of discussion was on a text or set of texts (including the ones students had written). Sometimes it was on students' experiences, and sometimes on relating information across texts and to students' experiences. Occasionally, students introduced into the discussion additional texts that they had encountered in their own experiences. The discussions provided opportunities for students to learn to construct and integrate and to do so across multiple

Table 13.2. Percentage of Class Time Devoted to Various Activities:
Ninth-Grade Classroom

Instructional time[a]	Literature discussion, reading texts, or interleaved	Writing, or interleaved with literature, read, or both	Grammar, vocabulary	Procedural, administrative
Week 1 (300)	33	6	20	40
Week 2 (270)	65	18	19	0
Week 3 (290)	24	65	0	10
Week 4 (230)	22	0	70	9
Week 5 (230)	26	34	22	17
Week 6 (260)	54	35	4	8
Week 7 (150)	73	27	0	0
Week 8 (290)	69	3	21	7
Week 9 (180)	62	17	0	22

[a] In minutes per week: Fluctuations in minutes of instructional time reflect out of class time due to other school activities and administrative and in-service days when students were not in class. There were five classes per week, except for Weeks 4 and 5 (4 days/week) and 7 and 9 (3 days/week).

texts. They were vehicles for creating public representations of text content, situation models, and thematically based intertext models.

The character of these discussions is exemplified by a series of lessons that occurred at the beginning of the 3rd week of school. Students had read aloud the *House on Mango Street* vignette titled *My Name*. For homework they had gotten information about the origin of their names from relatives. The next day VS had the students take out the *My Name* text and their writing about the origin of their names. After students had shared their information, VS asked "What is the importance of a name? Why is it important that you have a name?" The students offered ideas that VS wrote on the board, some of which reflected what they had found out from their relatives. She then had students read aloud a segment from a new text, *Where the Heart Is*, authored by Billy Letts (1995). This text segment had material on why names are important as well as why people changed their names, a topic the class was going to deal with in the next text VS used. When they had finished reading, VS reinstated the question but indicated that this time answers were to be constrained by the text they had just read:

> VS: Very good. Thank you. Good job you guys. What is the importance of a name, then? According to Moses Whitecotton in the book *Where the Heart Is,* what is the importance of a name?

The students responded with a number of reasons from the text and when one student said it described who you are, VS asked how, read aloud a relevant part of the text, and asked them to explain it. This pattern is similar to the one in the seventh-grade classroom. VS had the students attend to what the text said—its meaning—and then engaged them in interpreting that meaning. In this case the interpretation was relatively unconstrained by information in the text, and students offered opinions based on conceptual, emotive, and affective associations to specific words (e.g., "Candy's just all cute, and just, nothing really behind it"). The discussion continued in a similar fashion, and VS ultimately summed up the ideas that had come out in the discussion: that a name connected you to your history, gave you character, and described you. In the next phase of the lesson, VS returned to a focus on what was in the printed text, but this time it was for purposes of connecting across two printed texts. And VS provided students with the same kind of explicit instruction we saw AW provide for her seventh-grade students.

> VS: So what I want you to do is take out *My Name*. Take out *My Name*. And look at both of these texts. The *Where the Heart Is* and *My Name*. And look at both of these texts. The *Where the Heart Is* and *My Name*. Look over them. And make comparisons to the two. Look at both of them. What ideas are the same? What ideas are different? . . . Look at both of them. And look at common themes. Is—how do they interact with one another. What would Moses Whitecotton think of Esperanza? What would Moses Whitecotton think of Esperanza? Or what would Esperanza think of Moses Whitecotton?

After students had worked on this task for several minutes, VS had them share what they had written. The comments reflected a mixture of opinions and opinions backed by specific references to ideas in the texts, some of which were offered spontaneously by students but others of which were prompted by VS. The sharing process externalized interpretations across the group and constituted public construction of situation models for each text (*My Name* and *Where the Heart Is*) and of an intertext model that connected the two around the theme of the relationship of one's name and one's character and identity.

This brief vignette is representative of the class sessions in VS's ninth-grade language arts class. VS orchestrated a complex interweaving of attention to text, students' ideas, and patterns of reasoning about and from information in texts. Subsequent class sessions further developed the academic discourse patterns for justifying conclusions with evidence from the texts. Students' contributions during these classes indicated that they also moved beyond the text to create interpretative levels that integrated information from their prior experiences with the meaning constructed from the text(s) per se (Goldman & Bloome, 2001).

Conclusion

In this chapter we analyzed classroom discourse to gain some insights into how students might learn to construct and integrate. Our claim is that discussions such as those that occurred in these classrooms and that explicitly and deliberately foster intertextual approaches to reading serve to introduce and support processes in readers that are analogous to the construction and integration phases of the CI model. We see in these classrooms not strategy instruction of the didactic sort but creation of environments for engaging in discussions of text, with text, and about text that serve to create a "public" situation model. The discursive practices of the teachers provided a way of externalizing comprehension so that it could be internalized.

The talk in these classrooms did not look much like the talk we have seen in other classrooms, even when teachers are doing comprehension strategy instruction. Comprehension instruction must go beyond simply telling students to make text-to-text, text-to-world, and text-to-self connections, the recommendations of one popular book on comprehension instruction (Keene & Zimmerman, 1997). Often teachers attempt to use such strategies, but they remain at superficial levels, typically governed by associative responding on the part of students and acceptance of these responses on the part of teachers. This superficiality may be due to limitations of the materials and the way the strategies are contextualized by traditional patterns of classroom discourse characterized by short answer, known-information questions (also known as initiation–response–evaluation sequences; cf. Cazden, 2003; Mehan, 1979). Our claim is that these forms of enactment are in part due to a view of reading as a single-reader, single-text endeavor in which such connections remain private and untested against either the text itself or the larger social context. The juxtaposition of multiple texts and the connections made by multiple readers in a shared context engenders the public confrontation of differences in meaning and interpretation and the reasoned resolution of such differences. In the two classrooms considered in this chapter, our analysis of the instructional discourse suggests that the teachers provide opportunities for students to learn to construct and integrate in ways that lead to mental representations that reflect appropriately constrained interweaving of text and knowledge. These instructional conversations make public inferential thinking and reasoning processes operating on texts and experiences, both past and present. In so doing, they externalize construction and integration processes in the public discourse of the classroom.

In the work described here we have depicted language arts classrooms from the standpoint of opportunities for learning to construct and integrate. In so doing, we show how Kintsch's research and theory, situated in experimental psychology, have contributed to reconceptualizing reading comprehension in actual classrooms. The insights emanating from this effort stimulate new theorizing and empirical investigations of teaching and learning in both experimental and naturally occurring situations.

References

Bloome, D. M. (1989). Beyond access: An ethnographic study of reading and writing in a seventh grade classroom. In D. M. Bloome (Ed.), *Classrooms and literacy* (pp. 53–107). Norwood, NJ: Ablex.

Bloome, D. M., & Goldman, S. R. (1999, April). *Reconceptualizing reading as intertextual practices.* Paper presented at the annual meeting of the American Educational Research Association, Montreal, Quebec, Canada.

Bloome, D. M., & Goldman, S. R. (2002, April). *Seeing intertextuality in classroom reading and writing*. Paper presented at the annual meeting of the American Educational Research Association, New Orleans, LA.

Bloome, D. M., & Goldman, S. R. (2004). *Using multiple texts for academic learning: Social and cognitive perspectives*. Final report submitted to the Spencer Foundation.

Bloome, D. M., Goldman, S. R., Coté, N., Meyerson, P., Mayfield-Stewart, C., & Wolfe, M. B. W. (1999, April). *Reconceptualizing reading as intertextual practice*. Paper presented at the annual meeting of the American Educational Research Association, Montreal, Quebec, Canada.

Cazden, C. (2003). *Classroom discourse: The language of teaching and learning* (2nd ed.). Portsmouth, NH: Heinemann.

Chi, M. T. H. (2000). Self-explaining: The dual processes of generating inference and repairing mental models. In R. Glaser (Ed.), *Advances in instructional psychology: Vol. 5. Educational design and cognitive science* (pp. 161–238). Mahwah, NJ: Erlbaum.

Cisneros, S. (1984). *House on Mango Street*. Houston, TX: Arte Público Press.

Coles, G. (2003). *Reading the naked truth: Literacy, legislation, and lies*. New York: Heinemann.

Coté, N. C., & Goldman, S. R. (1999). Building representations of informational text: Evidence from children's think-aloud protocols. In H. Van Oostendorp & S. R. Goldman (Eds.), *The construction of mental representations during reading* (pp. 169–193). Mahwah, NJ: Erlbaum.

Coté, N. C., Goldman, S. R., & Saul, E. U. (1998). Students making sense of informational text: Relations between processing and representation. *Discourse Processes, 25,* 1–53.

Goldman, S. R. (1997). Learning from text: Reflections on the past and suggestions for the future. *Discourse Process, 23,* 357–398.

Goldman, S. R. (in press). Cognitive aspects of constructing meaning through and across multiple texts. In N. Shuart-Ferris & D. M. Bloome (Eds.), *Intertextuality and research on classroom education*. Greenwich, CT: Information Age Press.

Goldman, S. R., & Bloome, D. M. (2001, July). *Construction of intertextual models in a ninth grade classroom*. Paper presented at the annual meeting of the Society for Text and Discourse, Santa Barbara, CA.

Halldorson, M., & Singer, M. (2002). Inference processes: Integrating relevant knowledge and text information. *Discourse Processes, 34,* 145–162.

Hinton, S. E. (1967). *The outsiders*. New York: Dell.

Hunt, I. (1976). *The lottery rose*. New York: Berkley Books.

Keene, E. O., & Zimmerman, S. (1997). *Mosaic of thought*. Portsmouth, NH: Heinemann.

Kintsch, W. (1974). *The representation of meaning in memory*. Hillsdale, NJ: Erlbaum.

Kintsch, W. (1988). The role of knowledge in discourse comprehension: A construction–integration model. *Psychological Review, 95,* 163–182.

Kintsch, W. (1998). *Comprehension: A paradigm for cognition*. New York: Cambridge University Press.

Kintsch, W., Britton, B. K., Fletcher, C. R., Kintsch, E., Mannes, S. M., & Nathan, M. J. (1993). A comprehension-based approach to learning and understanding. In D. L. Medin (Ed.), *The psychology of learning and motivation: Advances in research and theory* (Vol. 30, pp. 165–214). New York: Academic Press.

Kintsch, W., & Greeno, J. G. (1985). Understanding and solving word arithmetic problems. *Psychological Review, 92,* 109–129.

Kintsch, W., & van Dijk, T. A. (1978). Toward a model of text comprehension and production. *Psychological Review, 85,* 363–394.

Landauer, T. K., & Dumais, S. T. (1997). A solution to Plato's problem: The Latent Semantic Analysis theory of acquisition, induction and representation. *Psychological Review, 104,* 211–240.

Letts, B. (1995). *Where the heart is*. New York: Warner Books.

McNamara, D. S. (2001). Reading both high and low coherence texts: Effects of text sequence and prior knowledge. *Canadian Journal of Experimental Psychology, 55,* 51–62.

Mehan, H. (1979). *Learning lessons*. Cambridge, MA: Harvard University Press.

National Institute of Child Health and Human Development. (2000). *Report of the National Reading Panel—Teaching children to read: An evidence-based assessment of the scientific research literature on reading and its implications for reading instruction* (NIH Publication No. 00-4769). Washington, DC: U.S. Government Printing Office.

Perfetti, C. A., Rouet, J. F., & Britt, M. A. (1999). Toward a theory of documents representation. In H. van Oostendorp & S. R. Goldman (Eds.), *The construction of mental representations during reading* (pp. 99–122). Mahwah, NJ: Erlbaum.

Snow, C. (2002). *Reading for understanding: Toward an R & D program in reading comprehension.* Santa Monica, CA: Rand.

van Dijk, T. A., & Kintsch, W. (1983). *Strategies of discourse comprehension.* New York: Academic Press.

Wineburg, S. (1991). Historical problem solving: A study of the cognitive processes used in the evaluation of documentary and pictorial evidence. *Journal of Educational Psychology, 83,* 73–87.

Wolfe, M. B. W., & Goldman, S. R. (2003). Use of Latent Semantic Analysis for predicting psychological phenomena: Two issues and proposed solutions. *Behavior Research Methods, Instruments, and Computers, 35,* 22–31.

Yatvin, J. (2002). *Babes in the woods: The wanderings of the National Reading Panel.* Bloomington, IN: Phi Delta Kappa International. Retrieved from http://www.pdkintl.org/kappan/k0201yat.htm

14

Computerized Learning Environments That Incorporate Research in Discourse Psychology, Cognitive Science, and Computational Linguistics

Arthur C. Graesser, Xiangen Hu, and Danielle S. McNamara

One of the salient characteristics of the research by Walter Kintsch, Tom Landauer, and Lyle Bourne is that they have attempted to solve a three-body problem. Specifically, they have attempted to productively coordinate science, computation, and application. It takes considerable depth, breadth, intelligence, and creativity to solve the three-body problem—much more than possessed by nearly all of our colleagues in experimental psychology, cognitive science, and discourse processing. Their contributions in the area of computation have included analytical models in mathematical psychology, statistical algorithms, and computer models with diverse computational architectures. They have designed, implemented, and tested several pioneering applications, including computerized learning systems, automated essay graders, and human–computer interfaces that can be effectively used by humans. The interdisciplinary vision of the three honorees for this Festschrift has profoundly inspired our research agenda, as will be made apparent in this chapter.

The research on AutoTutor and QUAID was supported by the National Science Foundation (NSF; Grants SBR 9720314, SES 9977969, REC 0106965, REC 0126265, ITR 0325428) and the Department of Defense (DoD) Multidisciplinary University Research Initiative administered by the Office of Naval Research (ONR) under Grant N00014-00-1-0600. The research on QUAID was supported by the NSF (Grant SES 9977969), on iSTART was supported by the NSF Interagency Education Research Initiative (Grant REC 0089271), and on CohMetrix was supported by the Institute for Education Sciences (IES; Grant R3056020018-02). Any opinions, findings, and conclusions or recommendations expressed in this material are those of the authors and do not necessarily reflect the views of DoD, ONR, NSF, or IES. Kurt VanLehn, Carolyn Rose, Pam Jordan, and others at the University of Pittsburgh collaborated with us in preparing AutoTutor materials on conceptual physics.

This chapter presents highlights of computerized learning environments that we have recently built and are currently testing at the interdisciplinary Institute for Intelligent Systems at the University of Memphis. The primary focus is on *AutoTutor*, a computer tutor that helps students learn by holding a conversation with them in natural language. This Web-delivered learning environment is designed with an architecture that attempts to be faithfully close to what we know about human tutoring strategies, discourse processing, cognition, and comprehension. The links among science, computation, and application will hopefully be made apparent. We then briefly describe another computer application, called *iSTART* (Interactive Strategy Trainer for Active Reading and Thinking), a trainer that helps readers learn how to use deep comprehension strategies.

AutoTutor

Graesser, Hu, and their colleagues have designed, developed, and tested Auto-Tutor. AutoTutor is a tutoring system that helps students construct answers to computer literacy questions and qualitative physics problems by holding a conversation in natural language (Graesser, Person, Harter, & the Tutoring Research Group [TRG], 2001; Graesser, Person, & Hu, 2002; Graesser, VanLehn, Rose, Jordan, & Harter, 2001; Graesser, Wiemer-Hastings, Wiemer-Hastings, Kreuz, & TRG, 1999). AutoTutor asks questions or presents problems that require approximately three to seven sentences to produce an ideal answer. However, the initial answers to these questions by students are typically only one to two sentences in length. This is where tutorial dialog is particularly helpful. AutoTutor engages the student in a mixed initiative dialog that assists the student in the evolution of an improved answer, drawing out more of the student's knowledge relevant to the answer. The dialog between AutoTutor and the student typically lasts 30 to 100 *turns* (i.e., the student expresses something, then the tutor, then the student, and so on).

AutoTutor produces several categories of *dialog moves* that facilitate covering information that is anticipated by AutoTutor's *curriculum script*. Auto-Tutor delivers its dialog moves through an animated conversational *agent* (synthesized speech, facial expressions, gestures), whereas students enter their answers using a keyboard. AutoTutor provides *feedback* to the student (positive, neutral, negative feedback), *pumps* the student for more information ("What else?"), *prompts* the student to fill in missing words, gives *hints*, fills in missing information with *assertions*, identifies and corrects bad answers, *answers* students' questions, and *summarizes* answers. As the student expresses information over many turns, the information in the three to seven sentences is eventually covered and the question is answered. During the process of supplying the ideal answer, the student periodically articulates misconceptions and false assertions. If these misconceptions have been anticipated in advance and incorporated into the program, AutoTutor provides the student with information to correct the misconceptions. Therefore, as the student expresses information over the turns, this information is compared with anticipated correct information (called *expectations*) and incorrect information (called *misconcep-*

tions), and AutoTutor formulates its dialog moves in a fashion that is sensitive to the student input. We refer to this tutoring mechanism as *expectation and misconception tailored dialog* (EMT dialog).

It is important to acknowledge that the tutorial dialog patterns of Auto-Tutor were motivated by research in discourse processing and cognition. This design of AutoTutor was inspired by explanation-based constructivist theories of learning (Chi, deLeeuw, Chiu, & LaVancher, 1994; VanLehn, Jones, & Chi, 1992), by Anderson's cognitive tutors that adaptively respond to student knowledge (Anderson, Corbett, Koedinger, & Pelletier, 1995), and by previous empirical research that has documented the collaborative constructive activities that routinely occur during human tutoring (Chi, Siler, Jeong, Yamauchi, & Hausmann, 2001; Fox, 1993; Graesser & Person, 1994; Graesser, Person, & Magliano, 1995). This research has indicated that the process of actively constructing explanations and elaborations of the learning material produces better learning than merely presenting information to students. That is, constructivism is superior to mere instructionism (information delivery). This is where human tutors excel in scaffolding learning; they guide the students in productive constructive processes and simultaneously respond to the students' information needs.

The EMT dialog moves of AutoTutor and most human tutors are not particularly sophisticated from the standpoint of ideal tutoring strategies that have been proposed in the fields of education and artificial intelligence (Graesser et al., 1995). Graesser and colleagues videotaped over 100 hours of naturalistic tutoring, transcribed the data, classified the speech act utterances into discourse categories, and analyzed the rate of particular discourse patterns. These analyses revealed that human tutors rarely implement intelligent pedagogical techniques such as bona fide Socratic tutoring strategies, modeling–scaffolding–fading, reciprocal teaching, frontier learning, building on prerequisites, or diagnosis–remediation of deep misconceptions (Collins, Brown, & Newman, 1989; Palincsar & Brown, 1984; Sleeman & Brown, 1982). In Socratic tutoring, the tutor asks learners illuminating questions that lead the learners to discover and correct their own misconceptions in an active, self-regulated fashion. In modeling–scaffolding–fading, the tutor first models a desired skill, then has the learners perform the skill while the tutor provides feedback and explanation, and finally fades from the process until the learners perform the skill all by themselves. In reciprocal teaching, the tutor and learner take turns working on problems or performing a skill, giving feedback to each other along the way. Tutors who use frontier learning select problems and give guidance in a fashion that slightly extends the boundaries of what the learner already knows or has mastered. Tutors who build on prerequisites cover the prerequisite concepts or skills in a session before moving to more complex problems and tasks that require mastery of the prerequisites. Instead of implementing these and many other sophisticated tutoring strategies, tutors tend to coach students in constructing explanations according to the EMT dialog patterns.

The EMT dialog strategy is also substantially easier to implement computationally than are the sophisticated tutoring strategies. On this dimension, the computational and psychological solutions are perfectly compatible. AutoTutor

Exhibit 14.1.   Expectations and Misconceptions for the Earth–Sun Problem

Question	The sun pulls on the earth with the force of gravity and causes the earth to move in orbit around the sun. Does the earth pull equally on the sun? Why?
Ideal answer	The force of gravity between earth and sun is an interaction between these two bodies. According to Newton's third law of motion, if one body exerts a force on the other then the other body must exert an equal and opposite force on the first body. Therefore, the sun must experience a force of gravity due to the earth, which is equal in magnitude and opposite in direction to the force of gravity on earth due to the sun.
Expectations	1) The sun exerts a gravitational force on the earth. 2) The earth exerts a gravitational force on the sun. 3) The two forces are a third-law pair. 4) The magnitudes of the two forces are the same.
Anticipated misconceptions	5) Only the larger object exerts a force. 6) The force of earth on sun may be less than that of sun on earth.

uses latent semantic analysis (LSA) for its conceptual pattern-matching algorithm when evaluating whether student input matches the expectations and misconceptions. LSA is discussed in more detail within other chapters in this volume because Tom Landauer, Walter Kintsch, and their colleagues were pioneers in inventing, testing, and applying it (Foltz, Gilliam, & Kendall, 2000; E. Kintsch et al., 2000; W. Kintsch, 1998, 2001; Landauer & Dumais, 1997; Landauer, Foltz, & Laham, 1998). LSA is a high-dimensional, statistical technique that, among other things, measures the conceptual similarity of any two pieces of text, such as a word, sentence, paragraph, or lengthier document. To do so, a cosine between the LSA vector associated with expectation (E) or misconception (M) and the vector associated with student input (S) is calculated. An E or M is scored as covered if the match between E or M and the student's text input S meets some threshold, which has varied between .40 and .65 in previous instantiations of AutoTutor.

As an example, consider the question and ideal answer in Exhibit 14.1. The ideal answer has a paragraph of information that captures the reasoning behind the answer to the question. There are four key expectations embedded within the ideal answer; AutoTutor expects these answers to be covered in a complete answer and will direct the dialog in a fashion that finesses the students to articulate these expectations (through prompts and hints). AutoTutor stays on topic by completing the subdialog that covers Expectation E before starting a subdialog on another expectation. For example, suppose that Expectation 2 needs to be articulated in the answer. The following family of prompts is available to encourage the student to articulate particular content words in Expectation 2 (*The earth exerts a gravitational force on the sun*).

a) The gravitational force of the earth is exerted on the _____
b) The sun has exerted on it the gravitational force of the _____

       c) What force is exerted between the sun and earth? _____
       d) The earth exerts on the sun a gravitational _____

AutoTutor first considers everything the student expresses during Turns 1 through N to evaluate whether Expectation 2 is covered. If the student has failed to articulate one of the four content words (*sun, earth, gravitational, force*), AutoTutor selects the corresponding prompt (a, b, c, and d, respectively). Therefore, if the student has made three assertions at a particular point in the dialog, then all possible combinations of assertions X, Y, and Z would be considered in the matches (i.e., cosine [vector E, vector S]): X, Y, Z, XY, XZ, YZ, XYZ. The maximum cosine match score is used to assess whether Expectation 2 is covered. If the match meets or exceeds Threshold T, then Expectation 2 is covered. If the match is less than T, then AutoTutor selects the prompt (or hint) that has the best chance of improving the match (i.e., if the student provides the correct answer to the prompt). Only explicit statements by the student are considered to determine whether expectations are covered. As such, this approach is compatible with constructivist learning theories that emphasize the importance of the student generating the answer.

The conversation is finished for the question in Exhibit 14.1 when all four expectations are covered. In the meantime, if the student articulates information that matches Misconception 5 or 6, the misconception is corrected as a subdialog, and then the conversation returns to finishing coverage of the expectations. Again, the process of covering all four expectations and correcting misconceptions that arise normally requires a dialog of 30 to 100 turns (or 15–50 student turns).

In addition to asking questions, AutoTutor attempts to handle questions posed by the student. However, it is somewhat surprising that students rarely ask questions in classrooms, human tutoring sessions, and AutoTutor sessions (Graesser & Olde, 2003; Graesser & Person, 1994; Otero & Graesser, 2001). The rate of student questions is one student question per 6 to 7 hours in a classroom environment and one per 10 minutes in tutoring. Although it is pedagogically disappointing that students ask so few questions, the good news is that this aspect of human tutor interaction makes it easier to build a dialog-based intelligent tutoring system such as AutoTutor. It is not computationally feasible to interpret any arbitrary student input from scratch and to construct a mental space that adequately captures what the student has in mind. Instead, the best that AutoTutor can do is to compare student input with expectations through pattern matching operations. Therefore, what human tutors and students do is compatible with what currently can be handled computationally within AutoTutor.

At this point, our research group is fine-tuning the LSA-based pattern matches between student input and AutoTutor's expected input. The good news is that LSA does a moderately impressive job of determining whether the information in student essays matches particular expectations associated with an ideal answer. For example, in one of our recent studies, we asked experts in physics or computer literacy to make judgments concerning whether particular expectations were covered within student essays. A coverage score was computed as the proportion of expectations in the student essay that judges believed were covered, using either stringent or lenient criteria. Similarly, LSA was used to compute the proportion of expectations covered, using varying thresholds of cosine values on whether information in the student essay matched each expectation. Correlations between the LSA scores and the judges' coverage scores were approximately .50 for both conceptual physics (Olde, Franceschetti, Karnavat, Graesser, & TRG, 2002) and computer literacy (Graesser et al., 2000). Correlations generally increase as the length of the text increases, yielding correlations as high as .73 (Foltz et al., 2000). LSA metrics also did a reasonable job tracking the coverage of expectations and the identification of misconceptions during the course of AutoTutor's tutorial dialogs.

Unfortunately, sometimes the thresholds are not set right and there are undesirable consequences. If the threshold is set too low, then the expectations are considered as covered without the students articulating enough information. If the threshold is set too high, then students become extremely irritated. They believe they have covered an expectation (sometimes over several turns), but the threshold is not quite met so AutoTutor does not agree. One method to handle this problem is to compute different threshold values on the basis of the expectations that need to be covered. For example, the threshold should be set higher to the extent that the expectation has more words or a higher vector length. This approach takes into consideration chance probabilities of a match. That is, the chance value of the cosine match between two documents increases monotonically as a function of the size (number of words) of the documents, being as high as .50 for 256-word texts that have words randomly selected from a physics textbook (Penumatsa et al., 2003). However, there are alternative, more dynamic LSA evaluations of matches discussed below.

After examining the LSA spaces for a number of corpora, we realized, and later proved mathematically, that the first dimension of the LSA vector is always the same sign (Hu, Cai, Franceschetti, et al., 2003). We also discovered from various tests that the first dimension is not diagnostic in predicting matches between pairs of texts. Given these facts, we made several improvements in the use of LSA in AutoTutor. In one modification, we first applied some preprocessing of the LSA space. This includes (a) deemphasizing the first dimension of the LSA vector when computing cosine matches between documents, (b) weighting dimensions with a monotonic function of the singular values (from the singular value decomposition of the original co-occurrence matrix), and (c) normalizing dimensions of LSA space. We then used relative cosine values (that are compared with a threshold that is a function of the sizes of the contribution and expectation) rather than absolute cosine values when evaluating students' contributions. This approach is believed to improve the metric of similarity between pairs of texts (e.g., student input and expectations).

After examining the mathematics of LSA, we were able to identify formal relations between explicit similarity measures (such as weighted keyword matches between two documents) and LSA-based similarity measures (such as LSA cosine matches; Hu, Cai, Louwerse, et al., 2003, Theorem 2). This led us to improve LSA in AutoTutor in a different direction. First, in the EMT dialog in AutoTutor, the student usually makes several attempts to cover an expectation. AutoTutor uses LSA to evaluate every contribution from the student. If AutoTutor were using explicit similarity measures, then for every contribution the student makes to cover an expectation, AutoTutor should be able to explicitly decompose the contributions into four different types of information: (a) new and relevant, (b) new and irrelevant, (c) old and relevant, and (d) old and irrelevant. Such a decomposition for an LSA-based similarity measure can be approximated, on the basis of the relationship between LSA cosine matches and explicit similarity measures between documents. To approximate such a decomposition in EMT dialog, we used a method called the *span method*.

To better understand the span method, consider the LSA vector for the target (expectation) as $\mathbf{E}$, and contributions from the student as $\mathbf{C}_1,...,\mathbf{C}_n$. The first step is to decompose $\mathbf{C}_1$ into two vectors: one that is parallel to $\mathbf{E}$ (new and relevant) and another vector that is perpendicular to $\mathbf{E}$ (new and irrelevant). $\mathbf{C}_2$ is decomposed into two vectors: one that is parallel to $\mathbf{C}_1$ (*old*, because it is contained in $\mathbf{C}_1$) and another that is perpendicular to $\mathbf{C}_1$ (*new*, because it is not in $\mathbf{C}_1$). Furthermore, *old* information is decomposed into two vectors: parallel to $\mathbf{E}$ (old and relevant) and perpendicular to $\mathbf{E}$ (old and irrelevant). Similarly, *new* information is decomposed into two vectors: parallel to $\mathbf{E}$ (new and relevant) and perpendicular to $\mathbf{E}$ (new and irrelevant). For $\mathbf{C}_3$, there is a decomposition into two parts: perpendicular to the *span* of $\mathbf{C}_1$ and $\mathbf{C}_2$ (*new*, because it is not contained in $\mathbf{C}_1$ and $\mathbf{C}_2$) and parallel to the *span* of $\mathbf{C}_1$ and $\mathbf{C}_2$ (*old*, because it is contained in $\mathbf{C}_1$ and $\mathbf{C}_2$). For contribution $\mathbf{C}_i$, new information is the decomposed vector of $\mathbf{C}_i$ that is perpendicular to the span of $\mathbf{C}_1, \mathbf{C}_2,... \mathbf{C}_{i-1}$ and old information is the decomposed vector that is parallel to the span of $\mathbf{C}_1, \mathbf{C}_2,... \mathbf{C}_{i-1}$. We found that this span method performed much better in evaluating students' contributions (Hu, Cai, Louwerse, et al., 2003).

The question arises whether AutoTutor is successful in promoting learning gains. It is well established that one-to-one tutoring is a powerful method of promoting learning (Cohen, Kulik, & Kulik, 1982; Corbett, 2001), even though the vast majority of the human tutors have moderate domain knowledge and little or no training in pedagogy or tutoring. These unaccomplished human tutors enhanced learning with an effect size of .4 standard deviation units (called *sigmas*), which translates to approximately an improvement of half a letter grade (Cohen et al., 1982). According to Bloom (1984), accomplished human tutors produce effect sizes of 2 sigma (although the magnitude of this effect is suspect because of the relatively small number of studies that have looked at accomplished tutors). In the area of computer tutors, intelligent tutoring systems with sophisticated pedagogical tactics, but no natural language dialog, produce effect sizes of approximately 1 sigma (Corbett, 2001). Previous versions of AutoTutor have produced gains of 0.4 to 1.5 sigma ($M = 0.8$), depending on the learning performance measure, the comparison condition (either pretest scores or a control condition in which the learner reads the textbook for an equivalent amount of time as the tutoring session), the subject matter, and the version of AutoTutor (Graesser et al., 2003; Person, Graesser, Bautista, Mathews, & TRG, 2001). These results place previous versions of AutoTutor somewhere between an unaccomplished human tutor and an intelligent tutoring system. Moreover, one recent evaluation of physics tutoring remarkably reported that the learning gains produced by accomplished human tutors in computer-mediated communication were equivalent to the gains produced by AutoTutor.

We have focused on LSA in this section, but it is important to point out that AutoTutor has many other components that are needed to manage a mixed initiative dialog with the student. AutoTutor attempts to handle any input that the student types in, whether it is grammatical or ungrammatical. This is possible in part because of the recent advances in computational linguistics that have provided lexicons, corpora, syntactic parsers, shallow semantic interpreters, and a repository of free automated modules (Jurafsky & Martin, 2000). AutoTutor currently manages a surprisingly smooth conversation with the student, even though it does not deeply analyze the meaning of the student contributions, does not build a detailed common ground, and does not have an intelligent symbolic planner. We have tuned the dialog facilities of AutoTutor to the point where bystanders cannot accurately decide whether a particular dialog move was generated by AutoTutor or a human tutor (Person, Graesser, & TRG, 2002). Thus, it has surprisingly passed our bystander Tutoring test when assessing individual dialog moves. Our next steps include blending in deeper comprehension modules, dialog planners, and pedagogical strategies, and determining the extent to which these sophisticated components improve learning gains.

iSTART

Similar to AutoTutor, iSTART (Interactive Strategy Trainer for Active Reading and Thinking) is based on the assumption that actively constructing explanations and elaborations of written material produce better learning and comprehension than passive reading. Active, strategic reading processes are particularly critical when the reading material is difficult or less cohesive, such as science texts. Danielle McNamara and colleagues are developing this automated reading strategy trainer for high school and college classrooms to help students learn strategies that improve comprehension of challenging text material. The development of iSTART was largely inspired by work conducted by the three honorees. Walter Kintsch's construction–integration model of text comprehension provided the backbone and foundation of this research program (W. Kintsch, 1988). In addition, research showing that the inhibitory effects of text incohesion were accentuated for low-knowledge readers indicated a need to help struggling students better deal with these inevitable texts (McNamara, Kintsch, Songer, & Kintsch, 1996; McNamara & Kintsch, 1996). Work by Lyle Bourne (Healy & Bourne, 1995) emphasized the dependence of long-term, stable knowledge acquisition on learning situations that target cognitive processes that are needed to perform well on retention or comprehension tests. Finally, Tom Landauer's work on LSA (Landauer & Dumais, 1997) inspired the tools necessary to appropriately interact with students during reading strategy training (Magliano, Wiemer-Hastings, Millis, Muñoz, & McNamara, 2002; Millis, Magliano, Wiemer-Hastings, & McNamara, 2001).

iSTART is based on previous experiments that demonstrated that self-explanation coupled with reading strategy training (Self-Explanation Reading Training, or SERT) increases comprehension scores and course grades (McNamara, 2003; McNamara & Scott, 1999). SERT was inspired by previous research showing the benefits of strategy instruction (Bielaczyc, Pirolli, & Brown, 1995; Palincsar & Brown, 1984). The SERT intervention is much like techniques based on thinking aloud (Baumann, Seifert-Kessell, & Jones, 1992; Coté, Goldman, & Saul, 1998). However, SERT places greater emphasis on the use of active reading strategies to explain the text than have previous think-aloud interventions. The basis for SERT was a technique called *self-explanation*, the process of explaining the meaning of text while reading. Readers who explain the text either spontaneously or when prompted to do so understand more from the text and construct better mental models of the content (Chi et al., 1994). Unfortunately, some readers self-explain poorly. Reading strategy instruction within SERT (and iSTART) improves the quality and effectiveness of self-explanation. In turn, the process of self-explanation helps the reader to better learn the reading strategies by rendering them more tangible.

iSTART delivers reading strategy training using an interactive and adaptive format. Pedagogical agents interact with each other and with the user to increase active processing and participation by the student. Like SERT, iSTART begins with a brief instruction that includes definitions and examples of self-explanation and reading strategies. The strategies focus on the benefits of predicting what the text will say, making bridging inferences between separate ideas in the text, using prior knowledge and logic to understand the text, and monitoring comprehension. After this instructional phase, the student identifies which strategies are being used within examples of self-explanation. The student then types in explanations to sentences from science texts. The system analyzes the self-explanations and provides feedback to the user. Thus, iSTART includes four activities: instruction, modeling, strategy identification, and practice.

Closing Comments

As in the case of our three honorees, we have recognized the importance of interdisciplinary research and of integrating science, computation, and applications. The challenges of this vintage of research are profound and sometimes painful, but the products of our efforts are particularly rewarding. In addition to AutoTutor and iSTART, we have developed some additional computer-based applications. We have a Web site that helps military personnel learn and retrieve information about the ethical conduct of research on humans (called the *HURA Advisor*). We have developed a Web site that helps survey methodologists improve questions on questionnaires by critiquing questions with respect to comprehension difficulty (called *QUAID*). More recently, we developed a Web facility that analyzes texts on dozens of dimensions of language, cohesion, and comprehension difficulty (called *CohMetrix*). Our hope is that our research and applications will positively impact our field and society. We consider ourselves fortunate to be following the footsteps of scientists whose work will have a genuine impact on the world.

References

Anderson, J. R., Corbett, A. T., Koedinger, K. R., & Pelletier, R. (1995). Cognitive tutors: Lessons learned. *Journal of the Learning Sciences, 4,* 167–207.

Baumann, J. F., Seifert-Kessell, N., & Jones, L. A. (1992). Effect of think-aloud instruction on elementary students' comprehension monitoring abilities. *Journal of Reading Behavior, 24,* 143–172.

Bielaczyc, K., Pirolli, P. L., & Brown, A. L. (1995). Training in self-explanation and self-regulation strategies: Investigating the effects of knowledge acquisition activities on problem solving. *Cognition and Instruction, 13,* 221–252.

Bloom, B. S. (1984). The 2-sigma problem: The search for methods of group instruction as effective as one-to-one tutoring. *Educational Researcher, 13,* 4–16.

Chi, M. T. H., de Leeuw, N., Chiu, M., & LaVancher, C. (1994). Eliciting self-explanation improves understanding. *Cognitive Science, 18,* 439–477.

Chi, M. T. H., Siler, S., Jeong, H., Yamauchi, T., & Hausmann, R. G. (2001). Learning from human tutoring. *Cognitive Science, 25,* 471–533.

Cohen, P. A., Kulik, J. A., & Kulik, C. C. (1982). Educational outcomes of tutoring: A meta-analysis of findings. *American Educational Research Journal, 19,* 237–248.

Collins, A., Brown, J. S., & Newman, S. E. (1989). Cognitive apprenticeship: Teaching the craft of reading, writing, and mathematics. In L. B. Resnick (Ed.), *Knowing, learning, and instruction: Essays in honor of Robert Glaser* (pp. 453–494). Hillsdale, NJ: Erlbaum.

Corbett, A. T. (2001). Cognitive computer tutors: Solving the two-sigma problem. In *Proceedings of the Eighth International Conference on User Modeling* (pp. 137–147). London: Springer-Verlag.

Coté, N. C., Goldman, S. R., & Saul, E. U. (1998). Students making sense of informational text: Relations between processing and representation. *Discourse Processes, 25,* 1–53.

Foltz, P. W., Gilliam, S., & Kendall, S. (2000). Supporting content-based feedback in on-line writing evaluation with LSA. *Interactive Learning Environments, 8,* 111–127.

Fox, B. (1993). *The human tutorial dialog project.* Hillsdale, NJ: Erlbaum.

Graesser, A. C., Jackson, G. T., Mathews, E. C., Mitchell, H. H., Olney, A., Ventura, M., et al. (2003). Why/AutoTutor: A test of learning gains from a physics tutor with natural language dialog. In R. Alterman & D. Hirsh (Eds.), *Proceedings of the 25th Annual Conference of the Cognitive Science Society* (pp. 1–5). Boston: Cognitive Science Society.

Graesser, A. C., & Olde, B. A. (2003). How does one know whether a person understands a device? The quality of the questions the person asks when the device breaks down. *Journal of Educational Psychology, 95,* 524–536.

Graesser, A. C., & Person, N. K. (1994). Question asking during tutoring. *American Educational Research Journal, 31,* 104–137.

Graesser, A. C., Person, N. K., Harter, D., & the Tutoring Research Group. (2001). Teaching tactics and dialog in AutoTutor. *International Journal of Artificial Intelligence in Education, 12,* 257–279.

Graesser, A. C., Person, N., & Hu, X. (2002). Improving comprehension through discourse processes. *New Directions in Teaching and Learning, 89,* 33–44.

Graesser, A. C., Person, N. K., & Magliano, J. P. (1995). Collaborative dialogue patterns in naturalistic one-to-one tutoring. *Applied Cognitive Psychology, 9,* 1–28.

Graesser, A. C., VanLehn, K., Rose, C., Jordan, P., & Harter, D. (2001). Intelligent tutoring systems with conversational dialogue. *AI Magazine, 22,* 39–51.

Graesser, A. C., Wiemer-Hastings, P., Wiemer-Hastings, K., Harter, D., Person, N., & the Tutoring Research Group. (2000). Using latent semantic analysis to evaluate the contributions of students in AutoTutor. *Interactive Learning Environments, 8,* 129–148.

Graesser, A. C., Wiemer-Hastings, K., Wiemer-Hastings, P., Kreuz, R., & the Tutoring Research Group. (1999). Auto Tutor: A simulation of a human tutor. *Journal of Cognitive Systems Research, 1,* 35–51.

Healy, A. F., & Bourne, L. E., Jr. (Eds.). (1995). *Learning and memory of knowledge and skills: Durability and specificity.* Thousand Oaks, CA: Sage.

Hu, X., Cai, Z., Franceschetti, D. R., Penumatsa, P., Graesser, A. C., Louwerse, M., et al. (2003). LSA: The first dimension and dimensional weighting. In R. Alterman & D. Hirsh (Eds.), *Proceedings of the 25th Annual Conference of the Cognitive Science Society* (pp. 1–6). Boston: Cognitive Science Society.

Hu, X., Cai, Z., Louwerse, M., Olney, A., Penumatsa, P., Graesser, A. C., & the Tutoring Research Group. (2003). A revised algorithm for latent semantic analysis. In *Proceedings of the 18th International Joint Conference in Artificial Intelligence* (pp. 1489–1491). San Francisco: Morgan Kaufmann.

Jurafsky, D., & Martin, J. H. (2000). *Speech and language processing: An introduction to natural language processing, computational linguistics, and speech recognition.* Upper Saddle River, NJ: Prentice-Hall.

Kintsch, E., Steinhart, D., Stahl, G., Matthews, C., Lamb, R., & LSA Group. (2000). Developing summarization skills through the use of LSA-based feedback. *Interactive Learning Environments, 8,* 87–110.

Kintsch, W. (1988). The use of knowledge in discourse processing: A construction–integration model. *Psychological Review, 95,* 163–182.

Kintsch, W. (1998). *Comprehension: A paradigm for cognition.* Cambridge, England: Cambridge University Press.

Kintsch, W. (2001). Predication. *Cognitive Science, 25,* 173–202.

Landauer, T. K., & Dumais, S. T. (1997). A solution to Plato's problem: The latent semantic analysis theory of the acquisition, induction, and representation of knowledge. *Psychological Review, 104,* 211–240.

Landauer, T. K., Foltz, P. W., & Laham, D. (1998). An introduction to latent semantic analysis. *Discourse Processes, 25,* 259–284.

Magliano, J. P., Wiemer-Hastings, K., Millis, K. K., Muñoz, B. D., & McNamara, D. S. (2002). Using latent semantic analysis to assess reader strategies. *Behavior Research Methods, Instruments, and Computers, 34,* 181–188.

McNamara, D. S. (2003). *SERT: Self-Explanation Reading Training.* Unpublished manuscript, University of Memphis.

McNamara, D. S., & Kintsch, W. (1996). Learning from text: Effects of prior knowledge and text coherence. *Discourse Processes, 22,* 247–287.

McNamara, D. S., Kintsch, E., Songer, N. B., & Kintsch, W. (1996). Are good texts always better? Text coherence, background knowledge, and levels of understanding in learning from text. *Cognition and Instruction, 14,* 1–43.

McNamara, D. S., & Scott, J. L. (1999). Training reading strategies. In M. Hahn & S. C. Stoness (Eds.), *Proceedings of the 21st Annual Conference of the Cognitive Science Society* (pp. 387–392). Hillsdale, NJ: Erlbaum.

Millis, K. K, Magliano, J. P., Wiemer-Hastings, K., & McNamara, D. S. (2001). Using LSA in a computer-based test of reading comprehension. In J. D. Moore, C. Luckhardt-Redfield, & W. L. Johnson (Eds.), *Artificial intelligence in education* (pp. 583–585). Amsterdam: IOS Press.

Olde, B. A., Franceschetti, D. R., Karnavat, A., Graesser, A. C., & the Tutoring Research Group. (2002). The right stuff: Do you need to sanitize your corpus when using latent semantic analysis? In W. Gray & C. Schunn (Eds.), *Proceedings of the 24th Annual Conference of the Cognitive Science Society* (pp. 708–713). Mahwah, NJ: Erlbaum.

Otero, J., & Graesser, A. C. (2001). PREG: Elements of a model of question asking. *Cognition and Instruction, 19,* 143–175.

Palincsar, A. M., & Brown, A. L. (1984). Reciprocal teaching of comprehension fostering and comprehension monitoring activities. *Cognition and Instruction, 1,* 117–176.

Penumatsa, P., Ventura, M., Olde, B. A., Franceschetti, D. R., Graesser, A. C., & the Tutoring Research Group. (2003). The right threshold value: What is the right threshold of cosine measure when using latent semantic analysis for evaluating student answers? In *Proceedings of the 2003 Florida Artificial Intelligence Research Conference.* Menlo Park, CA: AAAI Press.

Person, N. K., Graesser, A. C., Bautista, L., Mathews, E. C., & the Tutoring Research Group. (2001). Evaluating student learning gains in two versions of AutoTutor. In J. D. Moore, C. L.

Redfield, & W. L. Johnson (Eds.), *Artificial intelligence in education: AI-ED in the wired and wireless future* (pp. 286–293). Amsterdam: IOS Press.

Person, N. K., Graesser, A. C., & the Tutoring Research Group. (2002). Human or computer? AutoTutor in a bystander Turing test. In S. A. Cerri, G. Gouarderes, & F. Paraguacu (Eds.), *Intelligent tutoring systems 2002* (pp. 821–830). Berlin: Springer.

Sleeman, D., & Brown, J. (Eds.). (1982). *Intelligent tutoring systems*. New York: Academic Press.

VanLehn, K., Jones, R. M., & Chi, M. T. H. (1992). A model of the self-explanation effect. *Journal of the Learning Sciences, 2,* 1–60.

Part VI

Knowledge Representation

15

On Quantifying and Characterizing Human Knowledge

Raymond S. Nickerson

It is a delight to be able to participate in a celebration of the distinguished careers of three such extraordinary experimenters as Lyle E. Bourne, Jr., Walter Kintsch, and Tom Landauer. The inspiration for this chapter is some work by Landauer. I am focusing on him simply because I know him best, having had the good fortune of interacting with him in many contexts over the years—always a pleasure and a learning experience for me.

Space constraints preclude even a cursory review of Landauer's work, which spans a most impressive range—from fundamental theoretical and empirical research on human memory to highly applied work on human–computer interaction. Given the need to focus, and because the invitation to participate in this volume indicated that authors were expected to describe some of their own work, I decided to try to make some connections between ideas expressed in some of Landauer's articles on human knowledge—or long-term memory if you prefer—and some data and thoughts of my own on the subject.

What do people know? What can people know? How is knowledge acquired? How is it organized in people's heads? Philosophers have reflected on these and related questions for centuries; more recently, psychologists have explored some of them by experimentation. Landauer has thought and written about questions of this sort. I note four articles in particular that I have found especially interesting: one on how knowledge may be represented biochemically (Landauer, 1964), another on how what is in one's memory is organized—or not (Landauer, 1975), a third on the question of how much knowledge people acquire and retain over a lifetime (Landauer, 1986), and one, with Susan Dumais, on how knowledge is acquired (Landauer & Dumais, 1997). What I find so inspiring about this work is that, besides providing insights into human

I am grateful to Susan Butler, Michael Carlin, Salvatore Soraci, and Yvonne Wakeford for help in collecting the previously unpublished data that are reported in this chapter.

cognition, it, like much of the best work in science, provokes a host of interesting questions.

One of the questions that Landauer's work prompts for me is, What is the character of human knowledge? I want to argue that knowledge has several identifiable characteristics that have implications for how we study it, measure it, and attempt to extend it though education. Some of these characteristics are obvious on reflection; some have been revealed by experimentation. In what follows I suggest what a few of these characteristics are, illustrating points, when possible, with data collected for a variety of purposes. Some of the suggestions, if correct, complicate the task of quantification, but perhaps they jointly capture something of the complex amalgam of facts, beliefs, assumptions, inferences, and uncertainties that knowledge is.

Limited, but How and Why?

That human knowledge is limited is painfully apparent to all of us. But how limited it is, and what determines its limit, are open questions. There are several estimates in the literature of how much individuals might know about specific topics. Landauer (1986) took the knowledge estimation game to another level by setting himself the task of estimating how much information a well-educated adult acquires and retains over a lifetime, which he defined (I wish he had been more generous) as 70 years. With several ingenious approaches to estimation, he converged on 1 billion bits—roughly the number of bits required to store the text of between 100 and 150 average-sized (300–400 page) books. There are two points I want to make about this estimate: First, it seems to me as plausible as any other I have seen, and, second, whatever the correct number is, we may be reasonably sure it does not represent a capacity limitation.

Simon and Gilmartin (1973) estimated that a chess master must have approximately 50,000 chunks of information stored in memory to be able to recognize frequently encountered chessboard configurations. What they meant by a chunk of information is not entirely clear, but suppose that a chunk is a particular board configuration. Given that it takes 3, 1, and 6 bits to identify respectively a chess piece, its color, and its location, and that during play there can be from 2 to 32 pieces on the board, it can take from 20 to 320 bits to represent a configuration. Assuming that, on average, there are about 20 pieces on the board, it takes, on average, about 200 bits to represent a configuration, or about 10 million to represent 50,000 of them.

Of course, a chess master has knowledge about chess that goes beyond the ability to recognize board configurations. He or she presumably knows the rules of the game and something of its history, how to select promising moves contingent on board configurations, and certain canonical strategies of attack and defense. He or she probably remembers various aspects of games played in the past, has some knowledge of the capabilities and vulnerabilities of opposing players, and so on. Let us assume, for the sake of argument, that this information requires roughly the same amount of storage as does the representation of the 50,000 board configurations. This gets us to about 20 million bits (about the equivalent of the text of two to three average-size books) as an estimate of what a master chess player knows (counting the 50,000 configurations) about chess. I certainly am not prepared to defend this estimate very vigorously, but it seems to me no less plausible than any other one might derive.

If we take these numbers semiseriously, the implication is that a 70-year-old holds in memory somewhere on the order of 50 times as much information as a chess master holds about chess. This does not mean, of course, that the average 70-year-old is an expert in 50 different areas, at least if an expert is taken to mean someone who knows a lot about an area that few other people know. However, it is easy to overlook how much everyone knows that does not qualify as expertise simply because everyone else knows it too. This estimate of what people may know in specific domains seems not inconsistent with Landauer's global estimate of what a person may acquire and retain over a lifetime.

One billion bits seems like quite a lot of information from one point of view, but as Landauer points out, to acquire one billion bits in 70 years, one must add to one's memory store (net of losses that occur) about two thirds of a bit per second when one is awake. From this chapter, assuming it takes about half an hour to read, you should retain indefinitely about 1,200 bits, or roughly the number it takes to represent about 20 to 25 words of printed text. If I could boil down what I would like you to remember into a not-long sentence expressed in a sufficiently dramatic way as to imprint it indelibly in your memory, this chapter could be reduced to about 1/300 of its actual length. Unfortunately for both of us, I do not know how to do that.

The estimate of 1 billion bits of information acquired and retained over a lifetime will seem to some intuitively to be too high and to others to be too low. It seems to me neither unreasonable nor inconsistent with anything else we know about cognition, and I am impressed with the multiavenue approach that Landauer took to arrive at it. In any case, I assume we would all agree that there is a limit to how much information people retain. A question the answer to which would have significant implications for education is: How does the amount of knowledge that the average person retains compare with what he or she is capable of retaining?

I think there are good reasons to believe, and am sure that Landauer does too, that whatever the amount of knowledge is that we typically acquire and retain, it does not come close to the maximum amount possible. In response to being criticized for not writing an article other than the one he wrote (Hunter, 1988), he made it clear that his estimate had to do not with how much information the brain is capable of holding, but with how much people, in fact, acquire (Landauer, 1988). Given what we currently know about the capacity of the physiological system or systems that may be involved in mediating memory— neuronal synapses and networks, glial cells (Landauer, 1964), hormones, cyclic AMP, molecules of DNA and RNA, and who knows what else—there is little reason to believe that many of us run up against anything like an insurmountable barrier to learning more than we do.

Fragmentary

Most of us, I suspect, know a little about many topics. If asked, we could name a few of the countries of the world, a few of the chemical elements, a few species of birds. We know a little about history, a little about astronomy, a little about first aid, a little about law. But a probe of our knowledge about most subjects would find it to be neither very broad nor very deep. Even with respect to subjects we know relatively well, our knowledge tends to be very spotty.

My colleagues and I have had people generate lists of items in specified categories from memory. Plots of the number of items produced by individuals as a function of time have generally been well fitted by an equation of the form

$$n(t) = n(\infty)(1 - e^{-\lambda t}),$$

where $n(t)$, is the number of words produced by time t, $n(\infty)$ is the curve's asymptote, and λ is the parameter representing the speed at which the curve approaches asymptote. Both parameters vary considerably with the type of lists that are produced and from person to person for any given type. I do not claim that an exponential always provides the best fit to the data, but it generally does a reasonably good job, and it is what a relatively simple model of the search process would predict (Nickerson, 1980). In most cases, people produce half of all the items they will eventually produce in a very few—5 or fewer—minutes.

Typically people are not able to produce large percentages of the items in the categories we have used. In one study (Nickerson, Smith, & Wallach, 1981), 62 subjects listed as many birds as they could and another 62 subjects listed countries. The study was focused on part-set cuing, but control subjects (who simply listed names without the benefit of cues) listed, on average, 32 birds and 71 countries. Consulting ornithology books and books on world facts, we estimated the number of possibilities for birds and countries to be approximately 347 and 165, respectively. So our subjects produced, on average, only about 9% of the names of birds and about 43% of the names of countries. We speculated that the larger percentage in the latter case could have been due in part to having more country names in memory, but that country names might also be easier to access because stored geographical–spatial representations might facilitate search.

In studies currently under way, *knowledge-probing* tasks that we have used include naming the chemical elements, presidents of the United States, musical instruments, mammals, and members of assorted other categories. Sometimes we have had people give confidence ratings on their answers. Sometimes we have asked them to estimate how well other people—peers—would do on the tasks described. And sometimes we have provided the answers to questions and asked subjects whether they would have been able to give the answer had they been asked.

One group of 46 college students listed chemical elements. The mean number listed was 20.4 (*Mdn* = 19). Individual lists varied in length from 1 to 53 (the latter was an outlier; the next largest number was 37). Very few of the

Table 15.1. Chemical Elements Most Frequently Appearing on Lists Produced by 46 College Students in the Order of Frequency of Their Appearance on the Lists

Hydrogen	44	Helium	34	Silver	32	Chlorine	28	Copper	22	Zinc	20
Oxygen	42	Sodium	33	Iron	30	Calcium	23	Boron	21	Neon	18
Carbon	39	Gold	32	Magnesium	29	Aluminum	22	Lithium	21	Fluorine	17
Nitrogen	35	Potassium	32	Sulfur	29	Argon	22	Uranium	21	Lead	16

Note. The number after each name is the number of lists on which that name appeared.

students could name more than a small percentage of the 109 elements in the periodic table as of 1982; none could list half and only 3 could list a third or more.[1] Table 15.1 shows the 24 elements listed by at least one third of the subjects, in the order of the frequency with which they appeared on the lists. Only 14 of the elements appeared on at least half of them. Two conclusions can be drawn from these results: (a) The knowledge of this group of students of the contents of the periodic table, at least as revealed by their ability to list the elements on request, is not very extensive; and (b) what a small random subset of the subjects in this study knows (and does not know) is likely to be reasonably representative of what other members of the group know (and do not know).

Another group of 29 students (all U.S. citizens) listed U.S. presidents. The mean number of presidents listed was 13.9 (*Mdn* = 14); individual lists varied in length from 8 to 28. As in the case of elements, the names of certain presidents appear to be relatively common knowledge among this group of students; those of certain others appear to be considerably less well-known. The more frequently listed names were G. Washington (29), W. Clinton (29), G. Bush (28), G. W. Bush (28), A. Lincoln (25), R. Nixon (25), J. Kennedy (24), R. Reagan (22), T. Roosevelt (19), F. Roosevelt (18), and T. Jefferson (17). The less frequently listed names were B. Harrison (0), J. Buchanan (0), W. Harrison (0), W. Harding (1), C. Arthur (1), R. Hayes (1), A. Johnson (1), Z. Taylor (1), M. Filmore (2), J. Tyler (2), and J. Madison (2).

Lists of other categories tend to show the same general properties: large individual differences among people with respect to the number of items they produce; production of a relatively small percentage of the members of the category (presumably people would recognize more items than they can produce on request); most of the items on a list being produced in the first few minutes, the rate of production falling roughly exponentially with time; large individual differences among category items with respect to the percentage of lists on which they appear; and considerable commonality among subjects with respect to the items they produce.

---

[1]The creation of several (at least four) ultra-heavy elements beyond Meitnerium (atomic number 109) has been announced by various research groups since 1994. As of 2002, these had not yet been named, except with the placeholder code used by the International Union of Pure and Applied Chemistry (Stwertka, 2002), and they are ignored in this chapter.

Content Addressable

People find it easy to search their memories on the basis of almost any criterion one might wish to state. Think of words that begin with *t*, or that have *r* in the third letter position, or that end in *ough*, or that have three syllables, or that have different meanings depending on which syllable is accented, or. . . . We have little difficulty in searching memory for specific items of knowledge we have, although we are not always able to find all that it is reasonable to assume is there. If asked to produce a list of the world's larger cities, major composers, vegetables, . . . , you would probably find it easy to produce items as fast as you could write them down at first, at least for a few moments. All of us can search memory on the basis of any of these, and other, criteria. We may not be able to come up quickly with a long list satisfying each of them, but we have no difficulty of fairly rapidly finding a few. I do not think we know a lot about how we do this. Saying that memory is associative does not really explain it.

I would be inclined to argue that the fact that we can search memory on the basis of many different criteria is relevant to the question of how information in memory is organized. However, in one of Landauer's (1975) classics, he proposed a model of memory that assumes neither organization nor directed search. According to this model, both the likelihood that a person would produce a given item in a list generation task and the speed with which he or she would produce it would be functions of the number of times the item was represented in the unorganized memory, which would be searched by an activation process spreading in all directions from wherever an incessantly roving pointer happened to be at the moment the search began.

I have not tried to make a careful assessment of whether this model can accommodate the kinds of results one gets in list generation tasks, but I suspect it probably can. That some items are more likely than others to be produced by a particular person would be expected on the assumption that some items are likely to be represented a greater number of times in that person's memory; that some items appear on many people's lists and others appear on few or none is to be expected if we assume that items differ considerably with respect to the frequency with which people encounter them in daily life and that there is a fair amount of commonality among people in this regard. Relevant to the last point, Table 15.2 shows, for the students mentioned above who listed as many elements as they could, the relationship between the number (or percentage) of lists on which an element appeared and its frequency of occurrence in Kucera and Francis's (1967) corpus of 1,014,232 words.

What may be more difficult for this model—or any other of which I am aware—to accommodate is the ease and speed with which we often can decide that something is not in memory. Is *deret* an English word? Or *piltic*? Or *murg*? Most of us would probably say no in each case very quickly, or, at least, if we were not sure whether these could be found as entries in a dictionary, we could say with confidence that they were not in our own lexicons. It seems highly unlikely that one typically decides that a letter string is not a word by searching one's entire lexicon and not finding the string there; but how does one do it? It is as though it were enough to check the single location where the string

Table 15.2. Average Number (Percentage) of Lists on Which Elements Occurred and Average Frequency of Occurrence in the Kucera and Francis (1967) Word Count

Average N (%) of lists	Average N in K-F count
≥ 30 (≥ 65)	25.3
20–29 (43–63)	9.7
10–19 (22–41)	3.6
0–9 (0–20)	0.2

Note. Lead, which appeared in the Kucera and Francis (K-F) count 129 times (and on our lists 16 times) was excluded from this analysis because of the assumed likelihood that a large percentage of the occurrences of the word in the K-F count were as the verb or as the noun meaning the first position.

would be if it were in the lexicon—much as one might check the location in a dictionary—to determine whether it is there. This is one illustration of what being "content addressable" might mean.

Implicit, Much of It

What each of us knows implicitly outweighs our explicit knowledge by a very large margin. Paradoxically, we are not aware of what we know implicitly until we have occasion to access that knowledge. Each of us knows, for example, that our great-great-grandparents lived beyond puberty, although probably few of us ever learned the fact explicitly; many of us probably do not even know the names of our great-great-grandparents or any of the distinguishing details of their lives, but by virtue of our knowledge of what it means to be a human being, we know, implicitly, a great deal about them.

Landauer and Dumais (1997) have presented a compelling case for inductive learning. They consider the question: How come we appear to know so much more than we explicitly learn? The answer, they suggest, is that much of what we know we induce from other things we know. I do not intend to discuss Landauer and Dumais's latent semantic analysis model here—I am still struggling to understand it—I simply want to make the observation that inference gives us the ability to leverage what we explicitly know, especially by applying generalizations to specific instances.

One can easily get into philosophical quicksand over the question of whether one should be said to know X, because one can infer X from other knowledge one has, if one has never entertained the thought X. If we grant that we should count as knowledge everything that one can infer from what one knows, we seem to be led to the conclusion that one can know a very great deal indeed. By virtue of knowing that all people are mortal—Socrates said it; it must be so—I know that Tom is mortal, that Lyle is mortal, that Walter is mortal, and so on. Give me the name of any of the 6 billion plus people alive on earth today, and I will tell you that I know that he or she is mortal. Better still, give me a number—any number—and I will tell you whether it is divisible by 2. It follows, if we allow that one can be said to know whatever one can infer, that I have knowledge of an infinity of numbers, which is to say an infinite amount of knowledge. Clearly, this is not a useful way to quantify knowledge, but it points up a real problem, which is that of specifying what is to count as knowledge and what is not to do so.

The billion bits of Landauer's estimate of the amount of information a mature memory holds is intended, I suspect, to pertain only to what is explicitly there (even if inductively derived). There must, of course, be the wherewithal to make the inferences, and perhaps some of that is learned, and therefore is included in the billion bits. Any effort to quantify what people know must limit attention to what they know explicitly, else the quantity becomes infinite and not very helpful; but we also need to recognize that the usefulness of explicit knowledge is magnified beyond measure by our ability to make inferences from it.

Approximate, Much of It

This point is closely related to the previous one. Much of what we know, explicitly or implicitly, is approximate. And we know a great deal—approximately. If asked how much the world weighs, I might be inclined to say that I have no idea. But in fact, that would not be entirely correct. I know that it weighs more than a few pounds and that it is lighter than the sun. Further, I am reasonably sure it is the heaviest of the inner planets and Mars, but lighter than the outer planets except Pluto. If pressed, I probably could do some calculations based on the size of the earth, which I do know approximately, and an estimate of how much a cubic foot of matter weighs on average, that would give me a number that would be an approximation, crude but not arbitrary.

Marilyn Adams and I once asked people to estimate a miscellany of quantities: the number of pounds of cane sugar consumed by the average American in a year, the weight of a dime, the length of the Amazon River, and so on. The study was never published, but Figure 2 in Nickerson (1980) shows a subset of the results. Over 80% of the answers that people gave to one set of such unlikely questions were correct to within a factor of 10 and 40% were correct to within a factor of 2. I am not sure how one would go about estimating how much approximate knowledge the average person has, but it must be the case that we know a great deal more approximately than we know precisely. And approximate knowledge is more than adequate for many applications. I need not know how much something weighs to know that it is too heavy for me to lift.

Varying in Certainty

When I learn a new "fact," whether I take it to be a fact depends strongly on whether it is consistent with what I already know, or think I know. Consequently, much of the "factual" information I take in—from books, from the media, from other sources—I take in not as facts but as claims that I may accept or question to varying degrees. And as time passes, accessibility to what

I have taken in changes, diminishing in some cases perhaps to the point of no return.

The result is that much of what is in my head is of a very uncertain nature. Some things I am relatively sure of—I am willing to behave as though they are facts. Many more, however, are less certain—I think they are facts but would not want to bet my life on them being so. It is of more than passing interest that we are able to introspect on the contents of our memories and make judgments about the trustworthiness of what we find there. The use of confidence judgments is commonplace in experiments, and the universal finding is that people have little difficulty in distinguishing different degrees of certainty in what they know or think they know.

Introspectively Gaugeable, Within Limits

Not only are people able to make judgments about the trustworthiness of what they find in their memories, but such judgments typically convey useful information regarding the reliability of the knowledge to which they pertain. If one plots the probability that a bit of presumed knowledge is accurate as a function of the degree of confidence one has that that bit of presumed knowledge is accurate, one typically gets a monotonically increasing curve—as confidence increases, so does the probability of being correct. Table 15.3 shows the relationship between confidence and correctness for data from a study in progress, in which each of 48 college students attempted to answer 50 questions selected to represent a range of difficulty from Nelson and Narens's (1980) norms, and rated their confidence in the correctness of each answer on a 4-point scale ranging from *certain it is correct* (4) to *pure guess* (1). The relationship between confidence and correctness has been the focus of a considerable amount of research, often discussed under the topic of "calibration." One is said to be well calibrated when the correlation between degree of confidence and accuracy is high.

Unfortunately, a given level of expressed confidence cannot be assumed to be context independent. This point is illustrated by the results of a study by Nickerson and McGoldrick (1963). Seventy-two college students judged the relative sizes (land areas) of states of the United States. Each of 100 items listed four states and the subjects' task was to identify the largest of the four in each case. In one (difficult) condition, the largest and next-largest state in each set of four were relatively close in size; in another (easy) condition, the

Table 15.3.   Probability That an Answer With the Indicated Confidence Was Correct

Confidence	Probability correct
1	.111
2	.356
3	.607
4	.926

largest and next-largest state in each set of four differed considerably in size; a third (mixed) set contained items from each of these sets and items with intermediate degrees of difficulty as well. Chance performance with this task is, of course, 25% correct. Our subjects got 30%, 51%, and 67% correct for the difficult, mixed, and easy sets, respectively.

What is most germane for present purposes is that, although the ratio of correct-to-total responses increased with expressed confidence under all three levels of difficulty, the correct-to-total ratio for a given confidence level differed depending on the mean difficulty of the questions that constituted the context in which the confidence judgments were made; confidence of a specific level was predictive of a much higher correct-to-total ratio when expressed in the context of relatively easy questions than when expressed in the context of relatively difficult ones.

Differentially Accessible to Cognition

I have been focusing on knowledge of the kind that can be brought into consciousness and, in most cases, described verbally. But people know many things that are not of this sort: how to walk, throw a ball, ride a bicycle, play a musical instrument, type. People who play a musical instrument and are able to play many pieces from memory may be unable to reproduce a piece that is in their repertoire any other way than by actually playing it. Recently I asked 30 touch typists, all of whom had typed for a minimum of 10 years (M = 26.9 years, Mdn = 26 years), to identify the letter keys on a drawing of the standard QWERTY keyboard on which the keys were not labeled. The drawing had blanks only for the letters—none for numerals, punctuation marks, or other functions. Only 6 of the group were able to do the task perfectly, and 3 of these had a number of scratch-outs and mark-overs. People expressed much frustration with this task and surprise at the fact that they could not easily do it. I invite you to try this yourself, if you touch type. Before you next look at a keyboard, draw a layout with 10, 9, and 7 boxes in the top, middle, and bottom rows, respectively, and try to fill in the letters as they appear on a keyboard.

If typists did not have an accurate memory of the keyboard's layout, they would not be able to type as they do. But for most touch typists, their memory of the keyboard is not visual, or at least not primarily so; rather the information is stored in memory in a way that facilitates its retrieval for use in typing, but not for humoring psychologists conducting experiments on memory. However the keyboard is represented in memory, the representation appears not to be readily accessible for identifying individual keys at a verbal level.

Pragmatic

There are a number of other characteristics of knowledge that might be discussed, but space does not permit. I end with one that will bring me back to Landauer's article on estimating how much people remember. Surely some of what we remember is trivia, but I want to claim, as a conjecture, that we tend to store and retain information that we typically find useful and tend not to store and retain information that we are unlikely to need.

The results of experimentation that Landauer used in making his estimate of 1 billion bits as the amount of information a person remembers included some on memory for pictures (Nickerson, 1965, 1968; Shepard, 1967; Standing, 1973). The common finding of these experiments was that people are pretty good at recognizing meaningful pictures that they have seen only once and for only a few seconds, both shortly after seeing them and after moderately long periods of time. I interpreted these results, as have others, as evidence of the capaciousness and retentiveness of visual memory; however, in his use of these results to estimate how much people know, Landauer estimated that the amount of information that would have to be stored to produce the kind of performance observed is probably not more than about 14 bits per picture.

When I first read this number, it struck me as almost surely wrong by several orders of magnitude. My article had the subtitle, after all, "A Demonstration of Capacity." At 14 bits per picture, the demonstration is not very impressive. And consider the following thought experiment. Imagine a pair of subjects, A and B. A looks at each of several hundred pictures and describes each of them to B, who is later shown a large set of pictures and asked to distinguish those that A described from those that A had not seen. We can only speculate on how A would describe the pictures for B's benefit. My guess is that he or she would have to use a lot more than 14 bits per picture to give B any reasonable idea of what he or she was seeing.

Or look at it this way. I have a pocket-sized digital camera. It has a resolution of 2048 × 1536 pixels, which means that, if one stored nothing but black or white for each pixel, one would need a little more than 3 million bits of storage per picture. Storing color requires many times this capacity. The human eye, with its 100 million receptors, each capable of firing at perhaps 1,000 times per second, can take in many times this much information in a glance. McCulloch (1951/1965), from whom I have appropriated this observation, pointed out that the disparity between the rate at which our visual system can process incoming information and the rate at which our motor system can put information out—via very rapid piano playing, for example, or by speech—is on the order of 100 million to one.

The input–output disparity is small, however, compared with the disparity between input and retention, using McCulloch's estimate for one and Landauer's for the other: According to McCulloch's estimate, the eye alone takes in 100 times as much information in 1 second as Landauer estimates that we retain after 70 years of experience of more or less continuous bombardment with visual and other types of input. What explains such an enormous disparity?

I make no pretense of attempting to answer this question but will make a few observations that are perhaps germane. First, the information in a visual scene can be quantified in various ways. Considering the scene as a bit map is only one of them, and by far the most demanding of storage. Compression techniques that take advantage of redundancies and contingencies in a scene can reduce the storage requirements in many cases by large amounts, although they do so at the cost of the need for space to store the compression algorithms.

Second, what people store of scenes or pictures may be greatly simplified abstractions that bear a relationship to the scenes or pictures themselves not unlike the relationship between a cartoon caricature of a face—recognizable from distinguishable features, but less informationally rich than the face itself or a photo thereof. Third, and this is the point I want to emphasize, there generally is little reason for us to store the details of visual patterns that we encounter in daily life, and, except on the rare instances in which there is a compelling reason to pay attention to details, we tend not to do so.

If this were not the case, it would be hard to account for the finding, reported by several investigators, that when people are asked to describe the visual details of objects that they presumably have seen frequently over many years, they often do not do very well at the task. This result was reported by Morton (1967), who found that people were unable to recall correctly the way letters were arranged on a (then circular) telephone dial. Several investigators have found that people typically are not able to recall all the features of common coins or even to specify the placement of inscriptions when they are told what the inscriptions are (Foos, 1989; Jones, 1990; Nickerson & Adams, 1979; Rubin & Kontis, 1983).

Readers who find the poor performance of people in these experiments surprising may wish to do an informal experiment. Try, without looking at the indicated objects, to draw the face of your watch, your automobile dashboard, the dial of your favorite radio, your TV remote control device, or the switches and control panel arrangement on some frequently used household appliance (stove, dishwasher, microwave oven). Chances are you will discover that you can get the general layout reasonably correct, but that you will have great difficulty with details.

So, while I still have trouble accepting Landauer's estimate of 14 bits per picture as the information one stores in performing picture recognition tasks of the kinds mentioned here, I readily accept the point that whatever the memory representations are, they are much—perhaps orders of magnitude—less rich in details than the images themselves.

Concluding Comment

Trying to come up with plausible answers to such questions as how much knowledge a well-educated person acquires over a lifetime, how much knowledge a person *could* acquire over a lifetime under ideal conditions, and what limits the amount of knowledge people typically acquire is a very interesting exercise from a theoretical point of view. Of course any answers that are proposed must be considered highly speculative at this stage of our very limited understanding of how the mind works, especially in view of the fuzziness of what it means to know something. But even making allowances for all the uncertainties, one cannot help being impressed by the enormous difference between what appears to be our very great ability to take information in and the relatively modest amount that we appear to retain. This seems to me to provide justification for working on the assumption that there may be much more effective ways of informing ourselves waiting to be discovered and implemented. I do not want to argue that acquiring as much knowledge as possible should necessarily be one's greatest objective in life, but I strongly suspect that most of us would be delighted to have acquired a few bits more than we have.

Tom Landauer's work includes some bold and creative excursions into this area. It gives us some insights into the acquisition and retention of knowledge, raises important questions, proposes some surprising answers, and provides challenges that can keep researchers busy for quite some time. I have greatly enjoyed reading his work and hope I have stored more than two-thirds bits per second in doing so, even without counting what was acquired inductively without my being aware of it. But then, being on the wrong side of Landauer's allotment of 70 years for a lifetime, I must consider anything I manage to retain even for a short while as a bonus.

References

Foos, P. W. (1989). Age differences in memory for two common objects. *Journal of Gerontology: Psychological Sciences, 44*, 178–180.

Hunter, L. (1988). Estimating human cognitive capacities: A response to Landauer. *Cognitive Science, 12*, 287–291.

Jones, G. V. (1990). Misremembering a common object: When left is not right. *Memory & Cognition, 18*, 174–182.

Kucera, H., & Francis, W. N. (1967). *Computational analysis of present-day American English.* Providence, RI: Brown University Press.

Landauer, T. K. (1964). Two hypotheses concerning the biochemical basis of memory. *Psychological Review, 71*, 167–179.

Landauer, T. K. (1975). Memory without organization: Properties of a model with random storage and undirected retrieval. *Cognitive Psychology, 7*, 495–531.

Landauer, T. K. (1986). How much do people remember? Some estimates of the quantity of learned information in long-term memory. *Cognitive Science, 19*, 477–493.

Landauer, T. K. (1988). An estimate of how much people remember, not of underlying cognitive capacities. *Cognitive Science, 12*, 293–297.

Landauer, T. K., & Dumais, S. T. (1997). A solution to Plato's problem: The latent semantic analysis theory of acquisition, induction, and representation of knowledge. *Psychological Review, 104*, 211–240.

McCulloch, W. S. (1965). Why the mind is in the head. In W. S. McCulloch (Ed.), *Embodiments of mind* (pp. 72–87). Cambridge, MA: MIT Press. (Original work published 1951)

Morton, J. (1967, September 2). A singular lack of incidental learning. *Nature, 215*, 203–204.

Nelson, T. O., & Narens, L. (1980). Norms of 300 general-information questions: Accuracy of recall, latency of recall, and feeling-of-knowing ratings. *Journal of Verbal Learning and Verbal Behavior, 19*, 338–368.

Nickerson, R. S. (1965). Short-term memory for complex meaningful visual configurations: A demonstration of capacity. *Canadian Journal of Psychology, 19*, 155–160.

Nickerson, R. S. (1968). A note on long-term recognition memory for pictorial material. *Psychonomic Science, 11*, 58.

Nickerson, R. S. (1980). Motivated retrieval from archival memory. In H. E. Howe, Jr. & J. H. Flowers (Eds.), *Nebraska Symposium on Motivation: Vol. 28. Motivation and cognitive processes* (pp. 73–119). Lincoln: University of Nebraska Press.

Nickerson, R. S., & Adams, M. J. (1979). Long-term memory for a common object. *Cognitive Psychology, 11*, 287–307.

Nickerson, R. S, & McGoldrick, C. C. (1963). Confidence, correctness, and difficulty with non-psychophysical comparative judgments. *Perceptual and Motor Skills, 17*, 159–167.

Nickerson, R. S., Smith, E. E., & Wallach, R. W. (1981). *Memory search of semantic categories following exposure to category instances* (BBN Report No. 4822). Cambridge, MA.

Rubin, D. C., & Kontis, T. C. (1983). A schema for common cents. *Memory & Cognition, 11*, 335–341.

Shepard, R. N. (1967). Recognition memory for words, sentences, and pictures. *Journal of Verbal Learning and Verbal Behavior, 6*, 156–163.

Simon, H. A., & Gilmartin, K. (1973). A simulation of memory for chess positions. *Cognitive Psychology, 5*, 29–46.

Standing, L. (1973). Learning 10,000 pictures. *Quarterly Journal of Experimental Psychology, 25*, 207–222.

Stwertka, A. (2002). *A guide to the elements* (2nd ed.). New York: Oxford University Press.

16

Finding Meaning in Psychology

Roger W. Schvaneveldt

In this chapter, I explore several themes in connection with a selective review of some research problems I have pursued over the years. The study of meaning is a major theme along with issues relating to the goals of scientific psychology and the demands of research on applied problems. Finally, I ponder the role of psychology in the broader scientific endeavor, and I propose a candidate for the psychological level of analysis.

Meaning

One of my enduring interests revolves around the study of meaning. Our everyday perception of the world appears direct and meaningful. Our ordinary encounters with language occur largely in dealing with the meanings expressed by language. Although meaning flows naturally from living, finding a rigorous scientific account of this natural ability is a difficult undertaking. My own pursuit of meaning in psychology has followed the path taken by experimental psychology in the last half century. That path curved away from the strict behaviorism that dominated the first half of the 20th century toward a new-found interest in mental processes and issues in cognitive psychology. Increased concern with applying scientific psychology has accompanied the empirical and theoretical developments. We have seen great strides in applying research in psychology to many practical problems, and the three honorees in this Festschrift—Lyle Bourne, Jr., Walter Kintsch, and Tom Landauer—have made many valuable contributions to increasing our understanding of concepts, language comprehension, and complex semantics. The honorees have also been leaders in moving their research into applications. The participants in the Festschrift have also contributed greatly to an enhanced understanding of cognition and the application of this knowledge. Now here comes my two-bits worth.

I am grateful to Lyle Bourne, Jr., Nancy Cooke, Rebecca Gomez, Alice Healy, Peder Johnson, David Meyer, Deb Roy, and Guy Van Orden for inspiration, stimulating discussions, comments, and criticisms. The responsibility is mine of course.

In the realm of signs and symbols, C. S. Peirce (1839–1914) proposed a triadic theory in the late 19th century. His theory provides a basic analysis of the meaning of signs, symbols, or representations. In Peirce's words (Buchler, 1940, p. 99), "a sign, or representamen, is something which stands to somebody for something in some respect or capacity." For Peirce, the triadic character of signs was irreducible. For signs to function, all three elements (the sign, the signified, and the interpretant) and the relations among them must be involved. Anything can stand for anything, but there must be an interpretation to bring about the sign function. Peirce's ideas are widely accepted by semiotic scholars (Eco, 1976; Morris, 1971; Ogden & Richards, 1946). In cognitive science, however, thought about mental representation seems to have lost track of the critical role of the interpretation in realizing a representation. Representations are postulated with abandon in theories and models, but interpretation often lies more in the perspective of the theorist than in the system being investigated. Representations are used to stand in for meaning, but there is no account of how representations acquire meaning aside from that attributed to them by theorists and modelers (Bickhard, 1998; Schvaneveldt & Van Orden, 2002).

Scientific Psychology

As a consequence of several historical and cultural factors, experimental psychology has placed great value on explanations of phenomena by identifying the efficient causal factors at work. In the pursuit of reductive explanations of perception and cognition, we often discover that the meaning that was so obvious at the outset has disappeared somewhere along the analytic way, and, like Humpty Dumpty, it cannot be recaptured by putting the reductive elements back together again. Nevertheless, reductive analyses are seductively appealing.

The study of perception provides a clear illustration of major advances following from a reductive approach. Modern textbooks on perception provide great detail about the physical basis of perception, including the structure of sensory systems and the details of neural processes involved in perception. We do understand a great deal about the neuroscience of perception, but I still have some nagging concerns that as this work progresses, we give less attention to certain critical psychological issues. Students may be learning less about perceptual phenomena (e.g., the constancies, contrast effects, motion, and coordination) as they learn more about brain function.

Am I alone in wondering about what is being left out as more and more effort of psychologists is devoted to neuroscience? Are we going to learn more about psychology this way, or should we just get used to the idea that with a good handle on neuroscience, we do not need psychology? I think we still need psychology, and I return to this concern in my discussion of a meaningful psychological level of analysis. First, let us look at some attempts to identify mental modules.

Semantic Priming: Searching for a Processing Account

Sternberg (1969) proposed the additive factors method to identify independent stages of information processing. The basic logic was that experimental factors (or variables) that produce additive effects on reaction time could be assumed to affect distinct stages of information processing, whereas factors that interact (are nonadditive) are presumed to be affecting at least one stage in common. Finding a set of additive factors could be used to support a model of independent stages. With some further interpretation as to the nature of these stages, underlying components of mental activity could be identified.

The application of this method can be illustrated by a collection of word recognition studies (Becker, 1979; Becker & Killion, 1977; Becker, Schvaneveldt, & Gomez, 1973; Meyer & Schvaneveldt, 1971; Meyer, Schvaneveldt, & Ruddy, 1975; Schvaneveldt & Meyer, 1973). A major focus of this work was to develop our understanding of the nature of semantic priming effects, but several of the studies can be interpreted in the additive factors framework. Figure 16.1 shows a summary of these experiments along with a possible interpretation. Recall that a priming experiment is performed by presenting a priming stimulus followed by a target stimulus. The target is either a word or a nonword, and the task is to determine which by pressing one key for a word or another key for a nonword as quickly as possible. Here we are only looking at reaction times for word targets. Three variables are of interest. Targets were presented under different quality conditions (e.g., varying intensity or varying clarity). The high-quality targets are responded to more rapidly than low-quality ones.

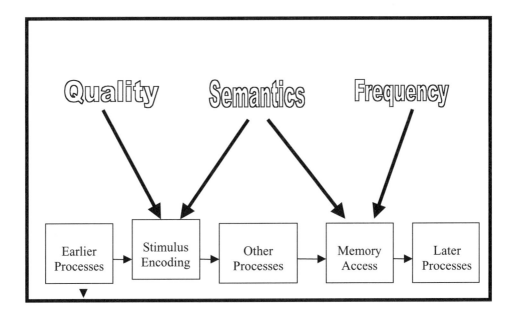

Figure 16.1.   Information processing stages and effects of experimental factors.

Semantics were manipulated by having targets either related to the priming stimulus (e.g., prime = *doctor* and target = *nurse*) or unrelated (prime is a word not related to the target). Responses are faster when targets are related to the primes. Finally, the target words were either relatively common words (high frequency) or relatively uncommon words (low frequency). Responses are faster to high-frequency words.

Of the possible interactions among these factors, one (Quality × Frequency) produced additive effects (no interaction). High- and low-frequency words showed the same effect of quality. The other two possible two-way interactions were observed. Semantic effects were larger for words presented with low quality compared with the effect for words presented with high quality. Also there is a larger effect of semantics for low-frequency words compared with the effect for high-frequency words. The Quality × Semantics interaction led us to suppose that semantic priming was affecting the encoding of the stimulus, a conclusion that was supported by other studies (Schvaneveldt & McDonald, 1981). We had long supposed that semantic priming would affect memory access, which seemed to be confirmed by the Semantics × Frequency interaction. However, the additivity of quality and frequency implied that these two factors affect different stages. This conclusion was contrary to the predictions of several models of word recognition.

At the time of this work there was some real enthusiasm over the prospects for the additive-factors methodology for providing insights into component mental processes. The enthusiasm waned, however, perhaps because additive factors are hard to come by. There are a number of reports of additive factors (see Sternberg, 1998, for several examples), but in some areas of research such as word recognition, it is more common to find interactions among variables. Also, different experiments sometimes disagree about additive and interactive effects. For example, Norris (1984) observed an interaction between quality and frequency that undermined our independent two-stage account. Theorizing in word recognition moved toward more interactive models with the verification model (Becker, 1979; Becker & Killion, 1977; Becker et al., 1973), the activation-verification model (Paap, Newsome, McDonald, & Schvaneveldt, 1982), and the dynamic resonance model (Grossberg & Stone, 1986).

In addition to these developments, consider the extensive discussion about the decidability of alternative models of mental processes on the basis of behavioral data (Anderson, 1978; Townsend, 1972; Utall, 1990). In short, it is possible to construct distinct models that equally fit any given set of data, making it difficult to argue that data uniquely support any particular model. Thus, like the fate of Donders's subtractive approach to the discovery of mental activities in the 19th century, Sternberg's additive factors method with all of its improvements did not provide the discovery tool we had hoped for. The problem is that additivity (and more generally, modularity) may be an inappropriate model for mental processes in general (Thelen & Smith, 1994; van Gelder, 1997; Van Orden, Holden, & Turvey, 2003). Perhaps cognition results from complex dynamics distributed over brain, body, and world operating over multiple time scales of evolution, development, and performance. If so, modularity would hold only under very limited conditions. I return to this point later.

Cognitive Psychology and Applied Research

An often-cited example of the failure of reductionistic psychology to scale up to real-world problems comes from the difficulties faced by psychologists brought into the war effort in World War II. Included among these psychologists are some of the giants of the field, for example, Donald Broadbent, Paul Fitts, and James Gibson. They found that their theories and findings were simply not up to the task of understanding and improving training, performance, or the human factors of technical systems. Having a reductionistic account of behavior did not illuminate the issues raised by actual people performing meaningful work. Some accounts (e.g., Lachman, Butterfield, & Lachman, 1979) attribute this demand for relevance as one of the primary factors leading to the development of cognitive psychology in the mid-20th century. Keeping questions about the relevance of research in mind does have an important impact on the course of the research. There are always choices to be made about the appropriate level of analysis for research. Trying to address an applied problem can exert powerful constraints on theory and experiment. My own experience with applications led to Pathfinder Networks.

Pathfinder: Applied Semantics

My first acquaintance with applied issues came when I undertook an analysis of the development of knowledge in fighter pilots around 1980 in collaboration with several colleagues (Schvaneveldt et al., 1985). With my interests in semantics in cognition, this seemed like a natural undertaking. Unfortunately, my earlier work in semantic priming proved to be of little use. Although we considered approaching the problem with those methods, the interesting questions in this applied domain seemed to demand methods for characterizing knowledge rather than identifying the details of mental processes.

In a way, we were in the position of the psychologists in World War II who had problems to solve, but the approaches they brought with them were inadequate. I did know a thing or two about multidimensional scaling and cluster analysis, so we devised a rating task that would produce judgments of proximity (or relatedness) for concepts found in the area of air-to-air combat. We began to see some interesting differences in the scaling solutions coming from the data of student pilots and instructors, but we also began to reflect on the fact that much theory in cognitive psychology was based on semantic networks, whereas our scaling solutions had other forms. The obvious next question was to ask how one would construct a network based on proximity data. Our answer was to develop what has come to be known as the Pathfinder scaling method (Schvaneveldt, 1990; Schvaneveldt, Durso, & Dearholt, 1989). The method basically defines a criterion for including links between concepts by preserving those links that maintain the shortest paths (or the links of greatest relatedness).

Examples of Pathfinder networks are shown in Figure 16.2. The top and bottom panels are derived from data obtained from subjects with differing

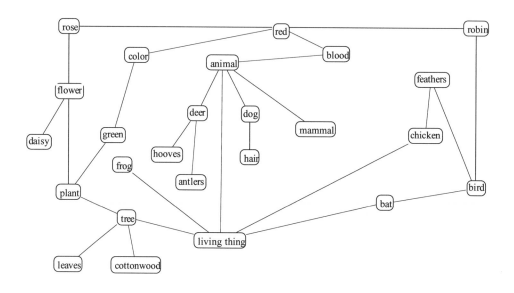

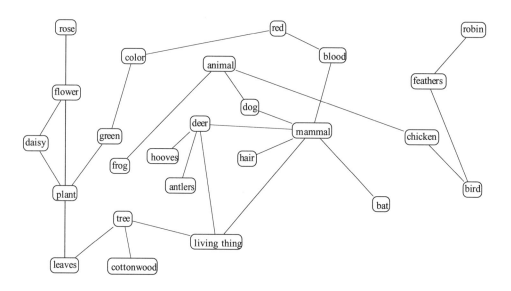

Figure 16.2. Networks from student ratings (see text).

expertise in biology. Can you tell which is which? The top comes from students in the introductory psychology participant pool, and the bottom comes from graduate students in biology. The differences in the networks appear to reflect differences in these concepts with increases in expertise. Most notable is the way *mammal* is connected in the two networks. In this set of concepts, *mammal* is more central for experienced biologists. Such differences have been the basis of numerous studies in aviation, medicine, computer programming, training, and education.

I wish to emphasize the way in which considerations of real problems led to a push toward increasing the complexity of the problem to be tackled, and by letting the demands of a real problem place constraints on what is meaningful. There was a push away from highly controlled laboratory tasks and variables toward less controlled but more relevant tasks and analyses. In this case, it was away from lexical-decision tasks and semantic priming toward direct judgments of relatedness and psychometric scaling of concepts and their relations. The Pathfinder scaling method has proved extremely fruitful with applications in many areas.

In summary, one of the strengths of much work in cognitive psychology is that it has addressed problems approaching the complexity found in the real world, and, as a result, the progress made in understanding cognition has had clearer implications for applied settings (see Durso et al., 1999). Some good examples are found in recent work of the Festschrift honorees. Bourne (2001) and Bourne, Healy, and Beer (2003) brought psychology to bear on understanding terrorism and military conflict. Kintsch (1998) extended his work on language comprehension to cognition more generally. Landauer and Dumais (1997) introduced a new method of deriving complex semantics with a wide array of applications. With so much to applaud, I should just stop here and celebrate, but there is more work to be done, so we continue.

The Psychological Level of Analysis

With some success in application and with the new enthusiasm of investigating the neural substrate of cognition, we might conclude that psychology has finally come of age and we can forge ahead in the established paradigms. Cognitive science can provide a functional account of behavior as well as a map of this account into the brain. This is a pretty picture, but there are some detractors. Do these endeavors exhaust the domain of psychology? Searle (1980, 1992) claimed that the functional approach to the mind misses the target. He was concerned with the general problem of getting semantics into (or out of?) a mechanical syntactic system of which contemporary computer models of mind consist. Dennett (1989) agreed that syntax does not determine semantics. Jerry Fodor is as strong an advocate of representational/computational theories of mind as can be found, but he, too, questioned the completeness of this approach for leading us to an adequate theory of mind (Fodor, 2000). He was particularly concerned that this approach would never come to grips with the adaptability of the human mind, or abductive reasoning (an idea traceable to Peirce). These and other concerns raise doubt about the possibility of finding a complete theory by following the most heavily trodden paths (Clark, 1997; Schvaneveldt & Van Orden, 2002). How might we confront such concerns?

Consider some thoughts from William James and from George Miller. James's view is perhaps most clearly expressed in his *Essays in Radical Empiricism,* which he developed later in his career as a capstone of his thought (James, 1912). In the essay, "A World of Pure Experience," he wrote:

> To be radical, an empiricism must neither admit into its constructions any element that is not directly experienced, nor exclude from them any element that is directly experienced. For such a philosophy, the relations that connect experiences must themselves be experienced relations, and any kind of relation experienced must be accounted as "real" as anything else in the system. (p. 42)

James was not proposing a new mental chemistry. Rather, he proposed taking pure experience as the ground of knowing while avoiding metaphysical assumptions that go beyond direct observation (Heft, 2001). By this means, James tried to avoid the dualism that leads to the mind–body problem among other thorny issues.

George Miller has long promoted the view that psychology is the science of mental life. In 1985, he argued that the constitutive problem of psychology is the explanation of conscious experience. He went on to say that this requires understanding affect, volition, and intention in addition to understanding cognition and intelligent systems.

Perhaps immediate experience is what is missing from scientific psychology. The desire to create an objective science has left aside subjectivity. To be sure, cognitive scientists rely on their subjective experience to deliver ideas and conjectures, but we seem to rapidly seek the security and objectivity of operational definitions and models, never again to make contact with the subjective source of these ideas. It seems to me that scientific psychology is the discipline where a science of the subjective should be found.

By following the lead of James and Miller, psychology should at least include a concern with immediate experience. Hasn't the field been there before? Isn't that where Wundt and introspection methods began? Well, yes and no. Yes, the mind can be the focus of psychology without the commitment to basic elements and their combination, and introspection is not the only avenue of investigation. By taking immediate experience as the raison d'etre of psychology, we may have a useful criterion for defining a unique psychological level of analysis. In this chapter, I can only begin to point to some of the implications of this way of thinking. A particularly difficult problem concerns the proper place of so-called *unconscious mental processes.* On James's view, the unconscious may be a problem for physiology rather than psychology. On the side of inclusion, we need to pay more attention to phenomena like those Miller said should be addressed. Volition, consciousness, and intention may not be easy problems, but they may be essential if we are to develop a psychology that is meaningful in the context of the actual lives of real people. There are promising ideas concerning intention and control that deserve attention.

Intention and Control

Darwin, himself, was something of a psychologist. He studied the adaptation of earthworms to experimentally imposed alterations of their environment. In the course of these studies, he discovered which properties of the environment the worms were capable of detecting, and how they adapted to sharpness, for example, by avoiding glass shards and by dealing with the blunt end of pine needles in preference to the sharp ends. Reed (1996) took such behavior as evidence of intentional action.

Although scientific psychology often approaches the study of intention through the incorporation of goals in models, we do not yet have an adequate account. Intentions are a major part of ordinary experience. Surely we encounter intentions in the laboratory whether we enjoy the contributions of a cooperative participant or despair at the behavior of an uncooperative one. Performing any laboratory task requires having intentions appropriate to engaging the task. If we fail to induce proper intentions, we probably end up discarding the data.

Work in cognitive science has generally dealt with intentions through the implementations of goal structures in cognitive models such as ACT-R (Automatic Components of Thought-Rational; Anderson, 1996) and EPIC (Executive-Process/Interactive Control; Meyer & Kieras, 1997). This general idea can be traced to the General Problem Solver proposed in the 1950s (Newell, Shaw, & Simon, 1958). These modeling efforts have produced useful results in the forms of models of complex behavior, often within applied settings. There are still some aspects of intention that need further investigation.

In everyday experience, understanding people's intentions enters crucially into our understanding of events as we negotiate a social world. As a clear example, consider the law. The same act can be punished as manslaughter or various degrees of murder depending on the intention of the perpetrator and when, if there was intent, the intent arose.

Despite the value of intentional attributions in everyday life, getting a scientific handle on intention has proved difficult. The difficulty seems to lie in our inability to reconcile the common concept of intentions with a causal account of behavior. Philosophers deal with this issue in an area of study known as *action theory* (Juarrero, 1999).

If we can have an account of behavior and the brain, why do we need to take intention into account (Churchland, 1989)? One reason is that it seems likely that useful generalizations about behavior are to be found at the psychological level of analysis. Dennett (1989) pointed out that treating systems as intentional (a broader notion than intentions to act) allows an observer to interpret behavior in rational terms. The crucial issue for Dennett is whether the intentional stance captures important generalizations. Because intentional thinking pervades common sense, it may be expected to be particularly relevant to contacting people's experience in applied settings. Applications often involve appreciating and affecting people's experience.

From considerations of intentions, we may have a basis for explaining behavior even if we cannot predict it because fulfilling intentions does not entail any specific behavior. I can satisfy an intention to communicate with a friend by calling, writing, e-mailing, or visiting. If you knew of that intention, you could use it to explain my behavior, but you could not predict it. You might have predicted that I would attempt to fulfill the intention. Just as in the law, intentions are often given more weight than behavior in assessing responsibility.

Juarrero (1999) offered an interesting account of intentional action by viewing intentions in the context of constraints operating in complex systems. On her view, an intention establishes a high-level constraint on behavior that serves to direct action in general toward the fulfillment of the constraint by creating certain attractors in the space of possible behaviors. Many other constraints, including physical and social factors acting on multiple time scales, also influence the flow of behavior, but the causal processes in such a system include circular causality resulting from "top–down (self-causal) control at work in intentional action" (Juarrero, 1999, p. 176).

The issue of intentional action can be seen in the context of a broader question about the locus of control for human activity, including human experience. Where lies such control? Behaviorism places control in the environment with the stimulus. Symbol systems localize control in the environment, homunculi, and the syntactic properties of symbols. Neuroscience tends to favor the brain as the locus of control. A complex systems account distributes control more widely, but control is generally seen as emerging from the interaction of people (considered at multiple levels) and environments (also at multiple levels) where multiple hierarchical constraints interact to bring about human activity (see Patee, 1973).

Thus, there are alternatives to taking mechanistic processes as the model for psychological theory. The mechanistic approach comes to us from the tradition of logic and positivistic philosophy. Psychology may be the only empirical science with entrenched bands of organized resistance still holding firmly to this tradition (Toulmin & Leary, 1985). This is not to say that models and formal systems are not valuable in trying to understand complex systems. It is to say, however, that we should not take such models as equivalent to the system being modeled, and we should be open to a broader view of causal processes such as that found in complex self-organizing systems. As a part of a broader view, consider some examples of what an ecological approach brings to the study of psychology.

Information and Aviation

In the tradition of William James, James Gibson has suggested an alternative approach to psychological theory. Consider his work on vision. He begins with a particular visual experience and asks which information in the optical array could support the experience. He emphasizes the importance of a dynamic view of the optical array. That is, information may unfold in time so perceptual processes must be sensitive to the dynamics of the flow to acquire the critical information. Compelling examples of such information come from Gibson's

(1979) analysis of information in optical flow as agents and objects move about in the world.

Gibson's perspective brings interesting changes in the way perception is understood. First, because environments are seen as providing sufficient information to specify perceptions, there is no need for "unconscious inferences" to fill the gap between sensation and perception. Second, rather than starting with the "facts" of anatomy and neurophysiology to arrive at perceptual experience, one starts by identifying environmental information that can support experience and then one looks to see how the nervous system can extract that information. Arguably, the Gibsonian account accords better with immediate experience. We do experience the world. James would likely approve.

Gibson's approach emphasizes characterizing the information in the environment as a first step in developing a psychological analysis. Some of my recent work in aviation focuses on trying to characterize the environment inhabited by pilots in terms of the information they need to perform successfully in various phases of flight (Schvaneveldt, Beringer, & Lamonica, 2001). This analysis has proved to be useful in a variety of ways. In the initial work, we discovered some interesting differences between the information deemed important by pilots with more expertise compared with novice pilots. In most cases, expert pilots gave higher priority to more information elements, which may stem from their ability to handle more information. There were a few cases in which novice pilots assigned higher priorities. An example is the priority of information about vertical velocity during takeoff and landing. To the uninitiated, it would seem that knowing about your rate of ascent or descent should be important as you depart or arrive at an airport. However, expert pilots say, "Get the pitch and power right, and the vertical velocity will take care of itself." Apparently, novices want to make sure it is taking care of itself. They are probably unsure about the pitch and power being right. The experts concentrate on the parameters they directly control.

Another use of our work in identifying information priorities comes from its relevance to evaluating aviation information systems. We developed an evaluation method that essentially compares the priority of information elements to their availability in various phases of flight (Schvaneveldt, Beringer, & Leard, in press). This method helps to identify where critical information is not as accessible as it should be as well as identifying clutter (information that is not needed but is present anyway). Our method should be useful to system designers as well as to certifiers of new information systems.

The Future

I can imagine a future scientific psychology that is more inclusive than what we find in the mainstream today. If we consider the core problem of psychological investigation to be the experience of evolved, animate, adaptive agents, we can develop a psychology that is continuous with biology even if it is not reducible to biology. From this perspective, immediate experience can be located at the interface between individuals and the world they inhabit (Heft, 2001; Reed, 1996). It is plausible that cognition, including consciousness, is not localized in the head but rather in the interaction of an observer and a world just as it appears to be in our experience (Clark, 1997; Hutchins, 1995; Velmans, 2000). This science of psychology will exploit models and formalisms acknowledged as such. It will also have room for bodies and environments along with the complexities of their interactions. Conscious experience will be a natural part of this scene because it is a natural property of various organisms, and the meaning I have been looking for will be central. I am eager for this future to arrive.

References

Anderson, J. R. (1978). Arguments concerning representations for mental imagery. *Psychological Review, 85,* 249–277.

Anderson, J. R. (1996). ACT: A simple theory of complex cognition. *American Psychologist, 51,* 355–365.

Becker, C. A. (1979). Semantic context and word frequency effects in visual word recognition. *Journal of Experimental Psychology: Human Perception and Performance, 5,* 252–259.

Becker, C. A., & Killion, T. H. (1977). Interaction of visual and cognitive effects in word recognition. *Journal of Experimental Psychology: Human Perception and Performance, 3,* 389–401.

Becker, C. A., Schvaneveldt, R. W., & Gomez, L. M. (1973, November). *Semantic, orthographic, and phonetic factors in word recognition.* Paper presented at the annual meeting of the Psychonomic Society, St. Louis, MO.

Bickhard, M. H. (1998). Levels of representationality. *Journal of Experimental and Theoretical Artificial Intelligence, 10,* 179–215.

Bourne, L. E., Jr. (2001, Fall/Winter). Terrorism and military conflict: General psychology informs international relations. *The General Psychologist, 36,* 53–55.

Bourne, L. E., Jr., Healy, A. F., & Beer, F. A. (2003). Military conflict and terrorism: General psychology informs international relations. *Review of General Psychology, 7,* 189–202.

Buchler, J. (1940). *The philosophy of Peirce: Selected writings.* London: Routledge & Kegan Paul.

Churchland, P. M. (1989). *A neurocomputational perspective.* Cambridge, MA: MIT Press.

Clark, A. (1997). *Being there: Putting brain, body, and world together again.* Cambridge, MA: MIT Press.

Dennett, D. C. (1989). *The intentional stance.* Cambridge, MA: MIT Press.

Durso, F. T., Nickerson, R., Schvaneveldt, R., Dumais, S., Chi, M., & Lindsay, S. (Eds.). (1999). *The handbook of applied cognition.* Chichester, England: Wiley.

Eco, U. (1976). *A theory of semiotics.* Bloomington: Indiana University Press.

Fodor, J. (2000). *The mind doesn't work that way: The scope and limits of computational psychology.* Cambridge, MA: MIT Press.

Gibson, J. J. (1979). *The ecological approach to visual perception.* New York: Houghton Mifflin.

Grossberg, S., & Stone, G. (1986). Neural dynamics of word recognition and recall: Attentional priming, learning, and resonance. *Psychological Review, 93,* 46–74.

Heft, H. (2001). *Ecological psychology in context: James Gibson, Roger Barker, and the legacy of William James's radical empiricism.* Mahwah, NJ: Erlbaum.

Hutchins, E. (1995). *Cognition in the wild.* Cambridge, MA: MIT Press.

James, W. (1912). *Essays in radical empiricism.* New York: Longmans.

Juarrero, A. (1999). *Dynamics in action: Intentional behavior as a complex system.* Cambridge, MA: MIT Press.

Kintsch, W. (1998) *Comprehension: A paradigm for cognition.* New York: Cambridge University Press.

Lachman, R., Butterfield, E., & Lachman, J. L. (1979). *Cognitive psychology and information processing.* Mahwah, NJ: Erlbaum.

Landauer, T. K., & Dumais, S. T. (1997). A solution to Plato's problem: The latent semantic analysis theory of acquisition, induction, and representation of knowledge. *Psychological Review*, *104*, 211–240.

Meyer, D. E., & Kieras, D. E. (1997). A computational theory of executive control processes and human multiple-task performance: Part 1. Basic mechanisms. *Psychological Review*, *104*, 3–65.

Meyer, D. E., & Schvaneveldt, R. W. (1971). Facilitation in recognizing pairs of words: Evidence of a dependence between retrieval operations. *Journal of Experimental Psychology*, *90*, 227–234.

Meyer, D. E., Schvaneveldt, R. W., & Ruddy, M. G. (1975). Loci of contextual effects on visual word recognition. In P. Rabbitt & S. Dornic (Eds.), *Attention and performance V* (pp. 98–118). London: Academic Press.

Miller, G. A. (1985). The constitutive problem of psychology. In S. Koch & D. E. Leary (Eds.), *A century of psychology as science* (pp. 40–45). New York: McGraw-Hill.

Morris, C. (1971). *Writings on the general theory of signs*. The Hague, the Netherlands: Mouton.

Newell, A., Shaw, J. C., & Simon, H. A. (1958). Elements of a theory of human problem solving. *Psychological Review*, *65*, 151–166.

Norris, D. (1984). The effects of frequency, repetition and stimulus quality in visual word recognition. *The Quarterly Journal of Experimental Psychology*, *36A*, 507–518.

Ogden, C. K., & Richards, I. A. (1946). *The meaning of meaning* (8th ed.). New York: Harcourt, Brace & World.

Paap, K. R., Newsome, S. L., McDonald, J. E., & Schvaneveldt, R. W. (1982). An activation-verification model for letter and word recognition: The word superiority effect. *Psychological Review*, *89*, 573–594.

Patee, H. H. (1973). The physical basis and origin of hierarchical control. In H. Patee (Ed.), *Hierarchy theory: The challenge of complex systems* (pp. 73–108). New York: George Braziller.

Reed, E. S. (1996). *Encountering the world*. Oxford, England: Oxford University Press.

Schvaneveldt, R. W. (Ed.) (1990). *Pathfinder associative networks: Studies in knowledge organization*. Norwood, NJ: Ablex.

Schvaneveldt, R. W., Beringer, D. B., & Lamonica, J. (2001). Priority and organization of information accessed by pilots in various phases of flight. *International Journal of Aviation Psychology*, *11*, 253–280.

Schvaneveldt, R. W., Beringer, D. B., & Leard, T. M. (in press). *Evaluating aviation information systems: The role of information priorities* (Final Report, Federal Aviation Administration). Mesa: Arizona State University.

Schvaneveldt, R. W., Durso, F. T., & Dearholt, D. W. (1989). Network structures in proximity data. In G. Bower (Ed.), *The psychology of learning and motivation: Vol. 24. Advances in research and theory* (pp. 249–284). New York: Academic Press.

Schvaneveldt, R. W., Durso, F. T., Goldsmith, T. E., Breen, T. J., Cooke, N. M., Tucker, R. G., & DeMaio, J. C. (1985). Measuring the structure of expertise. *International Journal of Man-Machine Studies*, *23*, 699–728.

Schvaneveldt, R. W., & McDonald, J. E. (1981). Semantic context and the encoding of words: Evidence for two modes of stimulus analysis. *Journal of Experimental Psychology: Human Perception and Performance*, *7*, 673–687.

Schvaneveldt, R. W., & Meyer, D. E. (1973). Retrieval and comparison processes in semantic memory. In S. Kornblum (Ed.), *Attention and performance IV* (pp. 395–409). New York: Academic Press.

Schvaneveldt, R. W., & Van Orden, G. C. (2002). Dynamics or representational epicycles? A review of Dietrich, E., & Markman, A. (Eds.), *Cognitive dynamics: Conceptual and representational change in humans and machines. Contemporary Psychology: APA Review of Books*, *47*, 461–464.

Searle, J. R. (1980). Minds, brains, and programs. *Behavioral and Brain Sciences*, *3*, 417–424.

Searle, J. R. (1992). *The rediscovery of the mind*. Cambridge, MA: MIT press.

Sternberg, S. (1969). The discovery of processing stages: Extensions of Donders' method. *Acta Psychologica*, *30*, 276–315.

Sternberg, S. (1998). Discovering mental processing stages: The method of additive factors. In D. Scarborough & S. Sternberg (Eds.), *An invitation to cognitive science: Vol. 4. Methods, models, and conceptual issues* (pp. 703–863). Cambridge, MA: MIT Press.

Thelen, E., & Smith, L. (1994). *A dynamic systems approach to the development of cognition and action*. Cambridge, MA: MIT Press.

Toulmin, S., & Leary, D. E. (1985). The cult of empiricism in psychology and beyond. In S. Koch & D. E. Leary (Eds.), *A century of psychology as science* (pp. 594–617). New York: McGraw-Hill.

Townsend, J. T. (1972). Some results concerning the identifiability of parallel and serial processes. *Perception & Psychophysics, 10*, 161–163.

Utall, W. R. (1990). On some two way barriers between theories and mechanisms. *Perception & Psychophysics, 48*, 188–203.

van Gelder, T. (1997). Dynamics and cognition. In. J. Haugland (Ed.), *Mind design II* (pp. 421–450). Cambridge, MA: MIT Press.

Van Orden, G. C., Holden, J. G., & Turvey, M. T. (2003). Self-organization of cognitive performance. *Journal of Experimental Psychology: General, 132,* 331–350.

Velmans, M. (2000). *Understanding consciousness*. London: Routledge.

17

Cultural Explorations of the Nature of Intelligence

Robert J. Sternberg and Elena L. Grigorenko

The same behavior that might get you compliments in one country—public criticism of a political regime, for example—might get you killed in another. What is considered intelligent clearly differs from one place to the next. Is it smart or fatally stupid to criticize the existing regime publicly, for example? Yet researchers often do their research as though culture does not matter. This research continues despite pervasive evidence that people in different cultures think and act differently (e.g., Greenfield, 1997; Laboratory of Comparative Human Cognition, 1982; Nisbett, 2003; Serpell, 2000). During recent years, investigators have been studying conceptions of intelligence, as well as intelligent behavior, around the world, with sometimes surprising results.

Lay Implicit Theories of Intelligence Around the World

In some cases, Western notions about intelligence are not shared by other cultures. For example, at the mental level, the Western emphasis on speed of mental processing (Sternberg, Conway, Ketron, & Bernstein, 1981) is not shared in many cultures. Other cultures may even be suspicious of the quality of work that is done very quickly. Indeed, other cultures emphasize depth rather than speed of processing. They are not alone: Some prominent Western theorists have pointed out the importance of depth of processing for full command of material (e.g., Craik & Lockhart, 1972).

Yang and Sternberg (1997a) reviewed Chinese philosophical conceptions of intelligence. The Confucian perspective emphasizes the characteristic of benevolence and of doing what is right. As in the Western notion, the intelligent person spends a great deal of effort in learning, enjoys learning, and persists in lifelong learning with a great deal of enthusiasm. The Taoist tradition, in contrast, emphasizes the importance of humility, freedom from conventional

The research in this chapter was supported primarily by the Partnership for Child Development.

standards of judgment, and full knowledge of oneself as well as of external conditions.

The difference between Eastern and Western conceptions of intelligence may persist even in the present day. Yang and Sternberg (1997b) studied contemporary Taiwanese Chinese conceptions of intelligence and found five factors underlying these conceptions: (a) a general cognitive factor, much like the g factor in conventional Western tests; (b) interpersonal intelligence (i.e., social competence); (c) intrapersonal intelligence; (d) intellectual self-assertion; and (e) intellectual self-effacement. In a related study but with different results, Chen (1994) found three factors underlying Chinese conceptualizations of intelligence: nonverbal reasoning ability, verbal reasoning ability, and rote memory. The difference may be due to different subpopulations of Chinese, to differences in methodology, or to differences in when the studies were done.

The factors uncovered in Taiwan differ substantially from those identified in U.S. people's conceptions of intelligence by Sternberg et al. (1981)— (a) practical problem solving, (b) verbal ability, and (c) social competence— although in both cases, people's implicit theories of intelligence seem to go quite far beyond what conventional psychometric intelligence tests measure. Of course, comparing Chen's (1994) study with Sternberg et al.'s (1981) study simultaneously varies both language and culture.

Studies in Africa, in fact, provide yet another window on the substantial differences. Ruzgis and Grigorenko (1994) argued that in Africa, conceptions of intelligence revolve largely around skills that help to facilitate and maintain harmonious and stable intergroup relations; intragroup relations are probably equally important and at times more important. For example, Serpell (1974, 1996) found that Chewa adults in Zambia emphasize social responsibilities, cooperativeness, and obedience as important to intelligence; intelligent children are expected to be respectful of adults. Kenyan parents also emphasize responsible participation in family and social life as important aspects of intelligence (Super & Harkness, 1982, 1986, 1993). In Zimbabwe, the word for intelligence, ngware, actually means to be prudent and cautious, particularly in social relationships. Among the Baoule, service to the family and community and politeness toward and respect for elders are seen as key to intelligence (Dasen, 1984).

It is difficult to separate linguistic differences from conceptual differences in cross-cultural notions of intelligence. In our own research, we use converging operations to achieve some separation. That is, we use different and diverse empirical operations to ascertain notions of intelligence. So we may ask in one study that people identify aspects of competence; in another study, that they identify competent people; in a third study, that they characterize the meaning of "intelligence," and so forth.

The emphasis on the social aspects of intelligence is not limited to African cultures. Notions of intelligence in many Asian cultures also emphasize the social aspect of intelligence more than does the conventional Western, or IQ-based, notion (Azuma & Kashiwagi, 1987; Lutz, 1985; Poole, 1985; White, 1985).

It should be noted that neither African nor Asian notions emphasize exclusively social notions of intelligence. These conceptions of intelligence much more emphasize social skills than do conventional U.S. conceptions of intelligence, at the same time that they recognize the importance of cognitive aspects of intelligence. In a study of Kenyan conceptions of intelligence (Grigorenko et al., 2001), it was found that there are four distinct terms constituting conceptions of intelligence among rural Kenyans—*rieko* (knowledge and skills), *luoro* (respect), *winjo* (comprehension of how to handle real-life problems), and *paro* (initiative)—with only the first directly referring to knowledge-based skills (including but not limited to the academic).

It is important to realize, again, that there is no one overall U.S. conception of intelligence. Indeed, Okagaki and Sternberg (1993) found that different ethnic groups in San Jose, California, had rather different conceptions of what it means to be intelligent. For example, Latino parents of school children tended to emphasize the importance of social-competence skills in their conceptions of intelligence, whereas Asian parents tended rather heavily to emphasize the importance of cognitive skills. Anglo parents also emphasized cognitive skills more. Teachers, representing the dominant culture, emphasized cognitive competence more than social competence. The rank order of children of various groups' performance (including subgroups within the Latino and Asian groups) could be perfectly predicted by the extent to which their parents shared the teachers' conception of intelligence. In other words, teachers tended to reward those children who were socialized into a view of intelligence that happened to correspond to the teachers' own. Yet, as we argue later, social aspects of intelligence, broadly defined, may be as important as or even more important than cognitive aspects of intelligence in later life. Some, however, prefer to study intelligence not in its social aspect but in its cognitive one.

Explicit-Theoretical Investigations of Intelligence Around the World

Many times, investigations of intelligence conducted in settings outside the developed world can yield a picture of intelligence that is quite at variance with the picture one would obtain from studies conducted only in the developed world. In a study in Usenge, Kenya, near the town of Kisumu, Sternberg and his colleagues were interested in school-age children's ability to adapt to their indigenous environment. They devised a test of practical intelligence for adaptation to the environment (see Sternberg & Grigorenko, 1997; Sternberg et al., 2001). The test of practical intelligence measured children's informal tacit knowledge of natural herbal medicines that the villagers believe can be used to fight various types of infections. At least some of these medicines appear to be effective (F. Okatcha, personal communication, 1999), and most villagers certainly believe in their efficacy, as shown by the fact that children in the villages use their knowledge of these medicines an average of once a week in medicating themselves and others. Thus, tests of how to use these medicines constitute effective measures of one aspect of practical intelligence as defined by the villagers as well as their life circumstances in their environmental contexts. Middle-class Westerners might find it quite a challenge to thrive or even survive in these contexts or, for that matter, in the contexts of urban ghettos often not distant from their comfortable homes.

The researchers measured the Kenyan children's ability to identify the medicines, where they come from, what they are used for, and how they are dosed. On the basis of work the researchers had done elsewhere, they expected that scores on this test would not correlate with scores on conventional tests of intelligence. To test this hypothesis, they also administered to the 85 children the Raven Colored Progressive Matrices Test (Raven, Court, & Raven, 1992), which is a measure of fluid or abstract-reasoning-based abilities, as well as the Mill Hill Vocabulary Scale (Raven et al., 1992), which is a measure of crystallized or formal-knowledge-based abilities. In addition, they gave the children a comparable test of vocabulary in their own Dholuo language. The Dholuo language is spoken in the home, English in the schools.

The researchers did indeed find no correlation between the test of indigenous tacit knowledge and scores on the fluid-ability tests. But to their surprise, they found statistically significant correlations of the tacit-knowledge tests with the tests of crystallized abilities. The correlations, however, were negative. In other words, the higher the children scored on the test of tacit knowledge, the lower they scored, on average, on the tests of crystallized abilities. This surprising result can be interpreted in various ways, but based on the ethnographic observations of the anthropologists on the team, Geissler and Prince, the researchers concluded that a plausible scenario takes into account the expectations of families for their children.

Many children drop out of school before graduation, for financial or other reasons, and many families in the village do not particularly value formal Western schooling. There is no reason they should, as the children of many families will for the most part spend their lives farming or engaged in other occupations that make little or no use of Western schooling. These families emphasize teaching their children the indigenous informal knowledge that will lead to successful adaptation in the environments in which they will actually live. Children who spend their time learning the indigenous practical knowledge of the community generally do not invest themselves heavily in doing well in school, whereas children who do well in school generally do not invest themselves as heavily in learning the indigenous knowledge—hence the negative correlations.

The Kenya study suggests that the identification of a general factor of human intelligence may tell us more about how abilities interact with patterns of schooling, especially Western patterns of schooling, than it does about the structure of human abilities. In Western schooling, children typically study a variety of subject matters from an early age and thus develop skills in a variety of skill areas. This kind of schooling prepares the children to take a test of intelligence, which typically measures skills in a variety of areas. Often, intelligence tests measure skills that children were expected to acquire a few years before taking the intelligence test. But as Rogoff (1990) and others have noted, this pattern of schooling is not universal and has not even been common for much of the history of humankind. Throughout history and in many places still, schooling, especially for boys, takes the form of apprenticeships in which children learn a craft from an early age. They learn what they will need to know to succeed in a trade, but not a lot more. They are not simultaneously engaged in tasks that require the development of the particular blend of skills measured by conventional intelligence tests. Hence it is less likely that one would observe a general factor in their scores, much as the investigators discovered in Kenya. Some years back, Vernon (1971) pointed out that the axes of a factor analysis do not necessarily reveal a latent structure of the mind but rather represent a convenient way of characterizing the organization of mental abilities. Vernon believed that there was no one "right" orientation of axes, and indeed, mathematically, an infinite number of orientations of axes can be fit to any solution in an exploratory factor analysis. Vernon's point seems perhaps to have been forgotten or at least ignored by later theorists.

We have found related, although certainly not identical, results in a study we have done among Yup'ik Eskimo children in southwestern Alaska (Grigorenko et al., in press). We assessed the importance of academic and practical intelligence in rural and urban Alaskan communities. A total of 261 children were rated for practical skills by adults or peers in the study: 69 children in Grade 9, 69 in Grade 10, 45 in Grade 11, and 37 in Grade 12. Of these children, 145 were girls and 116 were boys, and they were from seven different communities, six rural and one relatively urban. We measured academic intelligence with conventional measures of fluid and crystallized intelligence. We measured practical intelligence with a test of tacit knowledge as acquired in rural Alaskan Yup'ik communities. The urban children generally outperformed the rural children on a measure of crystallized intelligence, but the rural children generally outperformed the urban children on the measure of Yup'ik tacit knowledge. The test of tacit knowledge was superior to the tests of academic intelligence in predicting practical skills of the rural children (for whom the test was created) but not of the urban ones.

The test of practical intelligence developed for use in Kenya, as well as some of the other practically based tests described in this chapter, may seem more like tests of achievement or of developing expertise (see Ericsson, 1996; Howe, Davidson, & Sloboda, 1998) than of intelligence. But it can be argued that intelligence is itself a form of developing expertise—that there is no clearcut distinction between the two constructs (Sternberg, 1998, 1999). Indeed, all measures of intelligence, one might argue, measure a form of developing expertise.

An example of how tests of intelligence measure developing expertise rather than some fixed quantity emanates from work Sternberg, Grigorenko, and their colleagues have done in Tanzania. A study done in Tanzania (see Sternberg & Grigorenko, 1997, 2002; Sternberg et al., 2002) points out the risks of giving tests, scoring them, and interpreting the results as measures of some latent intellectual ability or abilities. The investigators administered to 358 school children between the ages of 11 and 13 years near Bagamoyo, Tanzania, tests including a form-board classification test, a linear syllogisms test, and a Twenty Questions Test, which measure the kinds of skills required on conventional tests of intelligence. Of course, the investigators obtained scores that they could analyze and evaluate, ranking the children in terms of their supposed general or other abilities. However, they administered the tests dynamically rather than statically (Brown & Ferrara, 1985; Feuerstein, 1979; Grigorenko & Sternberg, 1998; Guthke, 1993; Haywood & Tzuriel, 1992; Lidz, 1991; Sternberg & Grigorenko, 2002; Tzuriel, 1995; Vygotsky, 1978). Dynamic testing is like conventional static testing in that individuals are tested and inferences about their abilities are made. But dynamic tests differ in that children are given some kind of feedback to help them improve their scores. Vygotsky (1978) suggested that the children's ability to profit from the guided instruction they received during the testing session could serve as a measure of the children's zone of proximal development, or the difference between their developed abilities and their latent capacities. In other words, testing and instruction are treated as a whole rather than as distinct processes. This integration makes sense in terms of traditional definitions of intelligence as the ability to learn ("Intelligence and Its Measurement," 1921; Sternberg & Detterman, 1986). What a dynamic test does is directly measure processes of learning in the context of testing rather than measuring these processes indirectly as the product of past learning. Such measurement is especially important when not all children have had equal opportunities to learn in the past.

In the assessments, children were first given the ability tests. Then they were given a brief period of instruction in which they were able to learn skills that would potentially enable them to improve their scores. Then they were tested again. Because the instruction for each test lasted only about 5–10 minutes, one would not expect dramatic gains. Yet, on average, the gains were statistically significant. More important, scores on the pretest showed only weak although significant correlations with scores on the posttest. These correlations, at about the .3 level, suggested that when tests are administered statically to children in developing countries, they may be rather unstable and easily subject to influences of training. The reason could be that the children are not accustomed to taking Western-style tests and so profit quickly even from small amounts of instruction as to what is expected from them. Of course, the more important question is not whether the scores changed or even correlated with each other, but rather how they correlated with other cognitive measures. In other words, which test was a better predictor of transfer to other cognitive performance, the pretest score or the posttest score? The investigators found the posttest score to be the better predictor.

In interpreting results, whether from developed or developing cultures, it is always important to take into account the physical health of the subjects one is testing. In a study we did in Jamaica (Sternberg, Powell, McGrane, & McGregor, 1997), we found that Jamaican school children who suffered from parasitic illnesses (for the most part, whipworm or *Ascaris*) did more poorly on higher-level cognitive tests (such as of working memory and reasoning) than did children who did not suffer from these illnesses, even after controlling for socioeconomic status. Why might such a physical illness cause a deficit in higher-level cognitive skills?

Ceci (1996) has shown that increased levels of schooling are associated with higher IQ. Why would there be such a relation? Presumably, in part, because schooling helps children develop the kinds of skills that are measured by IQ tests and that are important in turn for survival in school. Children with whipworm-induced illnesses and related illnesses are less able to profit from school than are children without these illnesses. Every day they go to school, they are likely to be experiencing symptoms such as listlessness, stomachache, and difficulties in concentrating. These symptoms reduce the extent to which they are able to profit from instruction and in turn reduce their ultimate performance on higher-level cognitive tests.

The forms of developing expertise that are viewed as practically or otherwise intelligent may differ from one society to another or from one sector of a given society to another. For example, procedural knowledge about natural herbal medicines, on the one hand, or Western medicines, on the other hand, may be critical to survival in one society and irrelevant to survival in another (e.g., where one or the other type of medicine is not available). Whereas what constitutes cognitive components of intelligence is universal, the content that constitutes the application of these components to adaptation to, shaping, and selection of environments is culturally and even subculturally variable. But practical aspects of intelligence are important everywhere, as shown in a study conducted in Russia.

In this study, Grigorenko and Sternberg (2001) tested 511 Russian school children (ranging in age from 8 to 17 years) as well as 490 mothers and 328 fathers of these children. They used entirely distinct measures of analytical, creative, and practical intelligence. Consider, for example, the tests used for adults. Similar tests were used for children.

Fluid analytical intelligence was measured by two subtests of a test of nonverbal intelligence. The *Test of g: Culture Fair, Level II* (Cattell & Cattell, 1973) is a test of fluid intelligence designed to reduce, as much as possible, the influence of verbal comprehension, culture, and educational level, although no test eliminates such influences. In the first subtest, Series, individuals were presented with an incomplete, progressive series of figures. The subjects' task was to select, from among the choices provided, the answer that best continued the series. In the Matrices subtest, the task was to complete the matrix presented at the left of each row.

The test of crystallized intelligence was adapted from existing traditional tests of analogies and synonyms or antonyms used in Russia. Grigorenko and Sternberg (2001) used adaptations of Russian rather than American tests because the vocabulary used in Russia differs from that used in the United States. The first part of the test included 20 verbal analogies (internal consistency reliability = .83). An example is *circle—ball = square—? (a) quadrangular, (b) figure, (c) rectangular, (d) solid, (e) cube.* The second part included 30 pairs of words, and the subjects' task was to specify whether the words in the pair were synonyms or antonyms (internal consistency reliability = .74). Examples are *latent—hidden* and *systematic—chaotic*.

The measure of creative intelligence also comprised two parts. The first part asked the subjects to describe the world through the eyes of insects. The second part asked subjects to describe who might live and what might happen on a planet called *Priumliava*. No additional information on the nature of the planet was specified. Each part of the test was scored in three different ways to yield three different scores. The first score was for originality (novelty); the second was for the amount of development in the plot (quality); and the third was for creative use of prior knowledge in these relatively novel kinds of tasks (sophistication). The mean interstory reliabilities were .69, .75, and .75 for the three respective scores, all of which were statistically significant at the $p < .001$ level.

The measure of practical intelligence was self-report and also comprised two parts. The first part was designed as a 20-item, self-report instrument, assessing practical skills in the social domain (e.g., effective and successful communication with other people), in the family domain (e.g., how to fix household items, how to run the family budget), and in the domain of effective resolution of sudden problems (e.g., organizing something that has become chaotic). For the subscales, internal consistency estimates varied from .50 to .77. In this study, only the total practical intelligence self-report scale was used (Cronbach's α = .71). The second part had four vignettes, based on themes that appeared in popular Russian magazines in the context of a discussion of adaptive skills in the current society. The four themes were how to maintain the value of one's savings, what to do when one makes a purchase and discovers that the item one has purchased is broken, how to locate medical assistance in a time of need, and how to manage a salary bonus one has received for outstanding work. Each vignette was accompanied by five choices, and subjects had to select the best one. Obviously, there is no one "right" answer in this type of situation. Hence Grigorenko and Sternberg used the most frequently chosen response as the keyed answer. To the extent that this response was suboptimal, this suboptimality would work against the researchers in subsequent analyses relating scores on this test to other predictor and criterion measures.

In this study, exploratory principal-components analysis for both children and adults yielded very similar factor structures. Both varimax and oblimin rotations yielded clear-cut analytical, creative, and practical factors for the tests. Thus, a sample of a different nationality (Russian), a different set of tests, and a different method of analysis (exploratory rather than confirmatory analysis) again supported the theory of successful intelligence.

In the same study, the analytical, creative, and practical tests the investigators employed were used to predict mental and physical health among the Russian adults. Mental health was measured by widely used paper-and-pencil tests of depression and anxiety, and physical health was measured by self-report. The best predictor of mental and physical health was the practical-intelligence measure. (Or, because the data are correlational, it may be that health predicts practical intelligence, although the connection here is less clear.) Analytical intelligence came second, and creative intelligence came third. All three contributed to prediction, however. Thus, the researchers again concluded that a theory of intelligence encompassing all three elements provides better prediction of success in life than does a theory comprising just the analytical element.

Conclusion

We have argued that research in diverse cultures is important for understanding the nature of human intelligence. People from developed countries, and especially Western ones, can show and have shown a certain kind of arrogance in assuming that concepts (such as implicit theories of intelligence) or results (such as of studies based on explicit theories of intelligence) obtained in one culture—usually, their culture—apply anywhere. In all likelihood, they do not. Or at least, it cannot be assumed they do until this assumption is tested.

Many of the results we have described here are at variance with results typically obtained in Western countries. Other investigators as well have obtained results that differ dramatically from those obtained in the developed West. We believe, therefore, that cultural investigations of psychological constructs, such as intelligence, are crucial.

References

Azuma, H., & Kashiwagi, K. (1987). Descriptions for an intelligent person: A Japanese study. *Japanese Psychological Research, 29,* 17–26.

Brown, A. L., & Ferrara, R. A. (1985). Diagnosing zones of proximal development. In J. V. Wertsch (Ed.), *Culture, communication, and cognition: Vygotskian perspectives* (pp. 273–305). New York: Cambridge University Press.

Cattell, R. B., & Cattell, H. E. P. (1973). *Measuring intelligence with the Culture Fair Tests.* Champaign, IL: Institute for Personality and Ability Testing.

Ceci, S. J. (1996). *On intelligence . . . more or less* (Expanded ed.). Cambridge, MA: Harvard University Press.

Chen, M. J. (1994). Chinese and Australian concepts of intelligence. *Psychology and Developing Societies, 6,* 101–117.

Craik, F. I. M., & Lockhart, R. S. (1972). Levels of processing: A framework for memory research. *Journal of Verbal Learning and Verbal Behavior, 11,* 671–684.

Dasen, P. (1984). The cross-cultural study of intelligence: Piaget and the Baoule. *International Journal of Psychology, 19,* 407–434.

Ericsson, K. A. (Ed.). (1996). *The road to excellence.* Mahwah, NJ: Erlbaum.

Feuerstein, R. (1979). *The dynamic assessment of retarded performers: The learning potential assessment device theory, instruments, and techniques.* Baltimore, MD: University Park Press.

Greenfield, P. M. (1997). You can't take it with you: Why abilities assessments don't cross cultures. *American Psychologist, 52,* 1115–1124.

Grigorenko, E. L., Geissler, P. W., Prince, R., Okatcha, F., Nokes, C., Kenny, D. A., et al. (2001). The organisation of Luo conceptions of intelligence: A study of implicit theories in a Kenyan village. *International Journal of Behavioral Development, 25,* 367–378.

Grigorenko, E. L., Meier, E., Lipka, J., Mohatt, G., Yanez, E., & Sternberg, R. J. (in press). The relationship between academic and practical intelligence: A case study of the tacit knowledge of Native American Yup'ik people in Alaska. *Learning and Individual Differences.*

Grigorenko, E. L., & Sternberg, R. J. (1998). Dynamic testing. *Psychological Bulletin, 124,* 75–111.

Grigorenko, E. L., & Sternberg, R. J. (2001). Analytical, creative, and practical intelligence as predictors of self-reported adaptive functioning: A case study in Russia. *Intelligence, 29,* 57–73.

Guthke, J. (1993). Current trends in theories and assessment of intelligence. In J. H. M. Hamers, K. Sijtsma, & A. J. J. M. Ruijssenaars (Eds.), *Learning potential assessment* (pp. 13–20). Amsterdam: Swets & Zeitlinger.

Haywood, H. C., & Tzuriel, D. (Eds.). (1992). *Interactive assessment.* New York: Springer-Verlag.

Howe, M. J., Davidson, J. W., & Sloboda, J. A. (1998). Innate talents: Reality or myth? *Behavioral and Brain Sciences, 21,* 399–442.

Intelligence and its measurement: A symposium. (1921). *Journal of Educational Psychology, 12,* 123–147, 195–216, 271–275.

Laboratory of Comparative Human Cognition. (1982). Culture and intelligence. In R. J. Sternberg (Ed.), *Handbook of human intelligence* (pp. 642–719). New York: Cambridge University Press.

Lidz, C. S. (1991). *Practitioner's guide to dynamic assessment.* New York: Guilford Press.

Lutz, C. (1985). Ethnopsychology compared to what? Explaining behaviour and consciousness among the Ifaluk. In G. M. White & J. Kirkpatrick (Eds.), *Person, self, and experience: Exploring Pacific ethnopsychologies* (pp. 35–79). Berkeley: University of California Press.

Nisbett, R. E. (2003). *The geography of thought: Why we think the way we do*. New York: Free Press.

Okagaki, L., & Sternberg, R. J. (1993). Parental beliefs and children's school performance. *Child Development, 64*, 36–56.

Poole, F. J. P. (1985). Coming into social being: Cultural images of infants in Bimin-Kuskusmin folk psychology. In G. M. White & J. Kirkpatrick (Eds.), *Person, self, and experience: Exploring Pacific ethnopsychologies* (pp. 183–244). Berkeley: University of California Press.

Raven, J. C., Court, J. H., & Raven, J. (1992). *Manual for Raven's Progressive Matrices and Mill Hill Vocabulary Scales*. Oxford, England: Oxford Psychologists Press.

Rogoff, B. (1990). *Apprenticeship in thinking: Cognitive development in social context*. New York: Oxford University Press.

Ruzgis, P. M., & Grigorenko, E. L. (1994). Cultural meaning systems, intelligence and personality. In R. J. Sternberg & P. Ruzgis (Eds.), *Personality and intelligence* (pp. 248–270). New York: Cambridge University Press.

Serpell, R. (1974). Aspects of intelligence in a developing country. *African Social Research, 17*, 576–596.

Serpell, R. (1996). Cultural models of childhood in indigenous socialization and formal schooling in Zambia. In C. P. Hwang & M. E. Lamb (Eds.), *Images of childhood* (pp. 129–142). Mahwah, NJ: Erlbaum.

Serpell, R. (2000). Intelligence and culture. In R. J. Sternberg (Ed.), *Handbook of intelligence* (pp. 549–580). New York: Cambridge University Press.

Sternberg, R. J. (1998). Abilities are forms of developing expertise. *Educational Researcher, 27*, 11–20.

Sternberg, R. J. (1999). Intelligence as developing expertise. *Contemporary Educational Psychology, 24*, 359–375.

Sternberg, R. J., Conway, B. E., Ketron, J. L., & Bernstein, M. (1981). People's conceptions of intelligence. *Journal of Personality and Social Psychology, 41*, 37–55.

Sternberg, R. J., & Detterman, D. K. (1986). *What is intelligence?* Norwood, NJ: Ablex.

Sternberg, R. J., & Grigorenko, E. L. (1997). The cognitive costs of physical and mental ill health: Applying the psychology of the developed world to the problems of the developing world. *Eye on Psi Chi, 2*, 20–27.

Sternberg, R. J., & Grigorenko, E. L. (2002). Just because we "know" it's true doesn't mean it's really true: A case study in Kenya. *Psychological Science Agenda, 15*, 8–10.

Sternberg, R. J., Grigorenko, E. L., Ngrosho, D., Tantufuye, E., Mbise, A., Nokes, C., et al. (2002). Assessing intellectual potential in rural Tanzanian school children. *Intelligence, 30*, 141–162.

Sternberg, R. J., Nokes, K., Geissler, P. W., Prince, R., Okatcha, F., Bundy, D. A., & Grigorenko, E. L. (2001). The relationship between academic and practical intelligence: A case study in Kenya. *Intelligence, 29*, 401–418.

Sternberg, R. J., Powell, C., McGrane, P. A., & McGregor, S. (1997). Effects of a parasitic infection on cognitive functioning. *Journal of Experimental Psychology: Applied, 3*, 67–76.

Super, C. M., & Harkness, S. (1982). The development of affect in infancy and early childhood. In D. Wagnet & H. Stevenson (Eds.), *Cultural perspectives on child development* (pp. 1–19). San Francisco: Freeman.

Super, C. M., & Harkness, S. (1986). The developmental niche: A conceptualization at the interface of child and culture. *International Journal of Behavioral Development, 9*, 545–569.

Super, C. M., & Harkness, S. (1993). The developmental niche: A conceptualization at the interface of child and culture. In R. A. Pierce & M. A. Black (Eds.), *Life-span development: A diversity reader* (pp. 61–77). Dubuque, IA: Kendall/Hunt.

Tzuriel, D. (1995). *Dynamic-interactive assessment: The legacy of L. S. Vygotsky and current developments*. Unpublished manuscript.

Vernon, P. E. (1971). *The structure of human abilities*. London: Methuen.

Vygotsky, L. S. (1978). *Mind in society: The development of higher psychological processes*. Cambridge, MA: Harvard University Press.

White, G. M. (1985). Premises and purposes in a Solomon Islands ethnopsychology. In G. M. White & J. Kirkpatrick (Eds.), *Person, self, and experience: Exploring Pacific ethnopsychologies* (pp. 328–366). Berkeley: University of California Press.

Yang, S., & Sternberg, R. J. (1997a). Conceptions of intelligence in ancient Chinese philosophy. *Journal of Theoretical and Philosophical Psychology, 17*, 101–119.

Yang, S., & Sternberg, R. J. (1997b). Taiwanese Chinese people's conceptions of intelligence. *Intelligence, 25*, 21–36.

18

Word Association Spaces for Predicting Semantic Similarity Effects in Episodic Memory

*Mark Steyvers, Richard M. Shiffrin,
and Douglas L. Nelson*

A common assumption of theories of memory is that the meaning of a word can be represented by a vector that places a word as a point in a multidimensional semantic space (e.g., Burgess & Lund, 2000; Landauer & Dumais, 1997; Osgood, Suci, & Tannenbaum, 1957). Representing words as vectors in a multidimensional space allows simple geometric operations such as the Euclidian distance or the angle between the vectors to compute the semantic (dis)similarity between arbitrary pairs or groups of words. This representation makes it possible to make predictions about performance in psychological tasks in which the semantic distance between pairs or groups of words is assumed to play a role.

One recent framework for placing words in a multidimensional space is latent semantic analysis or LSA (Derweester, Dumais, Furnas, Landauer, & Harshman, 1990; Landauer & Dumais, 1997; Landauer, Foltz, & Laham, 1998). The main assumption is that the similarity between words can be inferred by analyzing the statistical regularities between words and text samples in which they occur. For example, a textbook with a paragraph that mentions *cats* might also mention *dogs, fur, pets,* and so on. This knowledge can be used to infer that *cats* and *dogs* are related in meaning. The technique underlying LSA is singular value decomposition (SVD). This procedure is applied to the matrix of word-context frequencies in a high-dimensional space (typically with 200–400 dimensions) in which words that appear in similar contexts are placed in similar regions of the space. It is interesting to note that some words that never occur in the same context might still be similar in LSA space if they co-occurred with other words that do occur together in text samples. Landauer and Dumais (1997) applied the LSA approach to over 60,000 words appearing in over 30,000 contexts of a large encyclopedia. More recently, LSA was applied to over 90,000 words appearing in over 37,000 contexts of reading material that an English reader might be exposed to from third grade up to the first year of college from various sources such as textbooks, novels, and newspaper articles. The LSA representation has been successfully applied to multiple-

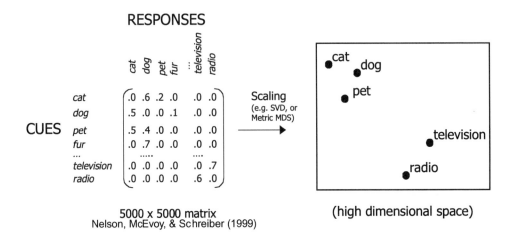

Figure 18.1. Illustration of the creation of word association spaces. By scaling the word associations of a large database of free-association norms, words are placed in a high-dimensional semantic space. Words with similar associative relationships are placed in similar regions of the space. SVD = singular value decomposition; MDS = multidimensional scaling.

choice vocabulary tests, domain knowledge tests, and content evaluation (see Landauer & Dumais, 1997; Landauer et al., 1998).

In this research, we apply scaling techniques such as SVD as well as multidimensional scaling (MDS) on a large database of free association collected by Nelson, McEvoy, and Schreiber (1999) containing norms for first associates for over 5,000 words. By applying scaling methods on the free-association norms, we hope to uncover the latent information available in the free-association norms that is not directly available by investigating simple measures for associative strengths based on the direct and indirect associative strengths through short chains of associates (e.g., Nelson & Zhang, 2000). The basic approach is illustrated in Figure 18.1. The free-association norms were represented in matrix form with the rows representing the cues and the columns representing the responses. The entries in the matrix are filled by some measure of associative strength between cues and responses. By applying scaling methods on the matrix, words are placed in a high-dimensional space such that words with similar associative patterns are placed in similar regions of the space. We refer to the resulting space as the *word association space* (WAS).

We believe such a construct will be very useful in the modeling of episodic memory phenomena because the associative structure of words plays a central role in recall (e.g., Bousfield, 1953; Deese, 1959a, 1959b, 1965; Jenkins, Mink, & Russell, 1958), cued recall (e.g., Nelson, Schreiber, & McEvoy, 1992), and recognition (e.g., Nelson, Zhang, & McKinney, 2001). For example, Deese (1959a, 1959b) found that the interitem associative strength of the words in a study list can predict the number of words recalled, the number of intrusions, and the frequency with which certain words intrude. In the present research, we compare the performance of LSA with WAS in three episodic memory tasks:

recognition memory, free recall, and cued recall. It was expected that the similarity structure in WAS is well suited to predict various semantic similarity effects in these episodic memory tasks.

Word Association Spaces

Deese (1965) asserted that free associations are not the result of haphazard processes and that they arise from an underlying regularity in preexisting associative connections. He laid the framework for studying the meaning of linguistic forms that can be derived by analyzing the correspondences between distributions of responses to free-association stimuli: "The most important property of associations is their structure—their patterns of intercorrelations" (Deese, 1965, p. 1). Deese applied factor analyses to the overlap in the distribution of free-association responses for a small set of words and argued that these analyses could be used to learn about the mental representation of words. In this chapter, we capitalized on Deese's ideas of using the pattern of intercorrelations in the free-association norms by placing a large number of word associations in a semantic space and then used this space to predict semantic similarity effects in memory. Instead of factor analyses, we used the techniques of SVD and metric MDS analyses.

The data for these procedures relied on free-association norms involving more than 5,000 words and 6,000 subjects (Nelson et al., 1999). An average of 149 ($SD = 15$) subjects were each presented with 100–120 English words. These words served as cues (e.g., *cat*) for which subjects had to write down the first word that came to mind (e.g., *dog*). For each cue the proportion of subjects who elicited the response to the cue was calculated (e.g., 60% responded with *dog*, 15% with *pet*, 10% with *tiger*, etc.).

Scaling by Singular Value Decomposition

The method of SVD can be applied to any matrix containing some measure of strength or co-occurrence between two words. Although many different ways have been proposed to calculate an index of associative strength between two words (e.g., Marshall & Cofer, 1963; Nelson & Zhang, 2000), we restrict ourselves to two simple measures of associative strength. Let A_{ij} represent the proportion of subjects who gave the response j to the cue i. The simplest measure would be to take A_{ij} itself. In the norms, the associative strengths A_{ij} are often highly asymmetric such that the associative strength in one direction is strong whereas it is weak or zero in the other direction. Even though SVD can be easily applied to asymmetric matrices, the results are more interpretable when it is applied to symmetric matrices. Therefore, in our first measure for associative strength we take:

$$S_{ij}^{(1)} = A_{ij} + A_{ji}$$

$S_{ij}^{(1)}$ is equivalent to adding forward strength to backward strength. This measure is of course symmetric so that $S_{ij}^{(1)} = S_{ji}^{(1)}$. This measure is based on only the direct association between i and j and involves only one associative step going from i to j (hence the index "1"). In the norms of Nelson et al. (1999), subjects were only allowed to give the first response that came to mind. The second strongest response in one subjects' mind might be elicited by another subject or it might not be elicited at all if the first response is a strong associate. Therefore, the $S^{(1)}$ measure might be underestimating the associative strength between two words especially in cases in which the measure is zero (Nelson et al., 1999). In the second measure for associative strength, we take:

$$S_{ij}^{(2)} = S_{ij}^{(1)} + \sum_k S_{ik}^{(1)} S_{kj}^{(1)}$$

This equals the forward plus backward plus mediated strength through other associates. Note that this measure involves the direct strength between i and j as well as the indirect strength by summing over all paths from i to k to j, the product of the symmetric associative strengths between i and k, and k and j. These indirect associative strengths involve the two-step probabilities of going from i to j and vice versa (hence the index "2"). Research has shown that the indirect associative strengths play a role in cued recall (Nelson & Zhang, 2000) and recognition (Nelson et al., 2001). For example, Nelson and Zhang (2000) found that including the indirect associative strengths in a measure for associative strength significantly increases the explained variance in the extralist cued recall task.

We applied SVD separately on these two measures of associative strength. The result of each SVD is the placement of words in a high-dimensional space, so that words that have similar associative structures are represented by similar vectors. Because of the SVD method, and on the basis of work in LSA (see Derweester et al., 1990), a suitable measure for the similarity between two words is the cosine of the angle between two word vectors. Let X represent the vector in WAS for word i. The similarity between words i and j is calculated by:

$$similarity\ (i, j) = \cos\ (\alpha) = \frac{X_i \cdot X_j}{\|X_i\|\ \|X_j\|},$$

where $\|X\|$ is the length of the vector and $X_i \cdot X_j$ represents the inner product between vectors i and j. Two words that are similar in meaning or that have similar associative structures are expected to have high similarity as defined by the cosine of the angle between the two word vectors. The SVD of the associative strengths can uncover the latent relationships between words. In the SVD of $S^{(1)}$, words that are not direct associates of each other can still be represented by similar vectors if their associates are related. In the SVD of $S^{(2)}$, words that are not directly associated or indirectly associated through one intermediate associate can still be represented by similar vectors if the associates of the associates of the words are related. In other words, the whole pattern of direct and indirect correlations between associations is taken into account when placing words in the semantic space.

An important variable is the dimensionality of the space. One can think of the dimensionality as the number of feature values for the words. The number of dimensions, which we varied between 10 and 500, will determine how much the information of the free-association database is compressed. With too few dimensions, the similarity structure of the resulting vectors does not capture enough detail of the original associative structure in the database. With too many dimensions or the number of dimensions approaching the number of cues, the information in the norms is not compressed enough so that we might expect that the similarity structure of the vectors does not capture enough of the indirect relationships in the associations between words. In the analyses of predicting performance in a variety of tasks (recognition, free and cued recall), we show that although the optimal number of dimensions depends on the specific task, intermediate values between 200 and 500 are appropriate for this method.

Scaling by Metric Multidimensional Scaling

An interesting comparison for the two WAS spaces based on SVD would be to construct a metric space in which the distance between two words (i.e., their dissimilarity) can be measured by the Euclidian distance between their vectors. Metric MDS is a classic method for placing stimuli in a space such that the Euclidian distance between points in the space approximates the Euclidian distances in the dissimilarity matrix. To apply metric MDS, one needs estimates for the distance between any two words. In fact, all nondiagonal entries in the matrix have to be filled with some estimate for the distance between words because no missing values are allowed in the method. This raises the problem of how to estimate the distance between i and j when the associative strength as measured by $S_{ij}^{(1)}$ is zero.

In our solution of this problem, we were inspired by network models for proximity data (e.g., Cooke, Durso, & Schvaneveldt, 1986; Klauer & Carroll, 1995). In these network models, dissimilarity between two stimuli is calculated by the shortest path between two nodes in a graph. In this research, we can use the word association norms as defining a graph: Two words are linked by an edge if they have nonzero associative strengths. We use the symmetric $S^{(1)}$ associative strengths because in the graph defined by $S^{(1)}$, it is possible to reach any word from any other word in the graph (in fact, the maximum number of steps between any pair of words is four). The distance between two words will be defined as the negative logarithm of the product of the associative strengths along the shortest path in the network defined by $S^{(1)}$. This is equivalent to the (negative) sum of the logs of the associative strengths along the shortest path:

$$T_{ij} = -\log\left(S_{ik}^{(1)}S_{kl}^{(1)} \cdots S_{qj}^{(1)}\right) = -\left[\log S_{ik}^{(1)} + \log S_{kl}^{(1)} + \ldots + \log S_{qj}^{(1)}\right]$$

Here, the shortest path between words i and j is from i to k to l through other words to q and finally j. With this distance measure, word pairs with weak or long associative paths are assigned large distances whereas word pairs with short or strong associative paths are assigned small distances. The distances T_{ij} were calculated for all word pairs in the word association database. Then, these distances were scaled by metric MDS. The result is that the words are placed in a multidimensional space and the dissimilarity or distance between two words is expressed by the Euclidian distance between the two corresponding word vectors:

$$distance\ (i,j) = \left[\sum_k (X_{ik} - X_{jk})^2\right]^{1/2}$$

Because of computational constraints, it was not possible to apply metric MDS to the full matrix T containing the distances for all word pairs. Instead, we chose 2,500 words from the original 5,018 words in the word association database. The words in this smaller set included words appearing in various experiments listed in the next section and included a selection of randomly chosen words from the original set. As with the SVD scaling procedure, the number of dimensions was varied between 10 and 500.

Predicting Semantic Similarity Effects in Memory

Since Deese's (1959b) classic study on intrusions in free recall, many studies have shown that memory errors are in part based on semantic overlap between the response and the contents of memory. We introduced WAS as a way of quantifying the semantic similarity between words that might help in predicting these memory errors. Three sets of data were taken to assess the performance of WAS: a recognition memory experiment, Deese's original free-recall experiment, and a cued-recall experiment. We tested three WAS-based measures for semantic similarity. The first two were based on the SVD of $S^{(1)}$, the one-step symmetric associative strengths, and on the SVD of $S^{(2)}$, the one- plus the two-step associative strengths involving indirect associative strengths. In these two semantic spaces (as in LSA) the cosine of the angle between two words expresses the similarity between two words. The last WAS measure was based on metric MDS of the shortest path associative strengths. In this space, the Euclidian distance between two word vectors is taken as a measure for the dissimilarity between two words. These WAS scaling solutions were contrasted with the (unscaled) associative strengths $S^{(1)}$ and $S^{(2)}$ that were taken as control comparisons. We also tested two LSA-based measures: one was based on a corpus of an encyclopedia and another on a corpus called *tasa* that included reading material that an English reader might be exposed to from third grade up to first year of college.

Recognition Memory: Semantic Similarity Ratings

In an unpublished study by the first author (Steyvers, 2000, Experiment 1), 89 subjects studied a list of words that contained 18 semantic categories of 5 words each. On the basis of a study by Brainerd and Reyna (1998), subjects gave two ratings for each of 100 test items. In one rating, they were instructed to judge whether the item was old or new and were told to judge semantically similar distractors as "new." In another rating, they were instructed to rate (on a 6-point scale) how semantically similar the item was to the studied items. We focused on the semantic similarity ratings for the new items from this study. For each subject, the 72 new test items were randomly selected from a larger pool of 144 words. An average of 44 (SD = 4.87) subjects rated the semantic similarity for each of the 144 words that might appear as new words in the test list. The semantic similarity ratings are theoretically interesting because they can be used to test models of semantic similarity. Subjects merely have to remember how similar the item was to the studied items without being forced to give old–new judgments that might be more influenced by various strategic retrieval factors (such as word frequency or previous retrievals).

Many memory models assume that a recognition memory judgment is produced by calculating the global familiarity involving the summed similarity between the test item and the episodic traces in memory (e.g., Gillund & Shiffrin, 1984; Hintzman, 1988). More recently, Shiffrin and Steyvers (1997, 1998) and McClelland and Chappell (1998) have proposed recognition memory models that produce recognition judgments with Bayesian decision processes. McClelland and Chappell (1998) proposed that the best match (i.e., maximum similarity) between the test item and the episodic traces in memory forms the basis for the recognition judgment. Shiffrin and Steyvers (1998) showed that in the Bayesian framework, a maximum similarity process produced results very similar to a summed similarity process. In this research, our aim is not to test these models specifically but to use and simplify the underlying mechanisms to predict semantic similarity ratings. Inspired by the global familiarity and Bayesian recognition memory models, we measured the correlations between the semantic similarity ratings in the recognition memory experiment with the *sum* or *maximum* of the WAS similarity between the test item and all study words. Because the results were very similar for the sum and maximum calculations, we list only the results for the maximum calculation.

The top left panel of Figure 18.2 shows the correlations between maximum similarity and number of dimensions (10–500) for the three WAS- and two LSA-based measures. For the SVD-based semantic spaces, increasing the number of dimensions in either WAS or LSA increases the correlation generally up to around 200–300 dimensions. For WAS, an additional data point was plotted for 2,500 dimensions, which is the maximum number of dimensions given that the matrix contained only 2,500 words (see previous section). This data point for 2,500 dimensions was included because it represents the case where none of the indirect relationships in the word association matrix are exploited and as such, no dimensionality reduction is performed. As can be observed, the correlation is lower for 2,500 dimensions indicating that some dimensionality reduction is needed to predict the semantic similarity ratings. Also, the SVD based on $S^{(2)}$ led to better correlations than the SVD based on $S^{(1)}$. This finding implies that adding the indirect associations in a measure for associative strength helps in predicting recognition memory performance. The two horizontal lines in the plot indicate the correlation when the associative strengths $S^{(1)}$ and $S^{(2)}$ are used as a measure for semantic similarity. The

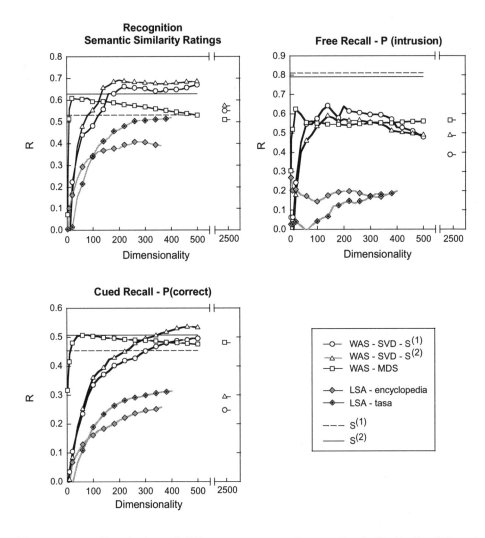

Figure 18.2. Correlations of different measures of semantic similarity for different dimensionalities. Data are taken from recognition memory, cued recall, and free recall. See text for details. WAS = word association space; SVD = singular value decomposition; MDS = multidimensional scaling; LSA = latent semantic analysis.

correlation is higher for $S^{(2)}$ than $S^{(1)}$, which again implies that in recognition memory, the indirect associative strengths help in predicting performance. It is interesting to note that the SVD scaling of $S^{(2)}$ gave higher correlations than associative strengths $S^{(2)}$ themselves. Even though $S^{(2)}$ includes the forward, backward, and all two-step associative strengths, applying the SVD and reducing the redundancies in the matrix of $S^{(2)}$ helped to increase the correlation. In other words, the indirect relationships and patterns of correlations that go beyond those of the two-step associative strengths were used by the SVD procedure and these were beneficial in predicting the ratings from this recognition memory experiment.

The metric-MDS solution shows quite a different pattern of results than the SVD solution. The best correlation was obtained with 20–40 dimensions, which is much lower than the number of dimensions typically needed in the SVD solutions of either WAS or LSA. Although the best correlation for metric MDS was .6 as opposed to .7 for the SVD-based solutions, it is interesting that relatively good performance can be achieved in semantic spaces that are of low dimensionality. Although specifying why this effect occurs is outside the scope of this chapter, it could be related to the estimates involving the shortest associative path between words. As described in the previous section, to apply metric MDS, one needs estimates for the distances between all word pairs in the vocabulary. The shortest associative path distance was proposed to meet this requirement; estimates were even generated for word pairs that were not associated directly or even indirectly through a chain of two associates. In SVD, no such estimates are required, and those entries were left at zero. It is possible, then, that the filling-in process of all word pair dissimilarities by the shortest associative path distances helped in the global placement of all words in the semantic space.

Of the two corpora in LSA, the tasa corpus led to much better performance than the encyclopedia corpus. This difference is not surprising because the tasa corpus includes material that reflects much more closely the reading material an English reader is exposed to, which in turn might lead to semantic spaces that are more psychologically plausible in terms of predicting semantic similarity effects in recognition memory. Comparing WAS with LSA, it becomes clear that WAS leads to much higher correlations than LSA.

Predicting Extralist Cued Recall

In extralist cued recall experiments, after studying a list of words, subjects are presented with cues that can be used to retrieve words from the study list. The cues themselves are novel words that were not presented during study, and typically each word is associatively or semantically related to one of the studied words. The degree to which a cue is successful in retrieving a particular target word is a measure of interest because this might be related to the associative/semantic overlap between cues and their targets. Research in this paradigm (e.g., Nelson, McKinney, Gee, & Janczura, 1998; Nelson et al., 1992; Nelson & Zhang, 2000) has shown that the associative strength between cue and target is one important predictor for the percentage of correctly recalled targets. Therefore, we expect that the WAS similarities between cues and targets are correlated with the percentages of correct recall in these experiments. We used a database containing the percentages of correct recall for 1,115 cue–target pairs from over 29 extralist cued recall experiments from Douglas Nelson's laboratory (Nelson, 2000; Nelson & Zhang, 2000).

The correlations between the various measures for semantic similarity and the observed percentage correct recall rates are shown in the bottom left panel of Figure 18.2. Overall, the results are very similar to the results obtained for the recognition memory experiment. The WAS space based on $S^{(2)}$ led to better performance than the WAS space based on $S^{(1)}$. Also, the associative strengths $S^{(2)}$ leads to better performance than the $S^{(1)}$ associative strengths. These findings are consistent with findings by Nelson and Zhang (2000) that show that the indirect relationships in word association norms can help in predicting cued recall performance. The plot also shows that the WAS space based on $S^{(2)}$ does somewhat better than the associative strengths $S^{(2)}$ it was based on (for high dimensionality). This advantage implies that applying dimensionality reduction to make greater use of the indirect associative connections helped in predicting cued recall. Finally, as with the recognition results, the WAS space correlates better with cued recall than LSA.

Predicting Intrusion Rates in Free Recall

In a classic study by Deese (1959b), the goal was to predict the intrusion rates of words in free recall. Fifty subjects studied the 12 strongest associates to each of 36 critical lures while the critical lures themselves were not studied. In a free-recall test, some critical lures (e.g., *sleep*) were falsely recalled about 40% of the time while other critical lures (e.g., *butterfly*) were never falsely recalled. Deese was able to predict the intrusion rates for the critical lures on the basis of the average associative strength from the studied associates to the critical lures and obtained a correlation of .80. Because Deese could predict intrusion rates with word association norms, the WAS vector space derived from the association norms should also predict them. Critical items with high average similarity (or low average distance) to the list words in the semantic space should be more likely to appear as intrusions in free recall. The average similarity (average distance) was computed between each critical lure vector and list word vectors, and the correlations were computed between these similarities and observed intrusion rates.

The top right panel in Figure 18.2 shows the results. The pattern of results is quite different from the pattern of results for either recognition or cued recall. The best correlation of .82 was obtained with $S^{(1)}$, the sum of backward and forward associative strength. This result is very similar to the correlation of .80 obtained by Deese with his word association norms. It is interesting to note that the plot shows that any manipulation that includes the indirect associations leads to worse performance than using the direct associations only. The WAS space based on $S^{(2)}$ now does worse than the WAS space based on $S^{(1)}$, and either space correlates more poorly than when using the associative strengths $S^{(1)}$ and $S^{(2)}$ themselves.

These findings imply that direct associative strengths are the best predictors of intrusion rates in free recall. One explanation for this finding is related to implicit associative responses (IARs). Underwood (1965) has argued that during study, the words associated with the study words are thought of and might be stored in memory as an implicit associative response. In Deese's study, it is likely that IARs were generated because the critical lures were all strongly associated to the list words. Therefore, during recall, the words that were actually presented and words that were thought of during study might be confused, leading in some cases to dramatic intrusion rates. Because free associations measure what responses are first thought of given specific cues, the direct associative strengths can be argued to be good predictors of the strength of implicit associative responses and subsequent intrusion rates.

Discussion

By a statistical analysis of a large database of free-association norms, WAS was developed. In this space, words that have similar associative structures are placed in similar regions of the space. In the first version of WAS, SVD was applied on the direct associations between words to place these words in a high-dimensional semantic space. In the second version of WAS, the same technique was applied on the direct and indirect associations between words. In the third version of WAS, metric MDS was applied on measures for the associative strength related to the shortest associative path between words (similar to the approach in Cooke et al., 1986; Klauer & Carroll, 1995).

Because the free-association norms have been an integral part in predicting episodic memory phenomena (e.g., Deese, 1965; Nelson et al., 1992), it was assumed that a semantic space based on free-association norms would be an especially useful construct to model memory phenomena. We compared WAS with LSA in predicting the results of several memory tasks: similarity ratings in recognition memory, percentage correct in extralist cued recall, and intrusion rates in free recall. In all these memory tasks, WAS was a better predictor for performance than LSA. This finding suggests to us that WAS forms a useful representational basis for memory models that are designed to store and retrieve words as vectors of feature values. Many memory models assume that the semantic aspects of words can be represented by collections of features abstractly represented by vectors (e.g., Hintzman, 1988; McClelland & Chappell, 1998; Shiffrin & Steyvers, 1997, 1998). However, in most memory modeling, the vectors representing words are arbitrarily chosen and are not based on or derived by some analysis of the meaning of actual words in our language. We expect that memory models based on these semantic vectors from WAS will be useful for making predictions about the effects of varying semantic similarity in memory experiments for individual words.

We propose that WAS is an approach that augments other existing methods available for placing words in a psychological space. It differs from the LSA approach in several ways. Because LSA operates on samples of text, it is relatively easy to apply LSA to large numbers of words. In contrast, the number of words that can be scaled by WAS depends on the number of words that can be normed. It took Nelson et al. (1999) more than a decade to collect the norms, highlighting the enormous human overhead of the method. Even though a working vocabulary of 5,000+ words in WAS is much smaller than the 70,000+ word long vocabularies of LSA, we believe it is large enough for the purpose of modeling performance in variety of memory experiments. In any event, we believe that WAS and LSA provide semantic spaces that are useful for both theoretical and empirical research.

The differences between the applications to different tasks certainly suggest that the usefulness of a particular semantic space will be task dependent. We speculate that the spaces differ in their semantic "reach." WAS is derived from the first associations provided, and thereby might emphasize local seman- tic domains and such things as two-word units in memory. The fact that it does well for judgments of similarity to an episodic list might suggest that such judgments are based on a few episodic recalls cued by the test word, and that such recalls reflect "nearby" associations. On the other hand, the fact that WAS does better than the associations themselves suggests that recalls involve additional semantic components beyond those "close by." The fact that free- recall intrusions favor associations over WAS suggests that this task favors very local semantics (perhaps through IARs). The fact that LSA lags behind the WAS-based measures suggests that LSA captures semantics with a wider reach than WAS or the associations themselves. If so, it ought to be possible to find other tasks that would favor LSA, but such research has not yet been carried out.

References

Bousfield, W. A. (1953). The occurrence of clustering in the recall of randomly arranged associates. *Journal of General Psychology, 49,* 229–240.

Brainerd, C. J., & Reyna, V. F. (1998). When things that were never experienced are easier to "remember" than things that were. *Psychological Science, 9,* 484–489.

Burgess, C., & Lund, K. (2000). The dynamics of meaning in memory. In E. Dietrich & A. B. Markman (Eds.), *Cognitive dynamics: Conceptual and representational change in humans and machines* (pp. 117–156). Mahwah, NJ: Erlbaum.

Cooke, N. M., Durso, F. T., & Schvaneveldt, R. W. (1986). Recall and measures of memory organiza- tion. *Journal of Experimental Psychology: Learning, Memory, and Cognition, 12,* 538–549.

Deese, J. (1959a). Influence of inter-item associative strength upon immediate free recall. *Psycho- logical Reports, 5,* 305–312.

Deese, J. (1959b). On the prediction of occurrences of particular verbal intrusions in immediate recall. *Journal of Experimental Psychology, 58,* 17–22.

Deese, J. (1965). *The structure of associations in language and thought.* Baltimore: Johns Hopkins University Press.

Derweester, S., Dumais, S. T., Furnas, G. W., Landauer, T. K., & Harshman, R. (1990). Indexing by latent semantic analysis. *Journal of the American Society for Information Science, 41,* 391–407.

Gillund, G., & Shiffrin, R. M. (1984). A retrieval model for both recognition and recall. *Psychological Review, 91,* 1–67.

Hintzman, D. L. (1988). Judgments of frequency and recognition memory in a multiple-trace memory model. *Psychological Review, 95,* 528–551.

Jenkins, J. J., Mink, W. D., & Russell, W. A. (1958). Associative clustering as a function of verbal association strength. *Psychological Reports, 4,* 127–136.

Klauer, K. C., & Carroll, J. D. (1995). Network models for scaling proximity data. In R. D. Luce, M. D'Zmura, D. Hoffman, G. J. Iverson, & A. K. Romney (Eds.), *Geometric representations of perceptual phenomena* (pp. 319–342). Mahwah, N J: Erlbaum.

Landauer, T. K., & Dumais, S. T. (1997). A solution to Plato's problem: The latent semantic analysis theory of acquisition, induction, and representation of knowledge. *Psychological Review, 104,* 211–240.

Landauer, T. K., Foltz, P. W., & Laham, D. (1998). An introduction to latent semantic analysis. *Discourse Processes, 25,* 259–284.

Marshall, G. R., & Cofer, C. N. (1963). Associative indices as measures of word relatedness: A summary and comparison of ten methods. *Journal of Verbal Learning and Verbal Behavior, 1,* 408–421.

McClelland, J. L., & Chappell, M. (1998). Familiarity breeds differentiation: A subjective-likelihood approach to the effects of experience in recognition memory. *Psychological Review, 105,* 724– 760.

Nelson, D. L. (2000). *The University of South Florida database on cued recall*. Retrieved January 1, 1999, from http://www.luna.cas.usf.edu/~nelson/

Nelson, D. L., McEvoy, C. L., & Schreiber, T. A. (1999). *The University of South Florida word association, rhyme and fragment norms*. Retrieved January 1, 1999 from http://www.luna.cas.usf.edu/~nelson/

Nelson, D. L., McKinney, V. M., Gee, N. R., & Janczura, G. A. (1998). Interpreting the influence of implicitly activated memories on recall and recognition. *Psychological Review, 105*, 299–324.

Nelson, D. L., Schreiber, T. A., & McEvoy, C. L. (1992). Processing implicit and explicit representations. *Psychological Review, 99*, 322–348.

Nelson, D. L., & Zhang, N. (2000). The ties that bind what is known to the recall of what is new. *Psychonomic Bulletin & Review, 7*, 604–617.

Nelson, D. L., Zhang, N., & McKinney, V. M. (2001). The ties that bind what is known to the recognition of what is new. *Journal of Experimental Psychology: Learning, Memory, and Cognition, 27*, 1147–1159.

Osgood, C. E., Suci, G. J., & Tannenbaum, P. H. (1957). *The measurement of meaning*. Urbana: University of Illinois Press.

Shiffrin, R. M., & Steyvers, M. (1997). A model for recognition memory: REM—retrieving effectively from memory. *Psychonomic Bulletin & Review, 4*, 145–166.

Shiffrin, R. M., & Steyvers, M. (1998). The effectiveness of retrieval from memory. In M. Oaksford & N. Chater (Eds.), *Rational models of cognition* (pp. 73–95). Oxford, England: Oxford University Press.

Steyvers, M. (2000). *Modeling semantic and orthographic similarity effects on memory for individual words*. Unpublished doctoral dissertation, Indiana University, Bloomington.

Underwood, B. J. (1965). False recognition produced by implicit verbal responses. *Journal of Experimental Psychology, 70*, 122–129.

Author Index

Numbers in italics refer to entries in the reference sections.

Subject Index

About the Editor

Alice F. Healy, PhD, received her AB degree summa cum laude in 1968 from Vassar College and her PhD in 1973 from The Rockefeller University. At Rockefeller, she worked under the guidance of George A. Miller and her dissertation advisor William K. Estes. She was assistant professor and then associate professor at Yale University from 1973 to 1981. She joined the faculty of the University of Colorado at Boulder in 1981 as a tenured associate professor and has held the position of professor since 1984. She is a fellow of the American Association for the Advancement of Science (AAAS), the American Psychological Association (APA), the American Psychological Society, and the Society of Experimental Psychologists. She served on the Governing Board and Publications Committee of the Psychonomic Society, on the Executive Committee and currently as president-elect of the APA Division 3 (Experimental Psychology) as chair of the Psychology Electorate of the AAAS, and as president of the Rocky Mountain Psychological Association. She has also served as associate editor of the *Journal of Experimental Psychology: Learning, Memory, and Cognition* and as editor of *Memory & Cognition*. She is presently principal investigator of grants from the National Aeronautics and Space Administration and the National Science Foundation and has a contract with the Army Research Institute, which has supported her research since 1986. She has published over 150 articles and chapters in professional journals and books, is coauthor of the textbook *Cognitive Processes* (1986), and is the senior editor of five volumes: the two-volume *Essays in Honor of William K. Estes* (1992), *Learning and Memory of Knowledge and Skills* (1995), *Foreign Language Learning* (1998), and the *Experimental Psychology* volume in the *Handbook of Psychology* (2003). Healy's research has focused on experimental cognitive psychology including learning, memory, reading, language, information processing, and decision making. Many of her recent studies explore principles to optimize the training, retention, and transfer of knowledge and skills. She has collaborated with numerous colleagues and students, most notably Lyle E. Bourne, Jr. She lives in Boulder, Colorado, with her husband Bruce, a noted cookbook author, and her 16-year-old daughter Charlotte.